Annals of Anthropological Practice

Biocultural Approaches to Health Disparities in Global Contexts

Thomas Leatherman

Volume Editor

Satish Kedia and David Himmelgreen

General Editors

NATIONAL ASSOCIATION FOR THE PRACTICE OF ANTHROPOLOGY
A SECTION OF THE AMERICAN ANTHROPOLOGICAL ASSOCIATION

Annals of Anthropological
Practice 38.2

Annals of Anthropological Practice (2153-957X) is published in May and November on behalf of the American Anthropological Association by Wiley Subscription Services, Inc., a Wiley Company, 111 River St., Hoboken, NJ 07030-5774.

Mailing: Journal is mailed Standard Rate. Mailing to rest of world by IMEX (International Mail Express). Canadian mail is sent by Canadian publications mail agreement number 40573520. POSTMASTER: Send all address changes to Annals of Anthropological Practice, Journal Customer Services, John Wiley & Sons Inc., 350 Main St., Malden, MA 02148-5020.

Publisher: Annals of Anthropological Practice is published by Wiley Periodicals, Inc., Commerce Place, 350 Main Street, Malden, MA 02148; Telephone: 781 388 8200; Fax: 781 388 8210. Wiley Periodicals, Inc. is now part of John Wiley & Sons.

Information for Subscribers: Annals of Anthropological Practice is published in two one-issue volumes per year. Institutional subscription prices for 2014 are: Print & Online: US$69 (US), US$68 (Rest of World), €45 (Europe), £36 (UK). Prices are exclusive of tax. Australian GST, Canadian GST and European VAT will be applied at the appropriate rates. For more information on current tax rates, please go to www.wileyonlinelibrary.com/tax-vat. The institutional price includes online access to the current and all online back files to January 1st 2008, where available. For other pricing options, including access information and terms and conditions, please visit www.wileyonlinelibrary.com/access.

Delivery Terms and Legal Title: Where the subscription price includes print issues and delivery is to the recipient's address, delivery terms are Delivered Duty Unpaid (DDU); the recipient is responsible for paying any import duty or taxes. Title to all issues transfers FOB our shipping point, freight prepaid. We will endeavour to fulfil claims for missing or damaged copies within six months of publication, within our reasonable discretion and subject to availability.

Copyright and Photocopying: © 2014 American Anthropological Association. All rights reserved. No part of this publication may be reproduced, stored or transmitted in any form or by any means without the prior permission in writing from the copyright holder. Authorization to photocopy items for internal and personal use is granted by the copyright holder for libraries and other users registered with their local Reproduction Rights Organization (RRO), e.g. Copyright Clearance Center (CCC), 222 Rosewood Drive, Danvers, MA 01923, USA (www.copyright.com), provided the appropriate fee is paid directly to the RRO. This consent does not extend to other kinds of copying such as copying for general distribution, for advertising or promotional purposes, for creating new collective works or for resale. Special requests should be addressed to: permissionsuk@wiley.com

Back Issues: Single issues from current and recent volumes are available at the current single issue price from cs-journals@wiley.com. Earlier issues may be obtained from Periodicals Service Company, 11 Main Street, Germantown, NY 12526, USA. Tel: +1 (518) 537-4700, Fax: +1 (518) 537-5899, Email: psc@periodicals.com.

Journal Customer Services: For ordering information, claims and any inquiry concerning your journal subscription please go to www.wileycustomerhelp.com/ask or contact your nearest office.

Americas: Email: cs-journals@wiley.com; Tel: +1 781 388 8598 or +1 800 835 6770 (toll free in the USA & Canada).

Europe, Middle East and Africa: Email: cs-journals@wiley.com; Tel: +44 (0) 1865 778315.

Asia Pacific: Email: cs-journals@wiley.com; Tel: +65 6511 8000.

Japan: For Japanese speaking support, Email: cs-japan@wiley.com; Tel: +65 6511 8010 or Tel (toll-free): 005 316 50 480.

Visit our Online Customer Get-Help available in 6 languages at www.wileycustomerhelp.com

Associate Editor: Shannon Canney
Production Editor: Muhammad Haider, Email: napa@wiley.com
Advertising: Kristin McCarthy, Email: kmccarthy@wiley.com

Print Information: Printed in the United States of America by The Sheridan Press.

Online Information: This journal is available online at *Wiley Online Library*. Visit www.wileyonlinelibrary.com to search the articles and register for table of contents e-mail alerts.

Access to this journal is available free online within institutions in the developing world through the AGORA initiative with the FAO, the HINARI initiative with the WHO and the OARE initiative with UNEP. For information, visit www.aginternetwork.org, www.healthinternetwork.org, and www.oarescience.org.

Aims and Scope: The Annals of Anthropological Practice (AAP) is dedicated to the practical problem-solving and policy applications of anthropological knowledge and methods. AAP is peer reviewed and is distributed free of charge as a benefit of NAPA (National Association for the Practice of Anthropology) membership. Through AAP, NAPA seeks to facilitate the sharing of information among practitioners, academics, and students, contribute to the professional development of anthropologists seeking practitioner positions, and support the general interests of practitioners both within and outside the academy. AAP is a publication of NAPA produced by the American Anthropological Association and Wiley-Blackwell. Through the publication of AAP, the AAA and Wiley-Blackwell furthers the professional interests of anthropologists while disseminating anthropological knowledge and its applications in addressing human problems.

Author Guidelines: For submission instructions, subscription and all other information visit: www.wileyonlinelibrary.com

Disclaimer: The Publisher, American Anthropological Association, and Editors cannot be held responsible for errors or any consequences arising from the use of information contained in this journal; the views and opinions expressed do not necessarily reflect those of the Publisher, American Anthropological Association, and Editors, neither does the publication of advertisements constitute any endorsement by the Publisher, American Anthropological Association, and Editors of the products advertised.

ISSN 2153-957X (Print)

ISSN 2153-9588 (Online)

Contents

INTRODUCTION: BIOCULTURAL CONTRIBUTIONS
TO THE STUDY OF HEALTH DISPARITIES

Thomas Leatherman
Department of Anthropology, University of Massachusetts, Amherst

Kasey Jernigan
Department of Anthropology, University of Massachusetts, Amherst

INTRODUCTION

The study of health disparities has emerged as an important theme in public health and the social sciences, and efforts to eliminate health disparities are a major thrust of governments and nongovernmental organizations in the United States and abroad. Initially, much work focused on identifying disparities with less emphasis on the contexts that create these disparities. An important shift over the past two decades has been the widespread recognition that health disparities have their roots in social and economic inequalities. Indeed, the World Health Organization (WHO) chose a theme issue on inequalities in health as the first issue for a new century and millennium. In an editorial for that issue, editor-in-chief Richard Feachem stated that "the gap in health between rich and poor ... (and) between other advantaged and disadvantaged groups defined, for example, by ethnicity, caste, or place of residence ... constitutes one of the greatest challenges of the new century" (Feachem 2000:1). This reality and the negative synergisms between inequalities and health have not diminished in the past decade and in many ways have grown.

In our current era of global capitalism, growing inequalities and unacceptably high levels of strife, hunger, malnutrition, and disease, there is a need for approaches that link human biology and health to social, cultural, and political-economic dynamics. Biocultural approaches to health can provide a fuller understanding of the ways large-scale forces and local-level lived realities "get under the skin." The premise that human health and health disparities are shaped by interwoven biocultural processes operating at multiple levels, and best understood through the combination of humanistic and scientific perspectives, is a foundational principle of medical anthropology. Yet biocultural approaches in medical anthropology have not always sought to link the local to broader global forces and provide an ethnographic lens on the lived realities and vulnerabilities in people's everyday lives. A more critical biocultural medical anthropology (Leatherman and Goodman 2011) has emerged to provide a framework for connecting history, political economy, and local biologies and health.

This collection of papers represents approaches to better understand health inequities from biocultural and critical biocultural perspectives. Biocultural anthropologists have been addressing issues of inequalities and health for decades in multiple environments

ANNALS OF ANTHROPOLOGICAL PRACTICE 38.2, pp. 171–186. ISSN: 2153-957X. © 2015 by the American Anthropological Association. DOI:10.1111/napa.12051

and ethnographic contexts. They have been in the vanguard of studies linking vulnerable environments and people to health outcomes, including but not limited to, studies of food insecurity, of psychosocial dimensions of health, of race, racism and health, of the consequences of environmental toxins on health, and the health costs of violence and trauma. In different ways and to different extents, the papers collected here address health disparities by exploring the contexts of inequality and the embodied processes linking inequalities to biology and health in local and regional contexts. They contribute perspectives and methodologies for addressing the way poverty and poor health are reproduced in local contexts; including the dynamics of "biosocial inheritance" (see Hoke and McDade in this issue). They provide case studies of health disparities within arenas of inequalities and structural violence, food insecurity and growing problems of global obesity and diabetes, and the syndemic of poverty, violence, and disease.

The contributors to this issue come from biological, sociocultural, nutritional, and medical anthropologies and share a commitment to a biocultural approach that seeks to understand the local in global contexts and histories. Contributors combine ethnographic, biological, and psycho-social field methods to better understand the embodiment of social and cultural realities into human biology and health in interdisciplinary fashion. To be sure, these papers represent only a slice of a broader range of biocultural and critical biocultural approaches in an anthropology of health, but amply illustrate the utility of these approaches.

HISTORICAL CONTEXT

Health disparities have puzzled observers for millennia, triggering responses from the afflicted and explanations from observers. James (2009) notes that Hippocrates, in his foundational text, *On Airs, Waters, and Places,* recognized that the physical environment— through its effects on food supply, body size, fertility, and social relationships— shaped disease susceptibility and mortality among ancient peoples (Hippocrates 2008). Gibbons' (2005) historical overview of health disparities cites other early examples of the epidemiology of health disparities including Bernardino Ramazzini's centuries-old observations of unusually high frequencies of breast cancer among Catholic nuns in Italy that led to an early association between socioenvironmental risk factors and health outcomes (Gibbons 2005; Wilson et al. 2002). British surgeon Sir Percival Potts reported a cluster of scrotal cancer cases among British chimney sweeps (Wilson et al. 2002). Further, since contact between Europeans and American Indians and Pacific Islanders, early explorers reported disparities in health as they observed epidemic disease spread though entire tribes while their own crews remained healthy (Jones 2009; Scheder 2006).

In the mid-19th century, nearly 2,000 years after Hippocrates' observations, large-scale epidemiological evidence began to corroborate these early observations, demonstrating clear associations between infectious diseases and sanitation, housing, and nutritional status, prompting social reform in the United Kingdom (Chadwick 2008; Macintyre 1997) and United States to improve health conditions (Dubos 1987; James 2009; Shattuck

2008; Sydenstricker 1933). Perhaps the most familiar account of an early epidemiological approach linking environments and health is of that John Snow and his analysis of cholera distribution in London, which prompted the disabling of the Broad Street pump (Snow 2008). Around the same time Frederich Engels published *Conditions of the Working Class in England* (1958) in which he analyzed the deplorable living and working conditions in Manchester during the industrial revolution and linked these conditions to higher rates of both morbidity and mortality. Another of the more socially and politically informed contributions to this early history was Rudolf Virchow's (1988) classic "Report on the Typhus Epidemic in Upper Silesia," in which he identified typhoid and other diseases afflicting miners and their families as "artificial" diseases to emphasize their direct links to poor housing, working conditions, and diet and lack of sanitation (Green and LaBonté 2008). He concluded that preserving health and preventing disease require broader social, economic, and political measures such as universal education and food cooperatives, improved wages and working conditions, and progressive taxation (LaBonté et al. 2005:6). Indeed, Virchow is credited with having written, "All disease has two causes, one pathological and the other political" (Bierman and Dunn 2006:99). Thus, by the end of the 19th century, there was clear evidence in the scientific literature (in Europe and the United States) of class variations in morbidity and mortality, as well as proposals to address these variations, including improved school and working conditions, better sanitation, and social interventions that aimed to reduce class differences in health outcomes (Amick et al. 1995; Gibbons 2005; Macintyre 1997).

In Europe, especially in Britain, studies of social class differences and health status continued throughout the 20th century, documenting how class inversely correlated with morbidity and mortality, prompting the British government to institute welfare policies in 1942 (Gibbons 2005; Macintyre 1997). Meanwhile in the United States, efforts to address health outcomes took a "race-based" (rather than class-based) approach. Sherman James (2009) notes that at the turn of the 20th century, "entrenched notions about the supposed biological superiority of whites over peoples of color meant that the sanitary reform movement would be applied unevenly in fast-growing, racially segregated cities . . . with the predictable result that tuberculosis—essentially a disease of poverty, crowded living quarters, and malnutrition—took an unnecessarily heavy toll on the health of city-dwelling African Americans" (James 2009:1). However, by the end of World War II, James observes that studies of racial/ethnic differences in health took on "a more socially-informed, multifactorial paradigm . . . in contrast to the nearly exclusive prewar emphasis on presumed innate biologic differences among races" (James 2009:1).

Of note, throughout the history of health disparities research, there has been little consensus on what actually constitutes health disparities (Braveman 2006; Carter-Pokras and Baquet 2002). Indeed, even the term *health disparities* is often used interchangeably with *health inequalities*, *health inequities*, or *health equity*. In the United States, *health disparities* is more commonly used, coming about in the mid-1990s (Braveman 2006), and is mostly studied as racial/ethnic differences in health, whereas *health inequalities* or *health inequity* are more familiar terms to public health professionals in Europe and elsewhere (Braveman 2006; Dressler 2009; Gibbons 2005; James 2009). Carter-Pokras and Baquet

(2002) and Braveman (2006) provide extensive reviews of the literature in the United States and abroad, pointing out differences among definitions and the potential policy implications. For example, the comparison population, areas of health, and population subgroups mentioned in health disparity definitions are small but important details. Lack of specification of these references can lead to inconsistency between funding priorities and program objectives. While it is difficult to trace the genesis of the term *health disparities*, scholars agree upon the lack of standardized definitions of the term and its interchangeable use as differences in health measures as well as health care service inequities. Braveman (2006) provides the following oft-cited definition for health disparities:

> A health disparity/inequality is a particular type of difference in health or in the most important influences on health that could potentially be shaped by policies; it is a difference in which disadvantaged social groups (such as the poor, racial/ethnic minorities, women, or other groups that have persistently experienced social disadvantage or discrimination) systematically experience worse health or greater health risks than more advantaged groups (Braveman 2006:180).

Despite government investment in welfare in Britain and a multifactorial approach to studying racial/ethnic health differences in the United States (as well as the 1965 enactment of Medicare and Medicaid), by the 1970s all evidence pointed to increasing disparities in morbidity and mortality in the United Kingdom and United States. The United Kingdom responded by forming the Research Working Group on Inequalities in Health with Sir Douglas Black as its chair. The Group issued the Black Report in 1980, which was "the first attempt by a national government to systematically study, understand, and explain health inequalities" (Gibbons 2005, International Origins). Although the publication of the Report was politically contested within the (then in power) Conservative government, its findings of widespread health inequalities warranted a call for the improvement of the physical and social environment of the poor and working classes.

In the United States, the Department of Health and Human Services issued a report in 1984 on the health of the nation that demonstrated major disparities in illness and death for African Americans and other minorities as compared to the nation's population as a whole (Gibbons 2005; National Center for Health Statistics [NCHS] 1983). In response to this report, a task force on black and minority health was formed to conduct a comprehensive study of minority health problems (Gibbons, 2005; Mayberry et al. 2000). The release of the "Report of the Secretary's Task Force on Black and Minority Health" in 1985 raised awareness of racial/ethnic health disparities, prompting large-scale epidemiological studies and systematic documentation of differential outcomes and health status (Brennan et al. 2004; Gibbons 2005; Mayberry et al. 2000) and later, large institutional goals to address health disparities (e.g., *Healthy People 2010*; the CDC's *REACH* in 1999; Institute of Medicine Report, *Unequal Treatment*).

Abroad, the Whitehall studies of British civil servants challenged associations that poor health status was limited to minorities and the poor by demonstrating that a class-based health gradient was present among even the well educated and employed (Marmot et al. 1978; Wilkinson 1996). This led to a more nuanced understanding of how relative as well as absolute levels of wealth and poverty in a society impacted health disparities. Wealthy countries and societies with greater income inequalities often demonstrate worse health outcomes than poorer ones with greater equality (Wilkinson 1996). Indeed, much recent work has focused on the role of income inequalities and its effect on a host of societal factors linked to local environments (e.g., environmental quality, exposure to violence, nutritional and health resources), social connectedness (e.g., levels of trust, social support, community engagement), and physical and psychosocial stress across the life cycle (including fetal environments) that lie at the root of much health disparity in morbidity and mortality (Coleman 1988; Dressler et al. 2005; Kuzawa and Sweet 2009; Marmot 1986; Sapolsky 2004; Tager et al. 1983; Wilkinson 1992, 1996).

Initially, and even up to the present, much work has focused on identifying disparities and reducing proximate risk factors that give rise to disproportionate negative health outcomes, with less focus on the contexts that create these socially patterned health disparities. Hence, a focus on patterns of health disparities has dominated over the focus on social inequalities that give rise to health disparities. An important shift from this earlier research has been the recognition that, rather than simply a matter of individual behavior or lifestyle choices, health disparities have their roots in the social, and economic inequalities that define some peoples' experience relative to others. Indeed, even the concept of "health disparities" is a great improvement over its predecessor of simply noting differences in health status by race, gender, social class, or place of residence (James 2009)—it shifts the focus of inequalities in health to outcomes rather than group traits. Chowkwanyun (2011:253) observes that the foundational works of Sherman James (James et al. 1987, 1992), Nancy Krieger (Krieger 1990, 2000; Krieger et al. 1993), David Williams (Williams 1999; Williams and Collins 1995; Williams et al. 1997), Thomas LaVeist (1992, 1993), and Arline Geronimus (Geronimus 2000; Geronimus and Bound 1990; Geronimus and Thompson 2004) are regularly cited in academic literature, leading to increased recognition and legitimization of the social and economic determinants of health, particularly within the field of public health. Indeed, the National Institutes of Health (NIH) recently developed the Network on Inequality, Complexity, and Health (2010) aimed to integrate cross-disciplinary approaches to address the complex problems of health disparities. Moreover, the WHO released a report in 2008 on the Social Determinants of Health.

FRAMEWORKS IN THE STUDY OF HEALTH DISPARITIES

Given the growing recognition in the field of public health that health disparities emerge as products of specific social, political, and economic structures, so too have "new" frameworks emerged that provide the discipline with a critical interpretive and analytical reframing for conceptualizing, investigating, analyzing, and addressing health disparities (e.g., Allacci and Chang 2009; Beckfield and Krieger 2003; Bowleg 2012; Chowkwanyun 2011; Gee and Ford 2011; James 2009; Kramer and Hogue 2009; Krieger 2001; Singh-Manoux et al. 2005). Quesada and colleagues (2011:341), however, note that a "logically consistent conceptual vocabulary or analytical approach" remains absent, resulting in a broad range of often overlapping terms including, for example, "social epidemiology" and Krieger's (1994) "ecosocial model"; the "risk environment framework" (Rhodes and Simic 2005); "social determinants of health" or "social determinants of health inequality" (Kawachi and Kennedy 1999; Marmot 2005; Marmot and Wilkinson 2006); and "political and economic determinants" (Navarro and Muntaner 2004; Singer 2001), to name a few.

Most of the "new" approaches stem from the understanding that health disparities emerge from complex and multifaceted processes and require collaboration across disciplines. Thus, many of the contemporary explanatory frameworks aim to weave together elements of biology, geography, political, social, cultural, historical, and economic processes responsible for health. Perhaps one of the most relevant approaches in public health is Nancy Krieger's (2001) ecosocial model that examines "how social influences become literally embodied into physio-anatomic characteristics that influence health and become expressed in societal disparities in health" (Krieger and Davey Smith 2004:92). Guided by the question "who and what drives current and changing patterns of social inequalities in health?" the ecosocial approach embraces a social production of disease perspective while aiming to bring in a comparably rich biological and ecological analysis (Krieger 2001). This approach integrates the political economic into the ecological and has four fundamental constructs: (1) embodiment; (2) pathways to embodiment; (3) cumulative interplay between exposure, susceptibility, and resistance; and (4) accountability and agency (Krieger 2001:672). Receiving the bulk of attention in the ecosocial model are the pathways to embodiment that are structured by arrangements of power, property, patterns of production, consumption, and reproduction, and human biology as it is shaped by evolution, ecology, and individual life histories (Krieger 2001; Yamada and Palmer 2007).

Krieger's ecosocial theory shares much in common with frameworks for studying inequalities and health in medical anthropology including political ecology of health (Baer et al. 2003), structural violence (Farmer 1999; Rylko-Bauer et al. 2009), critical biosocial and syndemics (Singer 2011; Singer et al. 2011), and critical biocultural medical (Leatherman and Goodman 2011) approaches. They differ somewhat in starting points and emphases, but all share a commitment to connecting history, political economy, biology, and human agency. They focus on macrosocial and historical factors that structure local-level environments and lived inequalities, shape biology and health, and constrained agency.

A critical biocultural approach reads health disparities along axes of vulnerabilities structured by macrosocial and political-economic processes and defined locally by exposure to disease or other health insult, inadequate coping resources or "constrained agency" (and thus greater impact of a health insult), and diminished resilience to recover from these impacts (Leatherman 2005; Leatherman and Goodman 2011; Singer 2011). As each of these dimensions converge in vulnerable groups, the very conditions that give rise to disparities are likely to persist and perpetuate a dialectical interaction of inequalities and health. In short, the goal is to link macro structures to local biologies in local contexts, utilizing ethnographic and biological field methods to expose and examine the grounded processes linking vulnerabilities and health. Attention is on how structural inequalities "get under the skin" to become embodied in biology and health. The embodiment of inequalities has been especially important in better understanding "how race becomes biology" (Gravlee 2009) and the generation of racial health disparities (Kuzawa and Sweet 2009).

Stress has long been an integrative concept for examining how inequalities become embodied in biology and health in biocultural anthropology (Goodman et al. 1988). New field-based biomarkers have led to a growth in research linking neuroendocrine stress response to immunity (McDade 2005). It is now well recognized that stress in fetal development and early life can impact adult health, and emerging epigenetic research provides insights into how biological response to environmental stressors in one generation can influence health outcomes in the next (Kramer and Hogue 2009; Kuzawa and Sweet 2009; Matthews and Phillips 2010; see Hoke and McDade in this issue). This work opens avenues to linking evolution and developmental plasticity to macrosocial forces that generate inequalities and stress, to constrained agency and the intergenerational transmission of responses to stress.

Much of the contemporary research on health disparities is seeking to better understand how certain populations are more vulnerable to poor health than others. For example, researchers are looking at the influence of the built environment on health disparities, including residential segregation (e.g., Acevedo-Garcia et al. 2003; Kramer and Hogue 2009), environmental pollution (Schell and Czerwinski 1998), food access and availability (e.g., Gordon-Larsen et al. 2006; Lovasi et al. 2009; Papas et al. 2007), and rurality (e.g., Hartley 2004; Phillips and McLeroy 2004; Wexler et al. 2014). However, even as health disparities emerge as the products of specific social, political, and economic structures, David Jones (2009) reminds us that they, too, enable actions that reproduce those structures. Thus, the links between inequalities and health disparities are bidirectional (see the contribution by Leatherman and Jernigan in this issue), and the connections are global, not just local and national. Indeed, what is at stake for and of interest to local communities sits within the context of national and international political and economic forces and determines how health disparities are explained and responded to (Jones 2009; Leatherman and Goodman 2011; Singer 2011).

BIOCULTURAL APPROACHES TO HEALTH DISPARITIES

It is now well accepted that social inequalities underlie health disparities in a variety of contexts. It is also clear that inequalities are growing in contexts of globalization and present a major challenge to public health (Farmer 1999; Feachem 2000; Kim et al. 2000; Sen 1992; Wilkinson 1996). Biocultural anthropology has much to offer studies of health disparities by employing critical biocultural approaches and rigorous field methods to link inequalities and health in global-local contexts. Most studies of health disparities measure inequalities through country comparisons, or broad in-country comparisons, using macrolevel economic measures (e.g., GINI coefficient of inequality) or health measures (e.g., life expectancy; mortality rate; DALYs). The focus usually does not reach down to subregions or social groups within a country, much less to more fine-grained pictures of how poverty, inequalities, and poor health affect people in local contexts. Biocultural field studies can do precisely what regional analyses and aggregate statistics cannot: demonstrate what these broad measures of inequality mean for real people living in conditions of vulnerability at the local level.

Biocultural anthropologists have contributed to research on inequalities and health through grounded research on the dialectical interactions among social inequalities, livelihoods, food security, nutrition, and illness. The contributions to this volume reflect a range of biocultural approaches that have emerged over the past two decades that aim to expose and illuminate the ways large-scale political-economic processes "get under the skin" and are hence both relevant and productive in addressing health disparities. It is obviously not the full range but they represent some of the important theoretical and methodological perspectives and present case studies in key areas of nutrition and health in global contexts.

The role of poverty and inequality in shaping health disparities operates across time and space—and differently in diverse national contexts. To assess variation in inequalities and health disparities, it is important to explain not just the persistence of vulnerabilities, poverty, and poor health but how lived experience is embodied in biology and health and how these local biologies and social inequalities are transmitted across the life course and generations. Hoke and McDade bring together perspectives from human plasticity and critical biocultural anthropology, developmental origins of health and disease, and research examining the long-term effects of early environments on social capital to formulate the notion of *biosocial inheritance*. Biosocial inheritance is the process whereby social adversity in one generation is transmitted to the next through reinforcing biological and social mechanisms that impair health and exacerbate social and health disparities. Their framework considers contemporary and historic political-economic forces that shape inequalities in human health, and across generations. It brings life history and evolutionary principles to the forefront and builds off recent work in epigenetics and the Developmental Origins of Health and Disease (DOHaD) that have emerged as important perspectives on health disparities in public health as well as biocultural anthropology. Using this framework, they examine the biosocial determinants of growth in the Andes, developing a model that seeks to illuminate more broadly the contemporary and historic sources of persistent poverty in the Andes and other low-income communities around the world. A central feature of the model is to illustrate how inequalities are embedded in biology and can be transmitted across life course and importantly across generations.

Absolute levels of wealth and poverty, access to basic needs, and ability to access medical care are recognized as key features shaping health disparities in many impoverished regions of the global south. Yet, relative deprivation and wealth inequalities are also important, and may be much more important in the less-impoverished regions around the world (Marmot and Wilkinson 2006). In part, this is because relative inequalities are reflected in social alienation and isolation, lack of trust and sense of belonging—and this makes life stressful and compromises health. Dressler and colleagues contribute a theoretical and methodological approach for dealing with relative inequalities and deprivation. They argue that what is meant by relative deprivation is "the inability of individuals to achieve the kind of lifestyle that is valued and considered normative in their social context." They make a compelling case using data collected over decades of research in urban Brazil that the concept and measurement of cultural consonance can be used to operationalize the notion of relative deprivation. Cultural consonance is the degree to which individuals approximate, in their own beliefs and behaviors, the prototypes for belief and behavior encoded in shared cultural models. Thus, lack of consonance reflects a loss of coherence in life and is associated with chronic stress and psychobiological distress that underlies health effects. This model provides a way for biocultural researchers to get at health disparities in general but moreover to specify and measure coherence in specific lifestyle contexts linked to different social, cultural, and economic contexts.

Absolute deprivation, nevertheless, remains important for many of the world's most vulnerable populations, as reflected in stark statistics on poverty, hunger, malnutrition, and disease. The Food and Agricultural Organization (FAO) estimated in 2002 that 840 million people in the world are undernourished and six million children under the age of five die each year from hunger (FAO 2002). Thus, an important focus in critical biocultural studies has been to explore links between economic vulnerability, food insecurity, diet, and nutrition. Ruiz and Himmelgreen focus on food systems and shifting patterns of food insecurity in the Monteverde Zone of Coast Rica, a farming zone going through rapid social and economic transition related to tourism. Hence, their work addresses another theme of much biocultural work in health disparities—populations in transition. Through a mixed methods approach and analysis, they demonstrate the statistical and ethnographic salience of two factors associated with food insecurity: levels of illness symptoms and food purchasing patterns—the more symptoms and more frequent purchases (related to limited or less-secure incomes), the greater the food insecurity. As they note, these findings conform to patterns seen in many different locations across the world where people with uncertain or limited access to essential resources are forced to cope with immediate stressors that reproduce the broader patterns of vulnerability in the long term. Exposure to food insecurity stressors—whether anxiety and worry or reductions in the quality and quantity of food consumed—seems to result in greater frequency of illness episodes.

The paper by Weaver, Meek, and Hadley focuses more directly on the psychosocial aspects of food insecurity, making the argument that if food is imbued with social and cultural meaning (as it clearly is), then food insecurity should be intimately connected to disruptions in these meanings and values and be related to social, mental, and physical effects on well-being. Indeed, among a Brazilian population, they demonstrate the relationships among food insecurity and poor physical (reduced arm fat) and mental health (higher depression scores) outcomes. But the specific reasons for mental health effects, which they posited would be related more strongly to the prestige value of foods eaten, were neither clearly evident nor easy to untangle. This leads to interesting observations for future and ongoing research in food security on the methods by which we conceive of and measure prestige and on the social importance not just of foods but related food behaviors such as patterns of eating, food sharing, and meeting other social obligations through food.

Another aspect of food systems and nutrition, and increasingly understood to be a different form of food insecurity, is the nutrition transition and globalization of overweight and obesity, the starting point of the paper by Brewis and Wutich. As they remind us, "Two thirds of all people live in countries where overnutrition kills more people than undernutrition." This globalizing trend is increasingly associated with structural inequalities and social vulnerabilities, and the spread of obesity among poor populations in the United States and less economically developed nations. A second, less well-known facet of the globalization of obesity, is the degree to which fat stigmas have been exported along with unhealthy nutrition. Recent research has demonstrated the proliferation of fat stigma across the globe, but little is known about the ways it impacts local populations or why some populations more than others. Brewis and Wutich employ a series of psychometric scales in groups of women from Paraguay, Bolivia, India, and among students and Muslim women in the United States that demonstrate high levels of fat stigma among all these women and local cultural contexts. Yet, measures of implicit stigma indicate that fat-stigma norms are not always internalized and suggest emotional vulnerabilities around being labeled medically or socially as "fat" may be very locale specific. Given that current approaches to obesity are more behaviorally based (and fat blaming) than structurally based, understanding the effects of and variation in stigmas around heavy bodies is important to create a better model of health care.

Biology and health are embodied in the lived experience of unequal life chances that shape so many lives and livelihoods in contexts of structural violence. A consistent theme within critical biocultural medical anthropology has been to explore the links among structural vulnerabilities, lived experience, and the uneven exposure to illness and its impacts, and the dialectical nature of these connections. The final two papers reflect this theme in different ways and contexts. Leatherman and Jernigan provide a case study set in the Andes of southern Peru that demonstrates the dialectical nature of the reproduction of poverty and poor health for rural populations whose lives are shaped by a series of local-level vulnerabilities located within a broader history of exploitation, oppression, and structural inequalities. They frame their presentation using models drawn from meta-analyses of health studies in Asia and Africa to illustrate how findings from multiple contexts resonate across a number of themes linking poverty and health, and specifically the social and economic costs of illness. It is clear that in these Andean populations, poverty and inequalities underlie poor nutrition and health, and that poor health is an important force in shaping lives, livelihoods, and household economies—the very conditions that underlie poor health. But how this works out on the ground is variable and complexly shaped by the different sorts of specific inequities people experience, and ethnography is needed for elucidating this variation. The goal is to demonstrate how a critical biocultural approach rooted in local ethnographic contexts can help explain why some people in a generally vulnerable population show greater and lesser degrees of vulnerability, resistance, and resilience.

The paper by Mendenhall explores these dialectical interactions in vulnerable populations in low- and high-income countries, where problems such as obesity, diabetes, and other related chronic conditions (cancer, heart disease, hypertension) occur in clusters and interact in a negative synergy, what Merrill Singer (2001) has termed "syndemics." Syndemics cluster in economically and socially vulnerable populations, and vulnerable groups not only suffer greater exposure to biological and social insults, but have fewer options with which to cope and often suffer greater impacts. Mendenhall's paper focuses on a violence, depression, diabetes syndemic (VIDDA) among women in South Africa, highlighting especially the role that structural violence and interpersonal violence plays in perpetuating and exacerbating this cluster of maladies. Living with these forms of violence limits access to healthy foods, creates psychobiological distress, and exacerbates diabetes and depression in these women's lives. Since the synergies among depression, diabetes, and violence move in all directions, it is critical to not simply recognize their co-occurrence but to try to map the social and biological paths of interaction. Through her grounded ethnography, Mendenhall illustrates how the multiple forms of violence do not emerge just as background context, but are co-constituted catalysts of both diabetes and depression.

Together these papers further the contributions of biocultural and critical biocultural approaches to health disparities. Theoretically, they draw insights from evolutionary, human plasticity, political economic, cognitive, psychological, and psychosocial approaches. Methodologically they employ mixed methods approaches while grounding much of their work in local ethnographic contexts. They confirm that biocultural approaches to health in anthropology do have much to offer in ongoing efforts to better understand and combat health disparities by exposing the myriad links between inequalities and illness and the complex ways inequalities are embodied in human biology and health.

REFERENCES CITED

Acevedo-Garcia, Dolores, Kimberly A. Lochner, Theresa L. Osypuk, and Sukanya V. Subramanian
    2003 Future Directions in Residential Segregation and Health Research: A Multilevel Approach. American Journal of Public Health 93(2):215–221.
Allacci, MaryAnn Sorensen, and Chung Chang
    2009 New Levels of Understanding: Methods for Revealing Structural Links to Chronic Disease. Critical Public Health 19(2):235–248.
Amick, Benjamin C., Sol Levine, Alvin R. Tarlov, and Diana Chapman Walsh
    1995 Introduction. *In* Society and Health. Benjamin C. Amick III, Sol Levine, Alvin R. Tarlov, and Diana Chapman Walsh, eds. Pp. 3–17. New York: Oxford University Press.
Baer, Hans A., Merrill Singer, and Ida Susser
    2003 *Medical anthropology and the world system.* Westport, CT: Praeger.
Beckfield, Jason, and Nancy Krieger
    2009 Epi+ Demos+ Cracy: Linking Political Systems and Priorities to the Magnitude of Health Inequities—Evidence, Gaps, and a Research Agenda. Epidemiologic Reviews 31(1):152–177.
Bierman, Arlene S., and James R. Dunn
    2006 Swimming Upstream: Access, Health Outcomes, and the Social Determinants of Health. Journal of General Internal Medicine 21(1):99–100.

Bowleg, Lisa
  2012 The Problem with the Phrase Women and Minorities: Intersectionality—An Important Theoretical
        Framework for Public Health. American Journal of Public Health 102(7):1267–1273.
Braveman, Paula
  2006 Health Disparities and Health Equity: Concepts and Measurement. Annual Review of Public Health
        27:167–194.
Brennan, Troyen A., Lucian L. Leape, Nan M. Laird, Liesi Hebert, A. Russell Localio, Ann G. Lawthers,
        Joseph P. Newhouse, Paul C. Weiler, and Howard H. Hiatt
  2004 Incidence of Adverse Events and Negligence in Hospitalized Patients: Results of the Harvard Medical
        Practice Study I. Quality and Safety in Health Care 13(2):145–151.
Carter-Pokras, Olivia, and Claudia Baquet
  2002 What Is a "Health Disparity"? Public Health Reports 117(5):426–434.
Centers for Disease Control (CDC)
  2013 Racial and Ethnic Approaches to Community Health. CDC REACH 2013. http://www.cdc.gov/
        nccdphp/dch/programs/reach/, accessed October 25, 2014.
Chadwick, Edwin
  2008 [1842] Report on the Sanitary Condition of the Laboring Population of Great Britain and On the
        Means of Improvement. In Public Health: The Development of a Discipline, Volume 1: from the Age
        of Hippocrates to the Progressive Era. Donna Schneider and David E. Lilienfeld, eds. Pp. 173–185.
        New Brunswick: Rutgers University Press.
Chowkwanyun, Merlin
  2011 The Strange Disappearance of History from Racial Health Disparities Research. Du Bois Review:
        Social Science Research on Race 8(1):253–270.
Coleman, James S.
  1988 Social Capital in the Creation of Human Capital. The American Journal of Sociology 94S: S95–S120.
Dressler, William W.
  2009 Explaining Health Inequalities. In Health, Risk, and Adversity, Volume 2 of Studies of the Biosocial
        Society. Catherine Panter-Brick and Agustín Fuentes, eds. Pp. 175–184. New York: Berghahn Books.
Dressler, William W., Kathryn S. Oths, and Clarence C. Gravlee
  2005 Race and Ethnicity in Public Health Research: Models to Explain Health Disparities. Annual Review
        of Anthropology 34: 231–252.
Dubos, Jean
  1987 Tuberculosis, Man, and Society: The White Plague. New Brunswick: Rutgers University Press.
Engels, Friedrich
  1958 [1845] The Condition of the Working Class in England. New York: Macmillan.
Farmer, Paul
  1999 Infections and Inequalities: the Modern Plagues. Berkeley: University of California Press. 2004 An
        Anthropology of Structural Violence. Current Anthropology 45(3):305–325.
Feachem, Richard G. A.
  2000 Poverty and Inequity: A Proper Focus for the New Century. Bulletin of the World Health Organiza-
        tion 78(1):1–2.
Food and Agricultural Organization of the United Nations (FAO)
  2002 State of Food Insecurity in the World. Rome: Food and Agriculture Organization of the United
        Nations.
Gee, Gilbert C., and Chandra L. Ford
  2011 Structural Racism and Health Inequities. Du Bois Review: Social Science Research on Race 8(1):115–
        132.
Geronimus, Arline T.
  2000 To Mitigate, Resist, or Undo: Addressing Structural Influences on the Health of Urban Populations.
        American Journal of Public Health 90(6):867–872.

Geronimus, Arline T., and John Bound
  1990 Black/White Differences in Women's Reproductive-Related Health Status: Evidence from Vital Statistics. Demography 27(3):457–466.
Geronimus, Arline T., and J. Phillip Thompson
  2004 To Denigrate, Ignore, or Disrupt: Racial Inequality in Health and the Impact of a Policy-Induced Breakdown of African American Communities. Du Bois Review 1(2):247–279.
Gibbons, Michael C.
  2005 A Historical Overview of Health Disparities and the Potential of eHealth Solutions. Journal of Medical Internet Research 7(5):e50.
Goodman, Alan, Brooke Thomas, Alan Swedlund and George Armelagos
  1988 Biocultural Perspectives on Stress in Prehistoric, Historic and Contemporary Population Research. Yearbook of Physical Anthropology 31:169–202.
Gordon-Larsen, Penny, Melissa C. Nelson, Phil Page, and Barry M. Popkin
  2006 Inequality in the Built Environment Underlies Key Health Disparities in Physical Activity and Obesity. Pediatrics 117(2):417–424.
Gravlee, Clarence
  2009 How Race Becomes Biology: Embodiment of Social Inequality. American Journal of Physical Anthropology 139(1): 47–57.
Green, Judith, and Ronald Labonté
  2008 Critical Perspectives in Public Health. New York: Routledge.
Hartley, David
  2004 Rural Health Disparities, Population Health, and Rural Culture. American Journal of Public Health 94(10):1675–1678.
Hippocrates
  2008 [c. 400 BCE] On Airs, Waters, and Places. In Public Health: The Development of a Discipline, Volume 1: From the Age of Hippocrates to the Progressive Era. Donna Schneider and David E. Lilienfeld, eds. Pp. 7–24. New Brunswick: Rutgers University Press.
James, Sherman A.
  2009 Epidemiologic Research on Health Disparities: Some Thoughts on History and Current Developments. Epidemiologic Review 31:1–6.
James, Sherman A., Nora L. Keenan, David S. Strogatz, Steven R. Browning, and Joanne M. Garrett
  1992 Socioeconomic Status, John Henryism, and Blood Pressure in Black Adults: The Pitt County Study. American Journal of Epidemiology 135(1):59–67.
James, Sherman A., David S. Strogatz, Steven B. Wing, and Diane L. Ramsey
  1987 Socioeconomic Status, John Henryism, and Hypertension in Blacks and Whites. American Journal of Epidemiology 126(4):664–673.
Jones, David S.
  2009 Rationalizing Epidemics; Meanings and Uses of American Indian Mortality Since 1600. Cambridge: Harvard University Press.
Kawachi, Ichiro, and Bruce P. Kennedy
  1999 Income Inequality and Health: Pathways and Mechanisms. Health Services Research 34(1):215–227.
Kim, Jim Yong, Joyce Millen, Alec Irwin, and John Gersham
  2000 Dying for Growth: Global Inequality and the Health of the Poor. Monroe, ME: Common Courage Press.
Kramer, Michael R., and Carol R. Hogue
  2009 Is Segregation Bad for Your Health? Epidemiologic Reviews 31(1):178–194.
Krieger, Nancy
  1990 Racial and Gender Discrimination: Risk Factors for High Blood Pressure? Social Science & Medicine 30(12):1273–1281.
  1994 Epidemiology and the Web of Causation: Has Anyone Seen the Spider? Social Science & Medicine 39(7):887–903.

2000 Discrimination and Health. *In* Social Epidemiology. Lisa Berkman and Ichiro Kawachi, eds. Pp. 36–75. New York: Oxford University Press.

2001 Theories for Social Epidemiology in the 21st Century: An Ecosocial Perspective. International Journal of Epidemiology 30(4):668–677.

Krieger, Nancy, Diane L. Rowley, Allen A. Herman, Byllye Avery, and Mona T. Phillips
1993 Racism, Sexism, and Social Class: Implications for Studies of Health, Disease, and Well-Being. American Journal of Preventive Medicine 9(Supplement 6):82–122.

Krieger, Nancy, and George Davey Smith
2004 Bodies Count, and Body Counts: Social Epidemiology and Embodying Inequality. Epidemiologic Reviews 26(1):92–103.

Kuzawa, Christopher W., and Elizabeth Sweet
2009 Epigenetics and the Embodiment of Race: Developmental Origins of US Racial Disparities in Cardiovascular Health. American Journal of Human Biology 21(1):2–15.

LaBonté, Ronald, Michael Polanyi, Nazeem Muhajarine, Tom Mcintosh, and Allison Williams
2005 Beyond the Divides: Towards a Critical Population Health Research. Critical Public Health 15(1):5–17.

LaVeist, Thomas A.
1992 The Political Empowerment and Health Status of African Americans: Mapping a New Territory. American Journal of Sociology 97(4):1080–1095.

1993 Segregation, Poverty, and Empowerment: Health Consequences for African Americans. Milbank Memorial Quarterly 71(1):41–64.

Leatherman, Thomas L.
2005 A Space of Vulnerability in Poverty and Health: Political Ecology and Biocultural Analysis. Ethos 33(1):46–70.

Leatherman, Thomas L., and Alan H. Goodman
2011 Critical Biocultural Approaches in Medical Anthropology. *In* A Companion to Medical Anthropology. Merrill Singer and Pamela I. Erickson, eds. Pp. 29–47. Malden, MA: Wiley Blackwell.

Lovasi, Gina S., Malo A. Hutson, Monica Guerra, and Kathryn M. Neckerman
2009 Built Environments and Obesity in Disadvantaged Populations. Epidemiologic Reviews 31(1):7–20.

Macintyre, Sally
1997 The Black Report and Beyond: What Are the Issues? Social Science & Medicine 44(6):723–745.

Marmot, Michael G.
1986 Social Inequalities in Mortality: The Social Environment. *In* Class and Health: Research and Longitudinal Data. Richard G. Wilkinson, ed. Pp. 21–33. London: Tavistock.

2005 Social Determinants of Health Inequalities. The Lancet 365(9464):1099–1104.

Marmot, Michael G., and Richard G. Wilkinson
2006 Social Determinants of Health. Oxford: Oxford University Press.

Marmot, Michael G., Geoffrey Rose, Martin Shipley, and Peter J. Hamilton
1978 Employment Grade and Coronary Heart Disease in British Civil Servants. Journal of Epidemiology and Community Health 32(4):244–249.

Matthews, Stephen G., and David I. W. Phillips
2010 Minireview: Transgenerational Inheritance of the Stress Response: A New Frontier in Stress Research. Endocrinology 151(1):7–13.

Mayberry, Robert M., Fatima Mili, and Elizabeth Ofili
2000 Racial and Ethnic Differences in Access to Medical Care. Medical Care Research and Review 57(Supplement 4):108–145.

McDade, Thomas W.
2005 The Ecologies of Human Immune Function. Annual Review of Anthropology 34:495–521.

Navarro, Vicente, and Carles Muntaner
2004 Political and Economic Determinants of Population Health and Well-Being: Controversies and Developments. Amityville: Baywood Publishing Company, Inc.

National Center for Health Statistics (NCHS)

1983 Health, United States, 1983, DHHS Pub. No. (PHS) 84-1232. Public Health Service. Washington. U. S. Government Printing Office. http://www.cdc.gov/nchs/data/hus/hus83acc.pdf, accessed June 11, 2014.

Papas, Mia A., Anthony J. Alberg, Reid Ewing, Kathy J. Helzlsour, Tiffany L. Gary, and Ann C. Klassen

2007 The Built Environment and Obesity. Epidemiological Review 29(1):129–143.

Phillips, Charles D., and Kenneth R. McLeroy

2004 Health in Rural America: Remembering the Importance of Place. American Journal of Public Health 94(10):1661–1663.

Quesada, James, Laurie Kain Hart, and Philippe Bourgois

2011 Structural Vulnerability and Health: Latino Migrant Laborers in the United States. Medical Anthropology 30(4):339–362.

Rhodes, Tim, and Milena Simic

2005 Transition and the HIV Risk Environment. British Medical Journal 331(7510):220-223.

Rylko-Bauer, Barbara, Linda Whiteford, and Paul Farmer, eds.

2009 Prologue: Coming to terms with global violence and health, In Gobal Health in Times of Violence (School for Advanced Research Advanced Seminar Series). Pp. 3-16. Santa Fe: SAR Press.

Sapolsky, Robert M.

2004 Social Status and Health in Humans and Other Animals. Annual Review of Anthropology 33:393–418.

Scheder, Jo C.

2006 The Spirit's Cell: Reflections on Diabetes and Political Meaning. In Indigenous Peoples and Diabetes. Mariana Leal Ferreira and Gretchen Chesley Lang, eds. Pp. 335–355. Durham: Carolina Press.

Schell, Lawrence, and Stefan Czerwinski

1998 Environmental Health, Social Inequality and Biological Differences. In Human Biology of Social Inequality. Simon S. Strickland and Prakash P. Shetty, eds. Pp. 114–131. Cambridge: Cambridge University Press.

Sen, Amartya

1992 Inequality Re-examined. Cambridge, MA: Harvard University Press.

Shattuck, Lemuel

2008 [1850] Report of the Sanitary Commission of Massachusetts 1850. In Public Health: The Development of a Discipline Vol 1: From the Age of Hippocrates to the Progressive Era. Donna Schneider and David E. Lilienfeld, eds. Pp. 209–280. New Brunswick: Rutgers University Press.

Singer, Merrill

2001 Toward a Bio-Cultural and Political Economic Integration of Alcohol, Tobacco and Drug Studies in the Coming Century. Social Science and Medicine 53(2):199–213.

2011 Toward a Critical Biosocial Model of Ecohealth in Southern Africa: The HIV/AIDS and Nutrition Insecurity Syndemic. Annals of Anthropological Practice 35(1):8–27.

Singer, Merrill, Ann Herring, Judith Littleton, and Melanie Rock.

2011 Syndemics in Public Health. In A Companion to Medical Anthropology. Merrill Singer and Pamela Erickson, eds. Pp. 159–180. San Francisco: Wiley Press.

Singh-Manoux, Archana, Michael G. Marmot, and Nancy E. Adler

2005 Does Subjective Social Status Predict Health and Change in Health Status Better Than Objective Status? Psychosomatic Medicine 67(6):855–861.

Smedley, Brian D., Adrienne Y. Stith, and Alan R. Nelson

2003 Unequal Treatment: Confronting Racial and Ethnic Differences in Health Care. Washington, D.C.: National Academy Press.

Snow, John

2008 [1854] On the Mode of Communication of Cholera. In Public Health: The Development of a Discipline Vol 1: From the Age of Hippocrates to the Progressive Era. Donna Schneider and David E. Lilienfeld, eds. Pp. 286–370. New Brunswick: Rutgers University Press.

Sydenstricker, Edgar

1933 Health and Environment. New York: McGraw-Hill Press.

Tager, Ira B., Scott T. Weiss, Alvaro Muñoz, Bernard Rosner, and Frank E. Speizer

1983 Longitudinal Study of the Effects of Maternal Smoking on Pulmonary Function in Children. New England Journal of Medicine 309(12):699–703.

Virchow, Rudolf

1988 Report on the Typhus Epidemic in Upper Silesia. *In* Rudolf Virchow: Collected Essays on Public Health and Epidemiology, Vol. 1. Lelland J. Rather, ed. Pp. 205–220. Canton, MA: Science History Publications.

Wexler, Lisa, Kasey Jernigan, Janet Mazzotti, Elizabeth Baldwin, Megan Griffin, Linda Joule, and Joe Garoutte

2014 Lived Challenges and Getting Through Them: Alaska Native Youth Narratives as a Way to Understand Resilience. Health Promotion Practice 15(1):10–17.

Wilkinson, Richard G.

1992 Income Distribution and Life Expectancy. British Medical Journal 304(6820):165–168.

1996 Unhealthy Societies: The Afflictions of Inequalities. New York: Routledge.

Williams, David R.

1999 Race, Socioeconomic Status, and Health: The Added Effects of Racism and Discrimination. Annals of the New York Academy of Sciences 896:173–188.

Williams, David R., and Chiquita Collins

1995 US Socioeconomic and Racial Differences in Health: Patterns and Explanations. Annual Review of Sociology 21:349–386.

Williams, David R., Yan Yu, James S. Jackson, and Norman B. Anderson

1997 Racial Differences in Physical and Mental Health: Socio-economic Status, Stress and Discrimination. Journal of Health Psychology 2(3):335–351.

Wilson, Samuel H., Lovell Jones, Christine Couseens, and Kathi Hanna

2002 Cancer and the Environment: Gene-Environment Interaction. Washington, D.C.: National Academy Press.

World Health Organization (WHO)

2008 Closing the Gap in a Generation: Health Equity Through Action on the Social Determinants of Health. Commission on Social Determinants of Health Final Report. Geneva: World Health Organization.

Yamada, Seiji, and Wesley Palmer

2007 An Ecosocial Approach to the Epidemic of Cholera in the Marshall Islands. Social Medicine 2(2):79–88.

BIOSOCIAL INHERITANCE: A FRAMEWORK FOR THE STUDY OF THE INTERGENERATIONAL TRANSMISSION OF HEALTH DISPARITIES

Morgan K. Hoke
Northwestern University

Thomas McDade
Northwestern University

Proponents of global market expansion claim that economic growth brings prosperity and creates a more equitable global society, yet these efforts may result in the exacerbation of economic disparities that translates into significant disparities in health. These trends underscore the importance of research examining the social determinants of health in an increasingly unequal world. This article brings together concepts from biocultural anthropology, developmental origins of health and disease, and research examining the long-term effects of early environments on social capital to formulate the notion of biosocial inheritance. Biosocial inheritance is the process whereby social adversity in one generation is transmitted to the next through reinforcing biological and social mechanisms that impair health, exacerbating social and health disparities. Such a theoretical framework considers contemporary and historic political-economic forces that shape inequalities in human health, across generations. We examine the biosocial determinants of growth in the Andes as a case study of biosocial inheritance, developing a model that will illuminate the contemporary and historic sources of persistent poverty in low-income communities around the world. By highlighting the biosocial mechanisms underpinning the intergenerational transmission of poverty, this model allows for the formulation of interventions aimed at breaking the cycle of poverty and a reconsideration of the way we think about poverty and social mobility. [inequality, health disparities, intergenerational, biosocial inheritance, biocultural anthropology]

Advances in science, technology, and public health have led to a shift in global life expectancy from an average of 30 to 67 years between 1800 and 2000 (Riley 2001). Countries such as Japan and Switzerland now boast life expectancies of up to 82 years (Gapminder 2008). However, significant inequalities remain between nations, with life expectancies of just 45 and 47 years in Sierra Leone and Botswana respectively (Gapminder 2008). Further, beyond the obvious macrolevel disparities, rapidly growing inequities in health due to social and economic inequalities also exist "within" countries. While we have taken great steps forward in health and health technologies, access to these benefits has not been disseminated equally, and in many places, unequal access contributes to

ANNALS OF ANTHROPOLOGICAL PRACTICE 38.2, pp. 187–213. ISSN: 2153-957X. © 2015 by the American Anthropological Association. DOI:10.1111/napa.12052

TABLE 1. Generational Effect Definitions

Cross-generational: Refers to characteristics in one generation that affect outcomes in the next generation. The effects themselves may not be shared across generations. Example: The nonepigenetic effects incurred through the prenatal environment can largely be considered intergenerational. A mother's consumption of mercury-laden fish can lead to a higher mercury concentration in the developing fetus and thus reduce cognitive function. This process is the result of intergenerational effects, an act in one generation that significantly affects another. The exposure may have distinct effects on the two generations involved. In the case of mercury exposure, there may be little consequence for the mother but significant effects on the fetus.

Multigenerational: Refers to direct exposures that result in significant effects on more than two generations, simultaneously. Example: A gestating woman is exposed to an endocrine disruptor that affects herself, her gestating female fetus, and the germ line of the third generation whose primordial germ cells are present after two weeks of gestation. All three generations experience altered outcomes as a consequence of direct exposure to the endocrine disruptor.

Transgenerational: Refers to effects that are transmitted through the germ line or other mechanisms leading to affects in multiple generations without direct exposure and thereby may affect more than three generations. Example: Kuzawa's proposed model of "phenotypic inertia" (2005) wherein the metabolic phenotype of a given individual is understood as the product of a long-term, integrated signal of the nutritional environment over multiple matrilineal generations. Epigenetic changes made in one generation are passed onto the next without the subsequent generation experiencing the precipitating conditions directly, as would be the case in the fourth generation (no direct exposure, only epigenetic transmission) of the above scenario with exposure to an endocrine disruptor (Skinner 2008).

---

growing health disparities across different segments of the population (Olshansky et al. 2012).

The persistence of poverty in the face of market expansion and improving conditions around the world has led scholars to examine the pathways through which inequality perpetuates itself across generations (e.g., Harper et al. 2003). However, only recently has this cross-, multi-, or transgenerational work been extended to the examination of health disparities. With the proliferation of this work has come debate over the meanings of terms such as inter-, cross-, multi-, and transgenerational. In order to avoid confusion throughout this article, we utilize these terms in accordance with the definitions found in Table 1.

Research on population health emphasizes the role of early-life environments in shaping trajectories of health, thereby leading to a proliferation of work linking early-life experiences with later-life outcomes. While some of this work emerged out of research on health inequalities (Blane et al. 2007), it has yet to fully engage with research and methods from other disciplines (Richter and Blane 2013). Such engagement may allow for a better understanding of the ways in which macrosocial and political-economic forces structure the formation and perpetuation of disparities through early-life environments. Additionally, such a perspective has rarely been applied in the realm of global health, where it may be particularly useful in understanding and intervening in the cycle of poverty.

We argue in this article that it is necessary to conceptualize early-life environments as the product of intergenerational processes and contemporary political-economic contexts. Adult health is shaped by early life, which is in turn a product of early environments influenced by ongoing political and economic and intergenerational processes. By explicitly understanding early-life environments—and their role in shaping adult health—as the result of intergenerational or transgenerational forces, scholars can better situate contemporary patterns of health and disease in their political-economic and historic contexts and therefore intercede more effectively.

The purpose of this article is to put forth a coherent framework for examining the cross-, multi-, or transgenerational processes that lead to social disparities in health. We begin with a brief review of the relevant literature related to health disparities and transgenerational effects in the fields of biocultural anthropology, life-course epidemiology, and research examining the long-term effects of early environments and health on social capital. Next, we present the concept of biosocial inheritance, a framework that integrates the study of contemporary and past political-economic forces shaping inequalities in health with insights from the study of early life and transgenerational influences on health and disease across the life course. The biological mechanisms through which biosocial inheritance can occur will be described along with a brief discussion of their incorporation into anthropological practice. To demonstrate the utility of this concept, we present a case study in which the notion of biosocial inheritance is utilized to examine the influences of height among the high-altitude population of Nuñoa, Peru. Finally, a discussion of the implications of this framework and directions for future research will be presented.

BACKGROUND

Biocultural Anthropology and Health

The biocultural perspective in anthropology is one that acknowledges the myriad ways in which culture and biology are inextricably united in "a continuous feedback relationship of ongoing exchange" (Lock 1998:410). The holistic perspective of biocultural inquiry allows anthropologists to examine a diverse array of topics across time with human health often serving as a primary interest. It incorporates both evolutionary and social perspectives, with biological and social variables serving as cause and effect (Wiley 1992).

Since the late 1990s, the "new" biocultural synthesis has sought to foreground political-economic issues in the study of human biology. These scholars employed political-economic analysis in the study of "local biologies" (Lock and Kaufert 2001), thereby tying them to larger global and historical contexts (Goodman and Leatherman 1998a). In particular, these scholars called for a shift in the focus of biocultural anthropology and notions of health from evolutionary theory and adaptability to the inclusion of political economic analysis in the study of human biology both past and present. This increased consideration of historicized power and its dynamics (Roseberry 1998; Wolf 1982) allows for a more nuanced understanding of both social and cultural variables in biocultural analyses of human health. Prior to these changes, the exclusion of political-economic contexts led to discussions of human variation that relied too heavily on adaptationist explanations and that now appear somewhat simplistic.

Anthropologists utilizing a biocultural approach can be found in every subset of anthropological research from medical anthropology to DOHaD (developmental origins of health and disease). Because biocultural anthropology is still evolving, there are perspectives and lines of inquiry that it has yet to fully incorporate. For instance, while there has been a call for the production of biological ethnography (Wiley 2004) or the incorporation of more qualitative methods into the study of human biology, this new anthropological genre has yet to make its way into mainstream practice. As biocultural scholars, we continue to struggle to incorporate ethnographic insight and detail into our work. Other scholars argue that there has been a lack of attention to culture or that we operate with an unproblematized notion of culture (Dressler 2005). Finally, while biocultural work has long acknowledged the utility of a life-course perspective, there has been a lack of biocultural research examining the role of intergenerational and transgenerational forces on contemporary human variation and health. As we continue to address these gaps, increasingly incorporating methods and theory from cultural anthropology, perhaps we may gain greater understanding of these important processes.

Life-course Epidemiology and the DOHaD

Life-course epidemiology originated in the early 20th century with the early work of Kermack et al. (1934), and it expanded in the 1990s through three primary strands of research: the study of biological programming, birth cohort research, and health inequalities research (Blane et al. 2007; for additional reviews see also Ben-Shlomo and Kuh 2002; Gluckman and Hanson 2006; Kuh et al. 2003; Smith 2003). Key to the origin of life-course epidemiology is research examining biological programming or "the developmental origins of health and disease" (DOHaD, see Gluckman and Hanson 2006). Research from this field has suggested a significant role for early environments in the programming of outcomes ranging from hypothalamic–pituitary–adrenal (HPA) axis and immune function to behavior and temperament. While much of the work in this area is limited to animal research, revelations from the study of humans have yielded important insights regarding early metabolic programming and increased risk of cardiovascular disease later in life (Barker et al. 1992, 1993a, 2002). Such work has illuminated the importance of examining the process of human development in order to understand later-life outcomes, implying an important role for consideration of the principles of DOHaD in the study of health disparities.

Furthermore, DOHaD has dramatically shifted our understanding of the influence of genes, environment, and their interaction in phenotypic outcomes. Research on DOHaD has led to increased attention to and intervention during developmental periods on an international scale and includes nutritional and aid programs targeting gestating women and children under the age of five. However, the effectiveness of these interventions may be limited due to a lack of contextual depth within this research; it is rarely situated within the cultural, social, or political-economic context of the populations examined. Furthermore, the majority of work in the field of DOHaD relies heavily on experimental animal models, which reinforces the notion that political economy and other complicating factors can be ignored (for further consideration of the use of animal models see Williams et al. 2004). Finally, there is a lack of explicit intergenerational or transgenerational focus; rather the "prenatal environment" or the maternal environment is considered as if it emerged de novo. Rather than acknowledging the maternal body as the product of ongoing physiological, social, and political-economic processes, these influences on maternal physiology are often placed within an analytical black box and ignored.

Also crucial to the development of life-course epidemiology is the use of large birth-cohort studies, particularly the National Survey of Health and Development undertaken in Europe (Mann et al. 1992; Wadsworth 1991). In the 1990s, the members of this cohort were reaching the stage of life when chronic diseases begin to emerge allowing for the observation of correlations between early-life events and later-life outcomes. Such work was supported by findings from additional studies such as the Dutch famine study and others, which linked nutritional stress in utero with increased risk of cardiovascular disease later in life (Lumey 1992; Lumey et al. 2009; Roseboom et al. 2001, 2006). These findings have also led to proliferation of cohort studies, which although costly and time consuming continue to provide significant insight on the role of development and cumulative effects in health throughout the life course.

Finally, life-course epidemiology was largely influenced by research on health inequalities. A number of major studies have revealed the significant relationship between social class and socioeconomic status and health (Blane 1995; Goldblatt 1990; Marmot et al. 1984; Rose and Marmot 1981; Wilkinson 1996), some of which have explicitly considered their effect on health across the life course. Research in this area has revealed the social gradient in health whereby health improves incrementally, in step with increasing social and economic status (Adler et al. 1993). Research focusing on the social gradient has demonstrated an important role for objective and subjective, or perceived, status in determining health outcomes (Adler et al. 2000). While a life-course perspective may account for some intergenerational influences (Halfon and Hochstein 2002), explicit consideration of intergenerational variables is usually limited to some measure of in utero experience and possibly a consideration of parental anthropometrics. Furthermore, this research often lacks an explicit discussion of the cyclical nature of social inequalities and a framing that understands these inequalities as both trans- and intergenerational phenomena.

Relating Early Health and Environments to Socioeconomic Capital Later in Life

While research in the field of life-course epidemiology has demonstrated the relationship between early environments and health outcomes, research in the fields of economics, demography, and sociology has connected these early-life inputs with health and socioeconomic outcomes later in life. Like biocultural anthropology, much of this research considers the origins and perpetuation of poverty and inequality (Palloni 2006). This extensive body of work includes examinations of prenatal environments and experience (for review see Almond and Currie 2011 and Currie 2011) and early-childhood health and experience (for review see Elo and Preston 1992; Currie and Almond 2011). These bodies of work suggest that early health and experience have significant long-term effects on health and socioeconomic outcomes such as cognitive abilities, educational attainment, earnings, and employment (Almond et al. 2012). The relationship among prenatal/early nutrition, growth, and later socioeconomic outcomes is now well established and serves as an important example of this body of work (Behrman 1996; Martorell 1995, 1999; Martorell et al. 1995, Martorell et al. 2010a, 2010b).

Unlike research in life-course epidemiology and DOHaD that demonstrates a somewhat limited acknowledgement and engagement with intergenerational influences, scholarly work considering the effects of child health and early environments on social and economic capital has paid explicit attention to the reproduction of inequalities across generations (Currie and Moretti 2005; Palloni 2006) and the mechanisms through which it occurs. This body of work considers the effects of parental characteristics (Behrman and Wolfe 1987; Ermisch and Francesconi 2001), in utero exposures/prenatal health (Almond 2006; Figlio et al. 2013; Lin and Liu 2012; Neelson and Stratman 2010; Nelson 2010; Stein et al. 1975), and the multigenerational transmission of maternal health shocks or exposures experienced by the mother in early childhood (Almond and Chay 2006; Almond et al. 2011; Currie and Moretti 2005; Stewart et al. 1980) on health and socioeconomic outcomes. Research in this area has faced criticism for its limited ability to assign causality or directionality as well as a difficulty in measuring or operationalizing complicated variables such as child health status. While some scholars acknowledge these limitations (Almond et al. 2011; Palloni 2006), much of the work in this field continues to be riddled with hyperdeterministic and overly causal language and plagued by grainy measures of exposure. Furthermore, it is difficult to identify mechanisms in many of the large cohort studies utilized in this research. Still, this work makes an important contribution to our understanding of social mobility and the transmission of social status across generations. This contribution is made even stronger when synthesized with work from other disciplines.

BIOSOCIAL INHERITANCE: THE MODEL

We present the framework of biosocial inheritance, which is designed to facilitate the integration of political-economic analysis and sociohistorical variables into considerations of intergenerational health outcomes. We seek to unite work from the fields of biocultural anthropology and DOHaD with research on the long-term effects of early environments on socioeconomic attainment. It is only when these lines of inquiry meet that we gain a holistic and clearer understanding of issues of poverty, health disparities, and social mobility in this increasingly globalized world. Importantly, this approach highlights the intergenerational mechanisms, both social and biological, that lead to the transmission of socioeconomic status and health across generations. Further, these mechanisms are intimately connected such that deeming them either biological or social is highly misleading, thus we adopt the term biosocial.

Emerging research shows that these intergenerational forces have a major influence on an individual's health and social trajectory and, therefore cannot be ignored in contemporary considerations of population health and well-being. Specifically, our interest lies in examining the parental histories and political-economic contexts that create early offspring environments. These environments provide the basis for biological and social programming that affects and is in turn affected by socioeconomic status in adulthood, ultimately leading to disparate health outcomes and a potential reification of the cycle.

Above all else, this framework should help to ground biological work examining intergenerational and transgenerational influences on health within the larger sociocultural, historical, and political economic context of the population and people in question. We begin with a brief history of its individual components and a definition of biosocial inheritance. This is followed by a brief presentation of the framework and a discussion of the possible mechanisms through which biosocial inheritance may operate. We conclude a consideration of how biosocial inheritance extends previous biocultural research on health disparities.

On the Origin of Biosocial Inheritance

Before defining biosocial inheritance as a concept it is perhaps most useful to first consider the meaning of its component parts. In anthropology, the term biosocial has at times been a controversial one, in large part due to its semantic association with the field of sociobiology (Goodman and Leatherman 1998b). However, many scholars in anthropology have used the term successfully to describe phenomena that are not easily categorized as one or the other (Leonard and Thomas 1989; Panter-Brick 1998; Singer 2011; Thomas et al. 1988). Others have used the term to explicitly reference the inextricable nature of the social and the biological (Pike 2004; Pike and Williams 2006). In the 1990s, with the advent of the human genome project, Rabinow (1992, 1996) employed the term "biosociality" to describe the formation of new social relations around a biological condition; in the case of his work, a certain genotype or the possession of a certain gene. Within the framework of biosocial inheritance, we use the term biosocial as a way of dissolving the false dichotomy of the biological and social, acknowledging the mutually constitutive nature of these seemingly opposing categories, and recognizing the limits of our language and our past conceptualization of these issues.

The term biosocial also highlights our interest in the larger social, political, and economic structures that both facilitate and constrain contemporary human health. While culture plays an important role, the term biosocial reminds us to examine the larger structures of power at work in creating and maintaining health disparities, answering a call by political-economic scholars such as Wolf (1982) and Roseberry (1998). Furthermore, while cultural norms and traditions often play a significant role in population health, there is a tendency to culture blame, a form of victim blaming wherein a population's poor or poorer health status is blamed on either specific or general "cultural practices." Culture blaming is ineffective and counterproductive, as we have seen in the case of female genital cutting (Abusharaf 2006; Gruenbaum 2001; Shell-Duncan 2008). Additionally, culture blaming often overlooks the relations of power involved in the clash of cultures, particularly that occurs when the clash involves belief systems and actions based on the seemingly monolithic and impenetrable practice of science and empirics and those based in other world understandings. A similar problem is the conflation of inequality or poverty with culture or "otherness" and the discussion of "the culture of poverty"

(Farmer 2003). Such conflation can lead scholars and others to fail to acknowledge and engage with the dynamics of power that create and sustain inequality and poverty at local and global levels (Bourgois 2001). While biosocial inheritance lies squarely within the purview of biocultural anthropology, by employing the term biosocial rather than biocultural we hope to keep the aforementioned issues of power at the forefront of our analysis.

The second part of the term, inheritance, references the process through which traits, materials, and status are transferred from one generation to the next. The term inheritance can refer either to biological or genetic inheritance, such as a genetic disorder, a uterine environment, or phenotypic appearance (affected by both genetic and epigenetic influences). It can also refer to socioeconomic or material inheritance that one receives from parents, grandparents, or other relations such as wealth, land, or status that can affect life outcomes. Significantly, it also captures those cultural practices and norms that are shared across generations, as well as elements such as language, memory, and heritage that are passed on to help to make sense of the past. The term inheritance applied in this manner harkens back to Lamarck's (n.d.) theory of inheritance of acquired characteristics, which has received some renewed attention in light of our growing understanding of epigenetics and the existence of environmentally induced traits that may transfer across generational lines (Kuzawa 2005). It should be noted that inheritance does not necessarily imply a sort of static transference; the trait, material, or practice may shift or change somewhat between generations. Furthermore, biosocial inheritance can be positive, negative, or both depending on the environmental context. For example, a child who is born to a relatively poor family living in a small farming community in the Andes Mountains of Peru where nutrition is highly variable by season may benefit from the prenatal programming of a metabolic phenotype that allows for rapid fat storage. Fat stores built during and following the harvest season can buffer against periods of reduced food availability that precede the next harvest. A child whose family is relatively well-off may avoid the development of such a metabolic phenotype through supplementing the preharvest period with purchased foods, largely eliminating seasonal variability. However, as the community becomes incorporated into larger economic systems and begins the shift toward increasing wage labor, the nutritional highs and lows are replaced by consistent, readily available, calorie-dense, cheap foods and reduced physical activity. The poorer child with the "thrifty phenotype" is likely to be at greater risk for energy imbalance, obesity, diabetes, and other health issues.

Biosocial Inheritance: A Definition and Framework

We can thus define "biosocial inheritance" as the process through which social adversity or advantage is transmitted across generations through mechanisms both biological and social in nature. Health and health disparities play a key role in biosocial inheritance as outcome and mechanism. For example, poor health in adults can lead to the transmission of poor health to offspring, but it can also lead to reduced productivity and social capital in the following generation. Additionally, an impoverished environment inherited from parents can lead to poor child-health outcomes, reduced social capital in the form of education attainment, employment, and poor health outcomes when those children reach adulthood. Thus intergenerational influences often have the effect of perpetuating or amplifying biosocial traits across generations, thereby increasing the importance of an intergenerational perspective. Biosocial inheritance leads us to consider the generations prior to that generation with whom we are directly working. It forces us to think about what cultural practices, social norms, ideologies, and economic opportunities or constraints are transmitted from one generation to the next and how they interact with human biology to harm or enhance health. Furthermore, it brings to focus the ways in which health disparities and poverty interact to compound in a population across time, increasingly reducing the mobility for some and increasing the opportunity for success for others, thus contributing to the ever-widening disparities in contemporary society.

The many mechanisms of biosocial inheritance

Biosocial inheritance occurs though a number of different mechanisms. While many of them appear to be principally biological in nature, their activation, function, and cessation are often dependent on biological and social inputs. For example, although the pathways through which epigenetic changes occur and take affect are considered biological, these changes may be induced by endocrine signals stimulated by a social phenomenon such as stress, making them biosocial in nature. Many anthropologists are already examining the numerous mechanisms through which biosocial inheritance may occur (see Table 2). We will briefly review several key examples that represent important ways in which the social environment can "get under the skin" and stay there for generations.

Developmental programming represents a major mechanism of biosocial inheritance. Programming during development can affect numerous systems including metabolism, the HPA axis, and immune systems. Epigenetic changes, in the form of chromosomal alterations, histone modifications, and DNA methylation are the proposed mechanisms for much of the developmental programming that leads to adult disease (Callinan and Feinberg 2006; Peaston and Whitelaw 2006). However, it is possible, and even likely, that there are other undiscovered or unidentified mechanisms through which this programming can occur. It is also possible that rather than programming, allostasis or the body's constant adjustment to internal and external changes (Sterling 2004, 2012; Sterling and Eyer 1988) may lead to a more rapid decline of body systems and the emergence of disease states (Seeman et al. 1997), particularly when challenges to allostasis are frequent and severe. Primarily the result of one's immediate environment, this allostatic burden can be understood as, at least in part, a result of intergenerational forces acting through their influence on our current environment.

Nutrition represents a prime example of a factor in our immediate environment that is highly mediated by intergenerational influence. For instance, while an infant may express preferences for certain foods early on, what the infant eats is largely a result of the way caregivers (most often parents) navigate their own environments. How long a mother is able to breastfeed her infant may depend on her economic resources, occupation, education, cultural beliefs, length of maternity leave, spousal and/or family support, and access to her child or a private place to express and store milk during the workday. The

TABLE 2. Mechanisms of Biosocial Inheritance

Mechanism	Explanation	Citations
Epigenetics	Epigenetic modifications are changes induced by environmental exposures that can be transmitted to subsequent generations through the germ line. In certain contemporary environments, this may lead to disparate health outcomes.	Kuzawa and Sweet (2009), Anway and Skinner (2008), O'Brien (2007), Uddin et al. (2010)
Immune function	Immune function is often dependent on intergenerational inputs such as caretaker choices/restrictions regarding breastfeeding (antibody and microbiome transmission) and early microbial exposures.	Grindstaff et al. (2003), McDade (2002, 2003)
Growth and development	Growth and development are directly affected by caretaker status and genetics as well as long-term social and cultural factors that are inherited.	Ramakrishnan et al. (1999), Venkataramani (2011)
HPA axis function	Early environments, shaped by caretakers, may lead to the development of offspring who experience HPA activation easily, return to normal levels more quickly, or remain activated for long periods of time, all of which can have distinct implications for health.	Cottrell and Seckl (2009), Davis and Sandman (2010), Kapoor et al. (2008), Tegethoff et al. (2009)
Metabolic programming	Metabolic programming can take place during prenatal and early development as a result of intergenerational influences or it may be the result of long term transgenerational signaling.	Barker (1998), Barker et al. (1993b, 2002), Desai and Hales (1997), Kuzawa (2005)

range and quality of supplementary foods an infant is given depend on family income, access, education, and ecology among other things.

Additionally, political or civil conflict may cause individuals to flee conflict areas for the safety of a nearby city or other locations. Such movement drastically changes the nutritional environment the next generation is born into. This shift in nutritional environment also occurs during rapid economic transition when agriculture begins to take a back seat to the purchase of processed foods. In any of these cases, the change creates a mismatch of transgenerational metabolic programming and contemporary nutritional environment implicated in the rise of obesity in middle- and low-income countries (Hales and Barker 2001; Popkin 2001; Popkin and Nielsen 2003). This same mismatch can be created by larger social and economic structures, such as the food deserts that emerge when large corporations refuse to place stores in certain locations due to perceived low profitability. Even with a rapid shift in nutritional environment, children are often not the primary agents in the decisions about how and what they eat. These early nutritional inputs have significant impact on social and biological outcomes throughout the life course of the child and are largely governed by intergenerational influences. What is more, some scholars have proposed that these early nutritional inputs may be translated into epigenetic changes and metabolic programming that may have effects on subsequent generations (Kuzawa 2005). Therefore, one's nutritional environment is largely inherited from parents and other predecessors and also serves to inform the programming of future generations.

Immune function represents another important mechanism through which intergenerational social influences interact with biology to affect health. A person's immune system develops over the course of childhood and early exposures greatly impact immune function throughout the life course. For instance, a child's increased microbial exposure via contact with animals and soil can help to prime the child's immune system to develop regulatory networks necessary for effective immune responses in adulthood (McDade 2003, 2005). These exposures can even moderate the relationship between stress and inflammation in adulthood (McDade et al. 2012), which is in turn associated with increased risk of cardiovascular disease (Ridker et al. 1998), type II diabetes (Pradhan et al. 2001), late-life disability (Kuo et al. 2006), and mortality (Harris et al. 1999). These early-life exposures, as with nutrition, are largely dependent on the socioeconomic status and activities of the prior generation, parents, and caretakers. While microbes represent a biological exposure influenced by social factors, inherited social status and subsequent stress can also represent an important exposure. McDade's work (2001, 2002) in Samoa demonstrated that status incongruity between inherited, Samoan *matai* titles and material wealth, characterized by technology and Western prestige materials, led to increased psychosocial stress and reduced immune function. Without careful attention to local, cultural structures of status inheritance and globalized, Western ideas of prestige, this health outcome would have remained unexplained and unaddressed.

Beyond these more apparently biological mechanisms, there are also mechanisms appearing more social or economic that become biological as they begin to impact health. For example, an impoverished prenatal and childhood environment can lead to impaired adult productivity both physically through health (Barker et al. 1989, 1990, 1993b; Blane et al. 2007; Lawlor et al. 2006; Valdez et al. 1994) and cognitively (Richards et al. 2001), thereby reducing socioeconomic potential. This reduced economic potential/success can in turn compromise adult health or exacerbate pre-existing health problems. Poor adult health, specifically poor maternal health, can lead to adverse birth outcomes such as low birth weight and preterm birth (Dodd et al. 2011), thereby setting up negative biosocial trajectories for the next generation and thus reinforcing the cycle. Alternatively, social hierarchies based on race or ethnicity can create stressful environments for gestating women who may subsequently experience the same adverse birth outcomes noted above

(Collins et al. 2000, 2004; Collins and David 2009; Giurgescu et al. 2011; Mustillo et al. 2004), leaving their children the same negative trajectories.

The mechanisms of biosocial inheritance are not limited to these examples or those listed in Table 2, and certainly are more likely to come to light with increased research focus in this area. The mechanisms through which biosocial inheritance occurs allow for what can be considered both positive and negative health effects; just as there is a synergistic relationship between poor health and poverty, there is a similar relationship between health and material and social success. When compounded across generations, it is not difficult to see how such mechanisms allow for the concretization and deeper entrenchment of health disparities. Those individuals with an advantage continue to improve across generations while those at a disadvantage face significant obstacles that impede social, economic, and health-based improvements.

CASE STUDY: BIOSOCIAL INHERITANCE OF STATURE IN THE ANDES

We now present a case study that will apply some of the concepts discussed throughout this article (summarized in Table 3). We apply the notion of biosocial inheritance to better identify and understand the determinants of growth and adult stature in Nuñoa, Peru. Scholars and policy makers have been investigating the anthropometrics of Peruvians for nearly a century. The ideas regarding the most powerful determinants of growth have shifted dramatically across that time period with changing research agendas and shifting theoretical foci, making it an excellent case study for demonstrating the importance of incorporating biosocial inheritance in our considerations of contemporary health disparities.

Despite our knowledge of the immense plasticity of human phenotypes, scholars continue to seek a genetic explanation for the heritability of height (Weedon et al. 2008; Yang et al. 2010). This would appear to be a straightforward form of inheritance as one's genes represent direct biological inheritance passed from one generation to the next. However, it has become apparent that certain environmental conditions must be met for an individual to approach their genetic potential (Silventoinen et al. 2000). This complicates the conceptualization of genetic inheritance, making it largely dependent on the social environment as well as the biological environment, and thus biosocial.[1] Numerous explanations for reduced Andean stature have been offered through the years, including adaptation to high altitude (Frisancho 1969, 1976, 1977; Frisancho and Baker 1970) and chronic malnutrition as a result of poverty and marginalization (Leonard 1989; Leonard and Thomas 1989; Leonard et al. 1990, Leatherman et al. 1995). Indeed, this work has demonstrated shifts in levels of chronic malnutrition in communities in the district due to shifting economic circumstances, and irrespective of relative elevation in the district (Leatherman 1994). Thus, it has become increasingly clear that a complex constellation of macro and micro forces, reaching across generations, shape child growth in Nuñoa and it is to these forces that we now turn.

Nuñoa is currently segmented into three distinct ecological and economic zones, the lower valley, the upper valley, and the centrally located town. Though it has traditionally been a center for alpaca and sheep wool production, which supplied most of the wealth

TABLE 3. Sociocultural, Historical, and Political-economic Factors in Biosocial Inheritance

	Explanation	Example from the Case Study
Historical context	Analyses should include relevant historical context both recent and more long term as needed.	Despite having occurred more than 20 years ago, the civil conflict between the Shining Path and the military continues to have significant repercussions for the growth of the population of Nuñoa.
Political-economic context	Analyses should consider relevant political-economic factors such as government policies, international involvement, economic development efforts, and present political conflict.	Local and federal government programs that seek to provide economic and nutritional support to children at risk for stunting. Aid from NGOs that may alter a family's economic and nutritional circumstances. Mining companies providing wages, education, and nutritional supplementation to workers and their families.
Relations of power	Analyses should consider past and present social, political, and economic hierarchies that may affect or be affected by health disparities.	Due to their economic or racial/ethnic status, individuals may experience difficulty in finding work, receiving healthcare, and so on, because of inherited hierarchies present in the Andes for hundreds of years.

in the region, the last ten years have seen a major economic shift with the emergence of a dairy industry in some lower sectors. Though there have been some government aid and subsidies to this industry, the growth is largely driven by an increasing demand for cheese to be sold in markets and utilized in the restaurants, particularly pizzerias, catering to tourists in the nearby city of Cusco. This rapid economic change appears to have led to improvements in the nutritional and economic status of those families living in the lower valley where water is plentiful and alfalfa for dairy cattle can be grown easily. Families living in the upper valley have not had the same level of dairying success, as they are unable to sustain the alfalfa production and herd quality that allows for adequate milk production year round. Most of these families have continued to rely on herding alpacas for income, with very limited subsistence agriculture. A relatively low international price for alpaca fiber over the past decade has severely limited earnings. Important changes have also occurred for the population that lives in the main town of Nuñoa where most families now rely on wage labor or mercantile activities and foods purchased in markets for a large part of subsistence, rather than or in addition to agricultural fields outside of town. These economic differences, largely formed as a result of international political economic forces (including a recent 9 percent growth rate in the Peruvian economy largely driven by mining revenues and decentralization of income distribution by the state), may result in significant differential effects on several mechanisms of the biosocial inheritance of growth: nutrition, metabolic programming, and immune function. We will explore each of these mechanisms in turn.

Like elsewhere in the world, nutrition in Nuñoa is largely dependent on access to high-quality foods. Access implies proximity, availability, and ability to obtain these foods. Access in Nuñoa is largely influenced by where someone is born and/or where their family lives (in the upper, lower, or urban zones) and thus what economic activities, access to land, animals, and labor are available to them. Further, within each of the economic zones, inequalities may have emerged or perhaps been exacerbated by the activities of international NGOs who lend money or gift animals to a limited number of families. In addition to influencing economic activities, poor road conditions and weather during the rainy season make traveling between the upper zone and the town difficult and costly. This reduces the number of trips a family can make and thus the quantity of food they can purchase and bring home. Depending on a family's economic means, coming into town may require a six- to eight-hour walk, one way. Even if a family has sufficient money to purchase food, if they cannot afford transportation or to pay someone to care for their herds while they are away, they may not be able to spend it. What is more, infrequent trips mean that fresh produce often fails to last the full interval, leaving the family with only dried and stored foods for a period of time. However, if a family that lives far into the countryside and has transportation—as many wealthy landowners still do when they are not in their second or third homes in nearby cities—or a large social network that can be tapped into for labor, nutritional, or economic support, access to quality nutrition is generally good. Thus, it is not simply a matter of where one's parents live but also their economic and social means.

Beyond differential economic activities, historical and contemporary social hierarchies also play a role in influencing how and where people live, as do recent and more long-term historic events. For example, in the 1980s the civil conflict between the militant Maoist group the *Sendero Luminoso* or Shining Path and the Peruvian state brought a period of upheaval, violence, and fear to Nuñoa. In terms of nutritional effects, there was reduced food availability, increased hunger and malnutrition alongside trauma and high levels of psychosocial stress (Leatherman et al. 1995).

Scholarship is showing the ways in which these traumas can echo through generations. As we have seen in previous research, periods of food shortage, political strife, and ethnic discrimination can have significant effects on stature and other health outcomes, such as birth weight, in subsequent generations (Lauderdale 2006; Lumey 1992; Lumey et al. 2009, 2011; Roseboom et al. 2000, 2001). Thus, metabolic programming that can take place when an individual is exposed to starvation in utero or in early childhood, represents an important biosocial mechanism through which the experience of these traumas may have been transmitted across generations. This conflict also took a tremendous toll on human capital. One study has shown that within Peru, the presence of the civil conflict led to a reduction of human capital and particularly education in the areas hardest hit (León 2012). Furthermore, this period of turbulence brought with it additional reshuffling of property as large landholders and wealthier cooperatives saw much of their land and animals re-appropriated. While many of Nuñoa's inhabitants fled during this time, others lacked the means to do so. In some cases, this may have deepened the disparities between the wealthier population, who were able to seek shelter in the cities, and those poorer families who had to stay behind to experience hunger, violence, and trauma, all of which can leave intergenerational traces (O'Brien 2007; Uddin et al. 2010).

Immune function and the experience of illness are also mechanisms through which intergenerational forces affect growth in Nuñoa. First and foremost there is a direct connection between growth faltering and episodes of illness, particularly diarrheal illness (Moore et al. 2001; Rowland et al. 1988). In infants, these episodes often occur beginning with the introduction of complimentary foods depending on issues of caretaker hygiene, education, and resources. Adult illness can also take a toll on infant and child growth. Among the agro-pastoral families living in the upper and lower zones of Nuñoa, adult illness often leads to the removal of older children from school to complete the role in economic production that an ailing adult can no longer fulfill (Leatherman 2005; see also Leatherman and Jernigan this issue). This often leads to these children falling behind in school and eventually dropping out, significantly harming their chances of social mobility and leaving them in a similarly vulnerable position in the future. With incomplete educations and limited skills, they often opt to remain in the agricultural fields of their parents rather than obtaining their own or starting new careers. Further, when economic production falters, though there is effort on the part of mothers to shield their children (Leonard 1991), food insecurity rises and the nutritional status of the family may decrease leading to increased experience of stress and worry, compromised immune function, and growth faltering in children. All of these impacts affect health outcomes across both generations and have repercussions throughout the life course and in generations to follow. Stature itself is a part of this picture of reduced social mobility. Several studies have shown that physical height is linked to career success (Judge and Cable 2004), income (Bassino 2006; Steckel 1983), socioeconomic status, and education (Mayer and Selmer 1999).

Finally, we must acknowledge the longstanding racial and ethnic hierarchies in place since the colonial period that continue to play an important role in social mobility and status in Nuñoa. Markers of indigeneity, such as reliance on Quechua as a primary language or traditional dress, often inherited from one's parents, can reduce a person's status and potential for social mobility (de la Cadena 2000; Mannheim 1984) and thus health. Persistent and fierce hierarchies, which also represent inherited social ideas, mean that these markers are a social burden that children carry with them even as they adopt an increasingly Westernized lifestyle. The ethnicity and economic choices of their parents and family, combined with societal norms and ideas, can propel the next generation forward or limit their mobility and health. When the cycle is established and health disparities are exacerbated by years of inherited social hierarchies, limited social mobility, and constrained physiology, the situation cannot be overturned with targeted, single-point interventions. For example, Leonard (1989) demonstrated a slight improvement in rates of stunting for the most well-off children and Leatherman et al. (1995) noted a slight secular increase in growth when compared with the 1960s data. However, a restudy in the late 1990s by Pawson et al. (2001) following the political and economic upheaval associated with the Shining Path showed no improvement over the 1960s and indicated that positive growth trends may have in fact reversed during that period. Thus, eliminating malnutrition alone will not alleviate this cycle; political-economic and social instabilities must also be addressed. Tackling malnutrition may aid in improving certain aspects of population health. However, the weight of intergenerational forces, such as nutritional access, metabolic programming, illness, and ethnic or racial hierarchies, mean a more holistic understanding and intervention is needed.

One reason for the need of holism is that rather than growth based solely on his or her own individual conditions, the growth of this contemporary Peruvian cohort is heavily influenced by inheritance from previous generations. First, children are often bequeathed a similar socioeconomic status as their parents. Although, if aided by a strong kinship network and collective resources such as a wealthy aunt and uncle in a nearby city, children may have an opportunity to live away from home, experience a different nutritional environment, and attend school undisturbed by family illness. Either outcome functions as a form of biosocial inheritance. This status has a strong effect on their access to good nutrition and thus growth. Furthermore, their parents' occupation means the contemporary cohort may inherit an environment where the balance between survival and starvation, education or illiteracy, depends on one major incident of parental or family illness (Leatherman 2005). Second, they may have inherited metabolic programming based on their mother's experience of trauma and malnutrition during the 1980s and early 1990s under the threat of the Shining Path and counterinsurgency efforts. This programming, as in the case with previously researched famines, may have significant consequences for their metabolic health both in childhood and later in life (Lauderdale 2006; Lumey 1992; Lumey et al. 2009, 2011; Roseboom et al. 2000, 2001). They have also inherited a social hierarchy in place since the colonial period in which their dress, language, and lifestyle may earn them scorn and derision or ease their passage through society and thus their access to nutrition, health care, and social capital. Even if they adopt new ways of dressing and earning a living, the choices of their parents and family continue to mark them until they are able to move far enough away to hide their social inheritance. It is likely that there are additional elements of biosocial inheritance affecting the lives and growth of this contemporary Peruvian cohort; we have outlined a few of the most apparent here. These examples demonstrate the way in which intergenerational forces play an important role in contemporary health disparities, how these forces act through mechanisms that function on both social and biological levels, and how by examining these forces we can better incorporate political economic analysis and historical context in our biocultural work.

To begin to actually document the effects of biosocial inheritance on growth in Nuñoa, a multitiered study design incorporating population-level growth comparisons across time and more-detailed contemporary data collection could be employed. The long history of studying growth in Nuñoa may allow for the tracking of generational shifts in growth. Additionally, it may make feasible the consideration of growth before and after major political events such as the land reforms occurring just after the study period in the 1960s and preceding that of the 1980s or before and after the emergence of the Shining Path or the dairy industry. While datasets from each generation are limited in that they represent only a cross section and are somewhat variable in age range, they still lend themselves to meaningful analysis when placed in larger historical contexts.

Such analysis would be complemented by a study of early growth and infant feeding contextualized in relatively detailed family histories. This initial study would serve as a baseline for followup over the next 20 years and beyond with collection of anthropometric and dietary data as well as measures of immune function, incidence of illness, and other health-related biomarkers. Subsequent periods of data collection would include repetition of all biological and nutritional data but could also be expanded to include data on cognitive function, academic achievement, experience of psychosocial stress or life stressors, and other measures that may shed light on the ways in which early environments are connected to later-life social and health outcomes. While such studies do exist elsewhere, by beginning this study with attention to the nuances of social, economic, and political inequalities as they are in infancy and develop across the life course, this study would offer the opportunity to make a meaningful contribution to the biosocial inheritance theory and the study of health disparities.

DISCUSSION: THE PRACTICE OF STUDYING BIOSOCIAL INHERITANCE

Extending Our Understanding of Health Disparities

At this juncture we might ask how exactly the notion of biosocial inheritance moves forward the study of health disparities within biocultural anthropology and more broadly. First and foremost, biosocial inheritance helps to place bodies in their cultural context, space, and time, doing away with ideas of universality and instead highlighting their inextricability from larger historical, political-economic forces (Lock 2013). When we force ourselves to consider what a contemporary cohort has inherited from previous generations, we begin to blur the lines of the individual, thereby challenging concepts of the self and the body and questioning their status as clearly bounded entities (Lock 2013). But most importantly, by situating contemporary health outcomes in their generational context, we are forced to grapple with the larger historical and political-economic forces that have acted across those generations. Biosocial inheritance serves as a natural extension of work on the spaces of vulnerability and spaces of hope begun by Leatherman (2005) as well as the study of the biology of poverty (Goodman et al. 1988; Leatherman and Goodman 1997; Thomas 1998). Further, it compels us to reconsider the transmission of poverty, social mobility, and the popular rhetoric of independence, self-sufficiency, and pulling oneself up by one's bootstraps. What is more, biosocial inheritance helps to demonstrate how these multidimensional, intergenerational processes take place, highlighting the complexity of health phenomena that cannot be cured with a magic bullet. Rather, biosocial inheritance can be used to advocate for the evaluation of programs based on long-term results rather than immediate outcomes.

Additionally, biosocial inheritance can be understood as a form of embodiment, whereby the social, political, and economic world around us manifests and perpetuates itself through our physiology (Krieger 2005). In other words, as we move through life, our bodies are continually internalizing and then manifesting our social, political, ecological, and economic environments in the form of physiological phenomena, from the speed and extent of our growth to the darkness of our freckles or the way we comport ourselves around others. Anthropological scholars have already utilized the notion of embodiment to describe the process by which racial inequalities have led to highly disparate health outcomes between black and white Americans (Gravlee 2009; Kuzawa and Sweet 2009). Although much of the anthropological work on embodiment has paid limited attention to the biological body, the use of embodiment in the examination of health disparities represents a prime opportunity to redress much of the black boxing of physiology that has taken place in the social sciences and embodiment scholarship throughout the 20th century (Lock 2013). Furthermore, there has been a call from biocultural scholars to better engage with this important theoretical concept that has been largely limited to cultural and medical anthropology (Leidy Sievert 2006).

Biosocial inheritance forces us to reconsider the way we think about contemporary environments. Environments, be they social, ecological, or otherwise, must be understood in part as products of intergenerational forces. It is an age-old adage; you cannot choose your family. Each of us is born into an environment that we inherit from our parents, an environment that is constantly shaped by larger historical, political-economic forces that echo across generations. Just as early work in biocultural anthropology and political ecology complicated our understanding of nature by demonstrating that the "natural" is often a product of human action (Hvalkof and Escobar 1998; Neumann 2005), so must biocultural scholars reconsider contemporary environments as a form of biosocial inheritance. Certainly, individuals have the capacity to modify, manipulate, or seek out new social and ecological environments, but even when all social ties are cut, biosocial mechanisms cause us to carry our inheritance with us wherever we go. Furthermore, the tendency for perpetuation and even exacerbation of health disparities across generations can be strong, making their examination of the utmost importance to the study of health disparities.

Finally, rather than being bound by the limitations, semantic and historical baggage of notions of adaptation, pathology, and evolution, biosocial inheritance provides a greater context for physiological and cultural characteristics that can hinder or aid individuals and groups across a changing environment or throughout the life course. Since cultural and biological "adaptations" have been shown to bring about new challenges, creating new problems that must be adapted to (McDade and Nyberg 2010; Schell 1997), it is perhaps more useful to see them as a part of a larger, longer picture. When we contextualize them in this way, questions of adaptability may become less relevant, with focus on context and outcome rather than evaluation coming to the fore. Each of us carries with us generations of biosocial history. While we often know the names and stories of our grandparents and great grandparents, we rarely consider the ways in which our lives and bodies have been directly and indirectly shaped by theirs. The consideration of biosocial inheritance helps us to incorporate this intergenerational perspective as well as creating an opportunity for the further integration of historic, cultural, and political economic analysis into the work of biocultural anthropology.

NOTE

Acknowledgement. The authors would like to acknowledge Ruby Fried, Aaron Miller, Jared Bragg, Stephanie Levy, and Kim McCabe for their helpful comments on early drafts and throughout the conceptualization of this article. We would also like to thank our two anonymous reviewers for their helpful comments.

1. One step further would be the understanding that who procreates with whom, who is able to comingle their genetic material to be passed on to the next generation, is largely influenced by both social and physical geographies and thus, even our DNA can be considered largely biosocial.

REFERENCES CITED

Abusharaf, Rogaia Mustafa, ed.
  2006 Female Circumcision: Multicultural Perspectives. Philadelphia: University of Pennsylvania Press.
Adler, Nancy E., W. Thomas Boyce, Margaret A. Chesney, Susan Folkman, and S. Leonard Syme
  1993 Socioeconomic Inequalities in Health: No Easy Solution. JAMA 269(24):3140–3145.
Adler, Nancy E., Elissa S. Epel, Grace Castellazzo, and Jeannette R. Ickovics
  2000 Relationship of Subjective and Objective Social Status with Psychological and Physiological Functioning: Preliminary Data in Healthy, White Women. Health Psychology 19(6):586–592.
Almond, Douglas
  2006 Is the 1918 Influenza Pandemic Over? Long-term Effects of *In Utero* Influenza Exposure in the Post-1940 U.S. Population. Journal of Political Economy 114(4):672–712.
Almond, Douglas, and Kenneth Y. Chay
  2006 The Long-run and Intergenerational Impact of Poor Infant Health: Evidence from Cohorts Born during the Civil Rights Era. University of California-Berkeley. http://users.nber.org/~almond/chay_npc_paper.pdf, accessed September 21, 2014.
Almond, Douglas, and Janet Currie
  2011 Killing Me Softly: The Fetal Origins Hypothesis. Journal of Economic Perspectives 25(3):153–172.
Almond, Douglas, Janet Currie, and Mariesa Herrmann
  2012 From Infant to Mother: Early Disease Environment and Future Maternal Health. Labour Economics 19(4):475–483.
Almond, Douglas, Hilary W. Hoynes, and Diane Whitmore Schanzenbach
  2011 Inside the War on Poverty: The Impact of Food Stamps on Birth Outcomes. Review of Economics and Statistics 93(2):387–403.
Anway, Matthew D., and Michael K. Skinner
  2008 Epigenetic Programming of the Germ Line: Effects of Endocrine Disruptors on the Development of Transgenerational Disease. Reproductive Biomedicine Online 16(1):23–25.
Barker, David James Purslove
  1998 Mothers, Babies and Health in Later Life. Elsevier Health Sciences.
Barker, David J. P., Adrian R. Bull, Clive Osmond, and Shirley J. Simmonds
  1990 Fetal and Placental Size and Risk of Hypertension in Adult Life. BMJ 301(6746):259–262.
Barker, David J. P., Johan G. Eriksson, Tom Forsén, and Clive Osmond
  2002 Fetal Origins of Adult Disease: Strength of Effects and Biological Basis. International Journal of Epidemiology 31(6):1235–1239.
Barker, David J. P., Peter D. Gluckman, Keith M. Godfrey, Jane E. Harding, Julie A. Owens, and Jeffrey S. Robinson
  1993a Fetal Nutrition and Cardiovascular Disease in Adult Life. Lancet 341(8850):938–941.
Barker, David J. P., C. Nicholas Hales, Carolyn H. Fall, Clive Osmond, K. Phipps, and Penny M. Clark
  1993b Type 2 (Non-nsulin-dependent) Diabetes Mellitus, Hypertension and Hyperlipidaemia (Syndrome X): Relation to Reduced Fetal Growth. Diabetologia 36(1):62–67.
Barker, David J., Clive Osmond, and Brian Pannett
  1992 Why Londoners Have Low Death Rates from Ischaemic Heart Disease and Stroke. BMJ 305(6868):1551–1554.

Barker, David J., P. D. Winter, Clive Osmond, B. Margetts, and Shirley J Simmonds
  1989 Weight in Infancy and Death from Ischaemic Heart Disease. Lancet 334(8663):577–580.
Bassino, Jean-Pascal
  2006 Inequality in Japan (1892–1941): Physical Stature, Income, and Health. Economics and Human
       Biology 4(1):62–88.
Behrman, Jere R.
  1996 The Impact of Health and Nutrition on Education. World Bank Research Observer 11(1):23–37.
Behrman, Jere R., and Barbara L. Wolfe
  1987 How Does Mother's Schooling Affect Family Health, Nutrition, Medical Care Usage, and Household
       Sanitation? Journal of Econometrics 36(1–2):185–204.
Ben-Shlomo, Yoav, and Diana Kuh
  2002 A Life Course Approach to Chronic Disease Epidemiology: Conceptual Models, Empirical Challenges
       and Interdisciplinary Perspectives. International Journal of Epidemiology 31(2):285–293.
Blane, David
  1995 Social Determinants of Health–Socioeconomic Status, Social Class, and Ethnicity. American Journal
       of Public Health 85(7):903–905.
Blane, David, Gopalakrishnan Netuveli, and Juliet Stone
  2007 The Development of Life Course Epidemiology. Revue D'Épidémiologie et de Santé Publique
       55(1):31–38.
Bourgois, Phillipe
  2001 Culture of Poverty. In International Encyclopedia of the Social and Behavioral Sciences. Neil J.
       Smelser and Paul B. Baltes, eds. Pp. 11904–11907. Oxford: Pergamon.
Callinan, Pauline A., and Andrew P. Feinberg
  2006 The Emerging Science of Epigenomics. Human Molecular Genetics 15(Suppl. 1):R95–R101.
Collins, James W., Jr., and Richard J. David
  2009 Racial Disparity in Low Birth Weight and Infant Mortality. Clinics in Perinatology 36(1):63–73.
Collins, James W., Jr, Richard J. David, Arden Handler, Stephen Wall, and Steven Andes
  2004 Very Low Birthweight in African American Infants: The Role of Maternal Exposure to Interpersonal
       Racial Discrimination. American Journal of Public Health 94(12):2132–2138.
Collins, James W., Jr, Richard J. David, Rebecca Symons, Adren Handler, Stephen N. Wall, and Lisa Dwyer
  2000 Low-income African-American Mothers' Perception of Exposure to Racial Discrimination and Infant
       Birth Weight. Epidemiology 11(3):337–339.
Cottrell, Elizabeth C., and Jonathan R. Seckl
  2009 Prenatal Stress, Glucocorticoids and the Programming of Adult Disease. Frontiers in Behavioral
       Neuroscience 3(19):1–9.
Currie, Janet
  2011 Inequality at Birth: Some Causes and Consequences. NBER Working Paper 16798. National Bureau of
       Economic Research. http://ideas.repec.org/p/nbr/nberwo/16798.html, accessed September 21, 2014.
Currie, Janet, and Douglas Almond
  2011 Human Capital Development before Age Five. Handbook of Labor Economics 4(B):1315–1486.
Currie, Janet, and Enrico Moretti
  2005 Biology as Destiny? Short and Long-run Determinants of Intergenerational Transmission of Birth
       Weight. NBER Working Paper 11567. National Bureau of Economic Research. http://www.nber.org/
       papers/w11567, accessed September 21, 2014.
Davis, Elysia P., and Curt A. Sandman
  2010 The Timing of Prenatal Exposure to Maternal Cortisol and Psychosocial Stress is Associated with
       Human Infant Cognitive Development. Child Development 81(1):131–148.
de la Cadena, Marisol
  2000 Indigenous Mestizos: The Politics of Race and Culture in Cuzco, Peru, 1919–1991. Durham, NC:
       Duke University Press.
Desai, Mina, and C. Nicholas Hales
  1997 Role of Fetal and Infant Growth in Programming Metabolism in Later Life. Biological Reviews of
       the Cambridge Philosophical Society 72(2):329–348.

Dodd, Jodie M., Rosalie M. Grivell, Anh-Minh Nguyen, Annabelle Chan, and Jeffrey S. Robinson
 2011 Maternal and Perinatal Health Outcomes by Body Mass Index Category. Australian and New Zealand Journal of Obstetrics & Gynaecology 51(2):136–140.

Dressler, William W.
 2005 What's Cultural about Biocultural Research? Ethos 33(1):20–45.

Elo, Irma T., and Samuel H. Preston
 1992 Effects of Early-life Conditions on Adult Mortality: A Review. Population Index 58(2):186–212.

Ermisch, John, and Marco Francesconi
 2001 Family Matters: Impacts of Family Background on Educational Attainments. Economica 68(270):137–156.

Farmer, Paul
 2003 Pathologies of Power. Health, Human Rights, and the New War on the Poor. Berkeley: University of California Press.

Figlio, David N., Jonathan Guryan, Krzysztof Karbownik, and Jeffrey Roth
 2013 The Effects of Poor Neonatal Health on Children's Cognitive Development. NBER Working Paper 18846. National Bureau of Economic Research. http://www.nber.org/papers/w18846, accessed September 21, 2014.

Frisancho, A. Roberto
 1969 Human Growth and Pulmonary Function of a High Altitude Peruvian Quechua Population. Human Biology 41(3):365–379.
 1976 Growth and Morphology at High Altitude. Man in the Andes Paul T. Baker and Michael A. Little, eds. Pp. 180–207. Stroudsburg PA: Dowden, Hutchinson, & Ross.
 1977 Developmental Adaptation to High Altitude Hypoxia. International Journal of Biometeorology 21(2):135–146.

Frisancho, A. Roberto, and Paul T. Baker
 1970 Altitude and Growth: A Study of the Patterns of Physical Growth of a High Altitude Peruvian Quechua Population. American Journal of Physical Anthropology 32(2):279–292.

Gapminder
 2008 Wealth & Health of Nations. http://www.gapminder.org. Electronic database, accessed August 10, 2013.

Giurgescu, Carmen, Barbara L. McFarlin, Jeneen Lomax, Cindy Craddock, and Amy Albrecht
 2011 Racial Discrimination and the Black-White Gap in Adverse Birth Outcomes: A Review. Journal of Midwifery & Women's Health 56(4):362–370.

Gluckman, Peter D., and Mark A. Hanson
 2006 The Developmental Origins of Health and Disease: The Breadth and Importance of the Concept. *In* Early Life Origins of Health and Disease. E. Marelyn Wintour-Coghlan and Julie A. Owens, eds. Pp. 1–7. New York: Springer Science+Business Media.

Goldblatt, Peter
 1990 Longitudinal Study: Mortality and Social Organisation. London: Her Majesty's Stationery Office.

Goodman, Alan H., and Thomas L. Leatherman
 1998a Building a New Biocultural Synthesis: Political-Economic Perspectives on Human Biology. Ann Arbor, MI: University of Michigan Press.
 1998b Traversing the Chasm between Biology and Culture: An Introduction. *In* Building a New Biocultural Synthesis: Political-Economic Perspectives on Human Biology. Pp. 3–42. Ann Arbor, MI: University of Michigan Press.

Goodman, Alan H., R. Brooke Thomas, Alan C. Swedlund, and George J. Armelagos
 1988 Biocultural Perspectives on Stress in Prehistoric, Historical, and Contemporary Population Research. American Journal of Physical Anthropology 31(Suppl. 9):169–202.

Gravlee, Clarence C.
 2009 How Race Becomes Biology: Embodiment of Social Inequality. American Journal of Physical Anthropology 139(1):47–57.

Grindstaff, Jennifer L., Edmund D. Brodie III, and Ellen D. Ketterson
  2003 Immune Function across Generations: Integrating Mechanism and Evolutionary Process in Maternal Antibody Transmission. Proceedings of the Royal Society, Series B: Biological Sciences 270(1531):2309–2319.
Gruenbaum, Ellen
  2001 The Female Circumcision Controversy: An Anthropological Perspective. Philadelphia: University of Pennsylvania Press.
Hales, C. Nicholas, and David J. P. Barker
  2001 The Thrifty Phenotype Hypothesis. British Medical Bulletin 60(1):5–20.
Halfon, Neal, and Miles Hochstein
  2002 Life Course Health Development: An Integrated Framework for Developing Health, Policy, and Research. Milbank Quarterly 80(3):433–479.
Harper, Caroline, Rachel Marcus, and Karen Moore
  2003 Enduring Poverty and the Conditions of Childhood: Lifecourse and Intergenerational Poverty Transmissions. World Development, Chronic Poverty and Development Policy 31(3):535–554.
Harris, Tamara B., Luigi Ferrucci, Russell P. Tracy, M. Chiara Corti, Sholom Wacholder, Walter H. Ettinger Jr., Harley Heimovitz, Harvey J. Cohen, and Robert Wallace
  1999 Associations of Elevated Interleukin-6 and C-Reactive Protein Levels with Mortality in the Elderly. American Journal of Medicine 106(5):506–512.
Hvalkof, Søren, and Arturo Escobar
  1998 Nature, Political Ecology, and Social Practice: Toward an Academic and Political Agenda. In Building a New Biocultural Synthesis: Political-economic Perspectives on Human Biology. Alan H. Goodman and Thomas L. Leatherman, eds. Pp. 425–450. Ann Arbor, MI: University of Michigan Press.
Judge, Timothy A., and Daniel M. Cable
  2004 The Effect of Physical Height on Workplace Success and Income: Preliminary Test of a Theoretical Model. Journal of Applied Psychology 89(3):428–441.
Kapoor, Amita, Sophie Petropoulos, and Stephen G. Matthews
  2008 Fetal Programming of Hypothalamic-pituitary-adrenal (HPA) Axis Function and Behavior by Synthetic Glucocorticoids. Brain Research Reviews 57(2):586–595.
Kermack, William O., Anderson G. McKendrick, and Peter L. McKinlay
  1934 Death-rates in Great Britain and Sweden: Expression of Specific Mortality Rates as Products of Two Factors, and Some Consequences Thereof. Journal of Hygiene 34(4):433–457.
Krieger, Nancy
  2005 Embodiment: A Conceptual Glossary for Epidemiology. Journal of Epidemiology & Community Health 59(5):350–355.
Kuh, Diana, Yoav Ben-Shlomo, John Lynch, Johan Hallqvist, and Chris Power
  2003 Life Course Epidemiology. Journal of Epidemiology and Community Health 57(10):778–783.
Kuo, Hsu-Ko, Jonathan F. Bean, Chung-Jen Yen, and Suzanne G. Leveille
  2006 Linking C-reactive Protein to Late-life Disability in the National Health and Nutrition Examination Survey (NHANES) 1999–2002. Journals of Gerontology Series A: Biological Sciences and Medical Sciences 61(4):380–387.
Kuzawa, Christopher W.
  2005 Fetal Origins of Developmental Plasticity: Are Fetal Cues Reliable Predictors of Future Nutritional Environments? American Journal of Human Biology 17(1):5–21.
Kuzawa, Christopher W., and Elizabeth Sweet
  2009 Epigenetics and the Embodiment of Race: Developmental Origins of US Racial Disparities in Cardiovascular Health. American Journal of Human Biology 21(1):2–15.
Lauderdale, Diane S.
  2006 Birth Outcomes for Arabic-named Women in California before and after September 11. Demography 43(1):185–201.

Lawlor, D. A., G. Davey Smith, and S. Ebrahim

2006 Does the New International Diabetes Federation Definition of the Metabolic Syndrome Predict CHD Any More Strongly than Older Definitions? Findings from the British Women's Heart and Health Study. Diabetologia 49(1):41–48.

Leatherman, Thomas L.

1994 Health Implications of Changing Agrarian Economies in the Southern Andes. Human Organization 53(4):371–380.

2005 A Space of Vulnerability in Poverty and Health: Political-ecology and Biocultural Analysis. Ethos 33(1):46–70.

Leatherman, Thomas L., James W. Carey, and R. Brooke Thomas

1995 Socioeconomic Change and Patterns of Growth in the Andes. American Journal of Physical Anthropology 97(3):307–321.

Leatherman, Thomas L., and Alan H. Goodman

1997 Expanding the Biocultural Synthesis toward a Biology of Poverty. American Journal of Physical Anthropology 102(1):1–3.

Leidy Sievert, Lynnette

2006 Menopause: A Biocultural Perspective. New Brunswick, NJ: Rutgers University Press.

León, Gianmarco

2012 Civil Conflict and Human Capital Accumulation: The Long-term Effects of Political Violence in Perú. Economics Working Paper 1333. Department of Economics and Business, Universitat Pompeu Fabra.

Leonard, William R.

1989 Nutritional Determinants of High-altitude Growth in Nuñoa, Peru. American Journal of Physical Anthropology 80(3):341–352.

1991 Household-level Strategies for Protecting Children from Seasonal Food Scarcity. Social Science & Medicine 33(10):1127–1133.

Leonard, William R., Thomas L. Leatherman, James W. Carey, and R. Brooke Thomas

1990 Contributions of Nutrition versus Hypoxia to Growth in Rural Andean Populations. American Journal of Human Biology 2(6):613–626.

Leonard, William R., and R. Brooke Thomas

1989 Biosocial Responses to Seasonal Food Stress in Highland Peru. Human Biology 61(1):65–85.

Lin, Ming-Jen, and Elaine M. Liu

2012 Does In Utero Exposure to Illness Matter? The 1918 Influenza Epidemic in Taiwan as a Natural Experiment. http://www.aeaweb.org/aea/2014conference/program/retrieve.php?pdfid=531, accessed September 26, 2014.

Lock, Margaret

1998 Menopause: Lessons from Anthropology. Psychosomatic Medicine 60(4):410–419.

2013 The Epigenome and Nature/Nurture Reunification: A Challenge for Anthropology. Medical Anthropology 32(4):291–308.

Lock, Margaret, and Patricia Kaufert

2001 Menopause, Local Biologies, and Cultures of Aging. American Journal of Human Biology 13(4):494–504.

Lumey, Lambert H.

1992 Decreased Birthweights in Infants after Maternal In Utero Exposure to the Dutch Famine of 1944–1945. Paediatric and Perinatal Epidemiology 6(2):240–253.

Lumey, Lambert H., Aryeh D. Stein, and Henry S. Kahn

2009 Food Restriction during Gestation and a Metabolic Syndrome in Later Life: Evidence from the Dutch Hunger Winter Families Study. Journal of Developmental Origins of Health and Disease 1(S1):S25.

Lumey, Lambert H., Aryeh D. Stein, and Ezra Susser

2011 Prenatal Famine and Adult Health. Annual Review of Public Health 32:237–262.

Mann, S. L., M. E. Wadsworth, and J. R. Colley

1992 Accumulation of Factors Influencing Respiratory Illness in Members of a National Birth Cohort and Their Offspring. Journal of Epidemiology and Community Health 46(3):286–292.

Mannheim, Bruce

    1984 Una Nación Acorralada: Southern Peruvian Quechua Language Planning and Politics in Historical Perspective. Language in Society 13(03):291–309.

Marmot, Michael G., M. J. Shipley, and Geoffrey Rose

    1984 Inequalities in Death-specific Explanations of a General Pattern? Lancet 323(8384):1003–1006.

Martorell, Reynaldo

    1995 Results and Implications of the INCAp Follow-up Study. Journal of Nutrition 125(4):11127s–1138s.

    1999 The Nature of Child Malnutrition and Its Long-term Implications. Food & Nutrition Bulletin 20(3):288–292.

Martorell, Reynaldo, Jean-Pierre Habicht, and Juan A. Rivera

    1995 History and Design of the INCAP Longitudinal Study (1969–77) and Its Follow-up (1988–89). Journal of Nutrition 125(Suppl. 4):1027S–1041S.

Martorell, Reynaldo, Bernardo L. Horta, Linda S. Adair, Aryeh D. Stein, Linda Richter, Caroline H. D. Fall, Santosh K. Bhargava, S. K. Dey Biswas, Lorna Perez, Fernando C. Barros, Cesar G. Victora, and Consortium on Health Orientated Research in Transitional Societies Group

    2010a Weight Gain in the First Two Years of Life Is an Important Predictor of Schooling Outcomes in Pooled Analyses from Five Birth Cohorts from Low- and Middle-income Countries. Journal of Nutrition 140(2):348–354.

Martorell, Reynaldo, Paul Melgar, John A. Maluccio, Aryeh D. Stein, and Juan A. Rivera

    2010b The Nutrition Intervention Improved Adult Human Capital and Economic Productivity. Journal of Nutrition 140(2):411–414.

Mayer, Haakon E., and Randi Selmer

    1999 Income, Educational Level and Body Height. Annals of Human Biology 26(3):219–227.

McDade, Thomas W.

    2001 Lifestyle Incongruity, Social Integration, and Immune Function in Samoan Adolescents. Social Science & Medicine 53(10):1351–1362.

    2002 Status Incongruity in Samoan Youth: A Biocultural Analysis of Culture Change, Stress, and Immune Function. Medical Anthropology Quarterly 16(2):123–150.

    2003 Life History Theory and the Immune System: Steps toward a Human Ecological Immunology. American Journal of Physical Anthropology 122(S37):100–125.

    2005 Life History, Maintenance, and the Early Origins of Immune Function. American Journal of Human Biology 17(1):81–94.

McDade, Thomas W., Morgan Hoke, Judith B. Borja, Linda S. Adair, and Christopher Kuzawa

    2012 Do Environments in Infancy Moderate the Association between Stress and Inflammation in Adulthood? Initial Evidence from a Birth Cohort in the Philippines. Brain, Behavior, and Immunity 31:23–30.

McDade, Thomas W., and Colleen H. Nyberg

    2010 Acculturation and Health. In Human Evolutionary Biology. Michael P. Muehlbein, ed. Pp. 581–602. Cambridge: Cambridge University Press.

Moore, S. R., A. A. M. Lima, M. R. Conaway, J. B. Schorling, A. M. Soares, and R. L. Guerrant

    2001 Early Childhood Diarrhea and Helminthiases Associate with Long-term Linear Growth Faltering. International Journal of Epidemiology 30(6):1457–1464.

Mustillo, Sarah, Nancy Krieger, Erica P. Gunderson, Stephen Sidney, Heather McCreath, and Catarina I. Kiefe

    2004 Self-reported Experiences of Racial Discrimination and Black–White Differences in Preterm and Low-birthweight Deliveries: The CARDIA Study. American Journal of Public Health 94(12):2125–2131.

Neelson, Sven, and Thomas Stratmann

    2010 Long-term Effects of Prenatal Influenza Exposure: Evidence from Switzerland. Social Science & Medicine 74(1):58–66.

Nelson, Richard E.

    2010 Testing the Fetal Origins Hypothesis in a Developing Country: Evidence from the 1918 Influenza Pandemic. Health Economics 19(10):1181–1192.

Neumann, Roderick P.

    2005 Making Political Ecology. London: Hodder Arnold.

O'Brien, Kenneth J.

    2007 The Uncounted Casualties of War: Epigenetics and the Intergenerational Transference of PTSD Symptoms among Children and Grandchildren of Vietnam Veterans in Australia. http://eprints.qut.edu.au/13794, accessed September 28, 2014.

Olshansky, S. Jay, Toni Antonucci, Lisa Berkman, Robert H. Binstock, Axel Boersch-Supan, John T. Cacioppo, Bruce A. Carnes, Laura L. Carstensen, Linda P. Fried, Dana P. Goldman, James Jackson, Martin Kohli, John Rother, Yuhui Zheng, and John Rowe

    2012 Differences in Life Expectancy Due to Race and Educational Differences Are Widening, and Many May Not Catch Up. Health Affairs 31(8):1803–1813.

Palloni, Alberto

    2006 Reproducing Inequalities: Luck, Wallets, and the Enduring Effects of Childhood Health. Demography 43(4):587–615.

Panter-Brick, Catherine

    1998 Biological Anthropology and Child Health: Context, Process and Outcome. *In* Biosocial Perspectives on Children. Catherine Panter-Brick, ed. Pp. 66–101. Cambridge: Cambridge University Press.

Pawson, Ivan G., Luis Huicho, Manuel Muro, and Alberto Pacheco

    2001 Growth of Children in Two Economically Diverse Peruvian High-altitude Communities. American Journal of Human Biology 13(3):323–340.

Peaston, Anne E., and Emma Whitelaw

    2006 Epigenetics and Phenotypic Variation in Mammals. Mammalian Genome 17(5):365–374.

Pike, Ivy L.

    2004 The Biosocial Consequences of Life on the Run: A Case Study from Turkana District, Kenya. Human Organization 63(2):221–235.

Pike, Ivy L., and Sharon R. Williams

    2006 Incorporating Psychosocial Health into Biocultural Models: Preliminary Findings from Turkana Women of Kenya. American Journal of Human Biology 18(6):729–740.

Popkin, Barry M.

    2001 The Nutrition Transition and Obesity in the Developing World. Journal of Nutrition 131(3):871S–873S.

Popkin, Barry M., and Samara Joy Nielsen

    2003 The Sweetening of the World's Diet. Obesity Research 11(11):1325–1332.

Pradhan, Aruna D., JoAnn E. Manson, Nader Rifai, Julie E. Buring, and Paul M. Ridker

    2001 C-Reactive Protein, Interleukin 6, and Risk of Developing Type 2 Diabetes Mellitus. JAMA 286(3):327–334.

Rabinow, Paul

    1992 Studies in the Anthropology of Reason. Anthropology Today 8(5):7–10.

    1996 Essays on the Anthropology of Reason. Princeton: Princeton University Press.

Ramakrishnan, Usha, Reynaldo Martorell, Dirk G. Schroeder, and Rafael Flores

    1999 Role of Intergenerational Effects on Linear Growth. Journal of Nutrition 129(2):544S–549S.

Richards, Marcus, Rebecca Hardy, Diana Kuh, and Michael E. J. Wadsworth

    2001 Birth Weight and Cognitive Function in the British 1946 Birth Cohort: Longitudinal Population Based Study. BMJ 322(7280):199–203.

Richter, Matthias, and David Blane

    2013 The Life Course: Challenges and Opportunities for Public Health Research. International Journal of Public Health 58(1):1–2.

Ridker, Paul M., Julie E. Buring, Jessie Shih, Mathew Matias, and Charles H. Hennekens

    1998 Prospective Study of C-reactive Protein and the Risk of Future Cardiovascular Events among Apparently Healthy Women. Circulation 98(8):731–733.

Riley, James C.

    2001 Rising Life Expectancy: A Global History. Cambridge: Cambridge University Press.

Rose, Geoffrey, and Michael G. Marmot

    1981   Social Class and Coronary Heart Disease. British Heart Journal 45(1):13–19.

Roseberry, William

    1998   Political Economy and Social Fields. *In* Building a New Biocultural Synthesis. Alan H. Goodman and Thomas L. Leatherman, eds. Pp. 75–91. Ann Arbor, MI: University of Michigan Press.

Roseboom, Tessa, Susanne de Rooij, and Rebecca Painter

    2006 The Dutch Famine and its Long-term Consequences for Adult Health. Early Human Development. 82(8):485–491.

Roseboom, Tessa J., Jan H. van der Meulen, Clive Osmond, David J. Barker, Anita C. Ravelli, Jutta M. Schroeder-Tanka, Gert A. van Montfrans, Robert P. J. Michels, and Otto P. Bleker

    2000 Coronary Heart Disease after Prenatal Exposure to the Dutch Famine, 1944–45. Heart 84(6):595–598.

Roseboom, Tessa J., Jan H. van der Meulen, Anita C. Ravelli, Clive Osmond, David J. Barker, and Otto P. Bleker

    2001 Effects of Prenatal Exposure to the Dutch Famine on Adult Disease in Later Life: An Overview. Molecular and Cellular Endocrinology 185(1–2):93–98.

Rowland, Michael G., Suan G. J. Rowland, and Timothy J. Cole

    1988 Impact of Infection on the Growth of Children from 0 to 2 Years in an Urban West African Community. American Journal of Clinical Nutrition 47(1):134–138.

Schell, Lawrence M.

    1997 Culture as a Stressor: A Revised Model of Biocultural Interaction. American Journal of Physical Anthropology 102(1):67–77.

Seeman, Teresa E., Burton H. Singer, John W. Rowe, Ralph I. Horwitz, and Bruce S. McEwen

    1997 Price of Adaptation–Allostatic Load and Its Health Consequences: MacArthur Studies of Successful Aging. Archives of Internal Medicine 157(19):2259–2268.

Shell-Duncan, Bettina

    2008 From Health to Human Rights: Female Genital Cutting and the Politics of Intervention. American Anthropologist 110(2):225–236.

Silventoinen, Karri, Jaakko Kaprio, Eero Lahelma, and Markku Koskenvuo

    2000 Relative Effect of Genetic and Environmental Factors on Body Height: Differences across Birth Cohorts among Finnish Men and Women. American Journal of Public Health 90(4):627–630.

Singer, Merrill

    2011 Toward a Critical Biosocial Model of Ecohealth in Southern Africa: The HIV/AIDS and Nutrition Insecurity Syndemic. Annals of Anthropological Practice 35(1):8–27.

Skinner, Michael K

    2008 What Is an Epigenetic Transgenerational Phenotype?: F3 or F2. Reproductive Toxicology 25(1):2–6.

Smith, George Davey

    2003 Health Inequalities: Lifecourse Approaches. Bristol: Policy Press.

Steckel, Richard H.

    1983 Height and Per Capita Income. Historical Methods 16(1):1–7.

Stein, Zena, Mervyn Susser, Gerhart Saenger, and Francis Marolla

    1975 Famine and Human Development: The Dutch Hunger Winter of 1944–1945.

Sterling, Peter

    2004 Principles of Allostasis: Optimal Design, Predictive Regulation, Pathophysiology, and Rational Therapeutics. *In* Allostasis, Homeostasis, and the Costs of Physiological Adaptation. Jay Schulkin, ed. Pp. 17–64. Cambridge: Cambridge University Press. http://www.brown.edu/Departments/Human_Development_Center/Roundtable/Sterling.pdf.

    2012 Allostasis: A Model of Predictive Regulation. Physiology & Behavior 106(1):5–15.

Sterling, Peter, and Joseph Eyer

    1988 Allostasis: A New Paradigm to Explain Arousal Pathology. *In* Handbook of Life Stress, Cognition, and Health. Shirley Fisher and James Reason, eds. Pp. 629–649. Oxford: John Wiley & Sons.

Stewart, R. J. C., Hilda Sheppard, R. Preece, and J. C. Waterlow
  1980 The Effect of Rehabilitation at Different Stages of Development of Rats Marginally Malnourished for Ten to Twelve Generations. British Journal of Nutrition 43(03):403–412.
Tegethoff, Marion, Christopher Pryce, and Gunther Meinlschmidt
  2009 Effects of Intrauterine Exposure to Synthetic Glucocorticoids on Fetal, Newborn, and Infant Hypothalamic-Pituitary-Adrenal Axis Function in Humans: A Systematic Review. Endocrine Reviews 30(7):753–789.
Thomas, R. Brooke
  1998 The Evolution of Human Adaptability Paradigms: Toward a Biology of Poverty. *In* Building a New Biocultural Synthesis: Political-Economic Perspectives on Human Biology. Alan H. Goodman and Thomas L. Leatherman, eds. Pp. 451–473. Ann Arbor, MI:University of Michigan Press.
Thomas, R. Brooke, Thomas L. Leatherman, J. W. Carey, and J. D. Haas
  1988 Biosocial Consequences of Illness among Small-scale Farmers: A Research Design. *In* Capacity for Work in the Tropics. K. J. Collins and D. F. Roberts, eds. Pp.249–276. Cambridge: Cambridge University Press.
Uddin, Monica, Allison E. Aiello, Derek E. Wildman, Karestan C. Koenen, Graham Pawelec, Regina de los Santos, Emily Goldmann, and Sandro Galea
  2010 Epigenetic and Immune Function Profiles Associated with Posttraumatic Stress Disorder. Proceedings of the National Academy of Sciences USA 107(20):9470–9475.
Valdez, R., M. A. Athens, G. H. Thompson, B. S. Bradshaw, and M. P. Stern
  1994 Birthweight and Adult Health Outcomes in a Biethnic Population in the USA. Diabetologia 37(6):624–631.
Venkataramani, Atheendar S.
  2011 The Intergenerational Transmission of Height: Evidence from Rural Vietnam. Health Economics 20(12):1448–1467.
Wadsworth, Michael Edwin John
  1991 The Imprint of Time: Childhood, History, and Adult Life. Oxford: Oxford University Press.
Weedon, Michael N., Hana Lango, Cecilia M. Lindgren, Chris Wallace, David M. Evans, Massimo Mangino, Rachel M. Freathy, John R. B. Perry, Suzanne Stevens, Alistair S. Hall, Nilesh J. Samani, Beverly Shields, Inga Prokopenko, Martin Farrall, Anna Dominiczak, Toby Johnson, Sven Bergmann, Jacques S. Beckmann, Peter Vollenweider, Dawn M. Waterworth, Vincent Mooser, Colin N. A. Palmer, Andrew D. Morris, Willem H. Ouwehand, Mark Caulfield, Patricia B. Munroe, Andrew T. Hattersley, Mark I. McCarthy, and Timothy M. Frayling
  2008 Genome-wide Association Analysis Identifies 20 Loci that Influence Adult Height. Nature Genetics 40(5):575–583.
Wiley, Andrea S.
  1992 Adaptation and the Biocultural Paradigm in Medical Anthropology: A Critical Review. Medical Anthropology Quarterly 6(3):216–236.
  2004 An Ecology of High-altitude Infancy: A Biocultural Perspective. Cambridge University Press.
Wilkinson, Richard G.
  1996 Unhealthy Societies: The Afflictions of Inequality. New York: Routledge.
Williams, Scott M., Jonathan L. Haines, and Jason H. Moore
  2004 The Use of Animal Models in the Study of Complex Disease: All Else Is Never Equal or Why Do So Many Human Studies Fail to Replicate Animal Findings? Bioessays 26(2):170–179.
Wolf, Eric R.
  1982 Europe and the People without History. Berkeley, CA: University of California Press.
Yang, Jian, Beben Benyamin, Brian P. McEvoy, Scott Gordon, Anjali K. Henders, Dale R. Nyholt, Pamela A. Madden, Andrew C. Heath, Nicholas G. Martin, Grant W. Montgomery, Michael E. Goddard, and Peter M. Visscher
  2010 Common SNPs Explain a Large Proportion of the Heritability for Human Height. Nature Genetics 42(7):565–569.

CULTURE AS A MEDIATOR OF HEALTH DISPARITIES: CULTURAL CONSONANCE, SOCIAL CLASS, AND HEALTH

WILLIAM W. DRESSLER
University of Alabama

MAURO C. BALIEIRO
Paulista University

ROSANE P. RIBEIRO
University of São Paulo-Ribeirão Preto

JOSÉ ERNESTO DOS SANTOS
University of São Paulo-Ribeirão Preto

Health disparities or health inequalities refer to enduring differences between population groups in health status, well-being, and mortality. Health inequalities have been described by race, ethnic group, gender, and social class. A variety of theories have been proposed to account for health inequalities, including access to medical care and absolute material deprivation. Several theorists (including Michael Marmot and Richard Wilkinson) have argued that relative deprivation is the primary factor. By this they mean the inability of individuals to achieve the kind of lifestyle that is valued and considered normative in their social context. In this article, we show that the concept and measurement of cultural consonance can operationalize what Marmot and Wilkinson mean by relative deprivation. Cultural consonance is the degree to which individuals approximate, in their own beliefs and behaviors, the prototypes for belief and behavior encoded in shared cultural models. Widely shared cultural models in society describe what is regarded both as appropriate and desirable in many different domains. These cultural models are both directive and motivating: people try to achieve the goals defined in these models; however, as a result of both social and economic constraints, some individuals are unable to effectively incorporate these cultural goals into their own lives. The result is an enduring loss of coherence in life, because life is not unfolding in the way that it, culturally speaking, "should." The resulting chronic stress is associated with psychobiological distress. We illustrate this process with data collected in urban Brazil. A theory of cultural consonance provides a uniquely biocultural contribution to the understanding of health inequalities. [cultural consonance, cultural consensus, relative deprivation, Brazil]

The Black Report (named for the chairman, Sir Douglas Black, of the commission that released it) was issued in Britain in 1980 (Black and Townsend 1982). It summarized the findings of a commission whose charge was to examine available health statistics and

ANNALS OF ANTHROPOLOGICAL PRACTICE 38.2, pp. 214–231. ISSN: 2153-957X. © 2015 by the American Anthropological Association. DOI:10.1111/napa.12053

determine if there were detectable and reliable inequalities in health in Britain. By this they meant systematic and enduring health differences between identifiable population groups. The commission found inequalities in health by age, gender, race, ethnicity, and, especially, social class.

These inequalities are now a focus of research in all parts of the world, although here in the United States we have seen fit to sanitize the topic under the rubric *health disparities*. As noted on the website for Healthy People 2020, the official policy blueprint for improving public health in the United States:

> If a health outcome is seen in a greater or lesser extent between populations, there is disparity. Race or ethnicity, sex, sexual identity, age, disability, socioeconomic status, and geographic location all contribute to an individual's ability to achieve good health. (Healthy People 2020, n.d.).

The question driving research is, what accounts for these disparities? Any number of structural and material factors could be relevant, as well as behavioral factors, including diet, physical activity, and health behaviors (e.g., smoking, drinking). There are also potential social selection processes, that is, individuals may assume a lower socioeconomic status as a result of their poor health, rather than their lower socioeconomic status leading to poor health. While all of these explanations have some merit, they still, in the final analysis, do not account for health disparities (Marmot 2004).

The major theorists in the area, notably Michael Marmot (2004), and Richard Wilkinson and Kate Pickett (2011), emphasize instead a psychosocial stress hypothesis. They argue that individuals in disadvantaged groups are deprived of meaningful participation in the wider society and that the stresses associated with that deprivation account for health disparities.

We will argue here that, while there is considerable evidence in support of this position, the evidence is not as strong as it could be, primarily because current models of health disparities fail to take culture and biocultural interactions into account. A biocultural approach in anthropology is uniquely situated to contribute to the study of health disparities precisely because it takes the concept of culture seriously, and is thus able to link the individual to collective representations of what a meaningful life is (Dressler 2005). The utility of this approach will be illustrated with data collected over the past 20 years in urban Brazil.

SOCIOECONOMIC DISPARITIES IN HEALTH

Arguably, the most important thinkers on the question of socioeconomic health disparities are Michael Marmot (2004) and Richard Wilkinson (1994; Wilkinson and Pickett 2006, 2007). Marmot is most well known for his direction of the Whitehall Studies. These prospective epidemiologic studies were designed to directly examine factors that accounted for the inverse association of social class and the risk of cardiovascular disease. British civil servants served as the study population. This controlled for access to health care, given that all members of the civil service (referred to as Whitehall in British vernacular) had access to high-quality care through the National Health Service and additional insurance. There was a clear social class hierarchy in Whitehall, formed by occupational categories. These included janitors and messengers at the bottom of the hierarchy, followed by clerical staff, then professional staff (statisticians, economists), and finally, at the top of the hierarchy, the administrative staff. These are individuals with elite British educations who help to set and direct policy.

After controlling for heart disease risk factors (blood pressure, cholesterol, and others), the lowest social class group was 50 percent more likely to die from heart disease than the highest social class group over a 25-year follow-up; furthermore, there was a gradient of increasing risk from the administrators down to the janitors, with no sharp break in the pattern. This is a particularly important part of the findings, because this was a study population in which no one could be considered "poor" in the sense that they lacked access to basic material resources for maintaining life. Rather, what is striking about the results in this and many other studies is that there is a continuous gradient, such that even doctoral level economists are at a slightly higher risk of mortality than the administrative staff who outrank them (Marmot 2004:60).

Much effort was invested in testing alternative hypotheses, such as diet, smoking, or other medical conditions, that could explain the gradient. Since nothing could explain the gradient, Marmot labeled it "The Status Syndrome" (2004). The main thrust of his argument is that increasing social status enables individuals to exercise greater autonomy in their lives, and this enhances their ability to live the life they value. Conversely, lower social status blocks these capabilities, resulting in long-term, chronic stress, and an increased risk of disease.

Richard Wilkinson (1994) is known for his studies of income inequality and health. Income inequality refers not to the differences in wealth or income between individuals, but rather to the entire range of socioeconomic variation within a system (community, U.S. state, or entire nation). It assesses the degree of inequality at the group level. As such, it is an "integral aggregate variable," or a variable that refers only to aggregates as units of observation. The Gini coefficient is a common way to measure income inequality. If everyone in a community had the same amount of money, the Gini coefficient would be equal to 0.0; if only one person in the community had all the money, the Gini coefficient would be equal to 1.0. Wilkinson (1994) first explored the association of income inequality and life expectancy in Western European societies, finding that as income inequality increased, life expectancy declined. This was striking, given that these are the world's most affluent nations. It was not the affluence, however, that was at issue, but rather how that affluence was distributed.

There have been numerous demonstrations of the association between income inequality and a variety of health, behavioral, and psychological outcomes (summarized in Wilkinson and Pickett 2011). For example, here in the United States, using states as units of analysis, the correlation between the state-level Gini coefficient and aggregate health outcomes are as follows: with overall mortality, $r = .403$ ($p < .01$); with homicide rates, $r = .695$ ($p < .01$); and, with mortality from coronary heart disease, $r = .521$ ($p < .01$; source: author's data). These correlations are large and impressive in part because they are based on aggregate data (hence, noise in the data gets averaged out); nevertheless, it is clear that income inequality is a potent correlate of our collective well-being.

In considering these findings, Wilkinson asks if it is an absolute (sometimes simply referred to as *material*) deprivation or a relative deprivation that is important. While these terms will be discussed in greater detail below, the primary distinction is between lacking the basic resources of food and shelter necessary for survival—or absolute/material deprivation—versus lacking what is considered to be customary in a given society— or relative deprivation. Wilkinson (Wilkinson and Pickett 2007) favors the relative deprivation argument, since so much of his work has dealt with social units that are not only affluent (Western European nations), but are also functioning welfare states. Marmot (2004:118) also invokes the concept in his explanation of the social gradient. The concept of relative deprivation has a long history in social thought, and a consideration of some of that history will be useful for the argument being constructed here.

DEPRIVATION: ABSOLUTE AND RELATIVE

Poverty, its nature and effects, has been the focus of social scientific inquiry since at least the 19th century and Engels' investigation of working class conditions in England (Engels 1958[1845]). At the turn of the century, Rowntree and other pioneering investigators in Britain attempted to objectively measure levels of poverty by estimating the nutritional needs of working families, and then estimating the amount of money required to fulfill both those nutritional needs and additional needs for clothing, heating, and household sundries (Townsend 1979:32–33). Current definitions of poverty in the United States are based on this approach (Weinberg 1995).

In a real sense, these estimates of poverty levels are based on a biological reductionist assumption: that human well-being is to be measured solely in terms of the minimum physiological requirements for growth, development, resistance to disease, and work capacity. As such, this approach to poverty ignores socially or culturally defined needs.

Townsend (1979), in his monumental *Poverty in the United Kingdom*, argued that this is a flawed approach to the definition of poverty for a variety of reasons. He noted the technical difficulties in estimating the nutritional requirements of individuals, as well as in determining the disposable income that is available to a household (Townsend 1979:32–39). But the primary flaw in this approach is the extent to which it ignores consensual social definitions of appropriate lifestyles. As Townsend put it:

> Individuals, families and groups in the population can be said to be in poverty when they lack the resources to obtain the types of diet, participate in the activities and have the living conditions and amenities which are customary, or are at least widely encouraged or approved, in the societies to which they belong. *Their resources are so seriously below those commanded by the average individual or family that they are, in effect, excluded from ordinary living patterns, customs and activities* (Townsend 1979:31, emphasis added).

What Townsend suggested was that poverty should be understood as the degree of relative deprivation experienced by individuals and groups. He distinguished three forms of deprivation: (1) objective deprivation, or the extent to which individuals are deprived of the material conditions of life; (2) conventionally acknowledged deprivation, or the extent to which persons are deprived of conditions socially defined as necessary or appropriate (see quote above); and (3) subjective deprivation, meaning the extent to which individuals feel themselves to be deprived (Townsend 1979:49). He regarded the second sense of the term relative deprivation to be the most important and useful, since it assesses the extent to which individuals are prevented from acting upon the social and cultural norms of their own group.

Townsend was not alone in regarding this normative sense of relative deprivation to be essential in understanding patterns of poverty (e.g., Bell 1995). There is, however, one difficulty that always arises in attempts to understand poverty in this sense. What are the "ordinary living patterns, customs, and activities" from which persons are excluded due to a lack of resources? How are such customs to be determined? It is this issue that has led many to adhere to a minimum income definition of poverty. As Weinberg notes in his rejection of relative deprivation: "Minimal consumption standards for all necessary commodities could in theory be established ... *but doing so would raise difficult ethical issues about which commodities to include (e.g., is a telephone a necessity?)*" (Weinberg 1995:6, emphasis added).

Townsend (1979:38) suggested that, as much as possible, the definition of relative deprivation should be based on independent or external criteria. Townsend argued that "style of life" is a sociocultural dimension by which deprivation could be assessed. Style of life includes the acquisition of basic consumer goods as well the awareness of culturally valued knowledge and the participation in culturally valued social activities. Since at least the work of Veblen (1918), lifestyle in this sense has been seen as a major component of social judgments regarding social worth or prestige, so much so that Veblen's term *conspicuous consumption* entered the vernacular. In recent years, however, investigators have argued that conspicuous consumption is only one aspect, perhaps relatively small, of the social meaning of consumption activities (Belk 1988; Bourdieu 1984; Douglas and Isherwood 1979; McCracken 1988). While recognizing the push of consumerism, this view sees style of life as a broadly patterned activity expressive of more than what Townsend (1979:58) referred to as "supercilious and derogatory distinctions." Rather, style of life as a dimension of social life expresses and reinforces in a concrete way a sense of belonging to and integration into a social group. And where an individual's or family's lack of consonance with the community is evident materially, to be demonstrated day in and day out, the sense of loss or failure may be profound.

In his empirical work in Britain, Townsend developed a lengthy inventory that included items dealing with material consumption (e.g., owning a television, refrigerator, and other similar items) and with social behaviors (e.g., being able to go out for a meal periodically). No justification for the inclusion of items was given other than the reasoned judgment of the investigator. A scale of deprivation was then developed in which an individual or household received one point for each item they lacked. The way in which this scale of relative deprivation covaried with other, more conventional indicators of poverty was then examined.

Later investigators expanded upon this approach, especially using survey data to define what a representative sample of the population defined as customary and approved consumption (Hallerod 1996; Mack and Lansley 1985). While these are reasonable approaches to the study of relative deprivation, they also tend to be arbitrary in choosing the cutoff point for what is thought to be important (e.g., 51 percent of the sample must say an item is important?). These approaches to the definition of consensual lifestyles rely solely on the statistical aggregation of individual responses (Shore 1991:11). There is no independent model that enables the investigators: (1) to test for the existence of a shared model of lifestyles; (2) to estimate the degree of sharing of the model; or (3) to estimate the content of that model.

Furthermore, why limit the investigation of relative deprivation to the specific domain of lifestyle? While Veblen's theory makes clear the importance of this domain, why would other domains not be important as well? Indeed, Marmot's (2004) argument suggests a broader range of aspirations that might be considered.

It would be useful to have a theory regarding how normative judgments might be structured within a society, and a related set of methodological procedures to assess the distribution of normative judgments and normative behaviors within a society. In this article, innovations in culture theory (D'Andrade, 1984, 1995) and ethnographic methods (Romney et al. 1986) are used that may provide the study of relative deprivation a more substantial theoretical and methodological foundation, and in turn contribute to an understanding of socioeconomic health disparities (Kawachi and Kennedy 1999). The cultural consensus model (Romney et al. 1986) and the related theory and measurement of cultural consonance provide a more solid conceptual and operational foundation for examining these processes.

CULTURAL CONSENSUS AND CULTURAL CONSONANCE

The foundation for the approach to be outlined here rests on a cognitive theory of culture. This theory starts with Goodenough's (1996) definition of culture: that which one must know to function adequately in a given social setting. This knowledge includes procedural understandings of how to do and make things, social understandings of how to interact appropriately with others, and the understanding of the world that underlies belief and opinion.

This knowledge is learned both through individual experience, resulting in idiosyncratic understandings, and through systematic interaction with others and socialization, resulting in shared understandings. Shared knowledge, or culture, is cognitively encoded in the form of cultural models: skeletal, stripped-down representations of some cultural domain (e.g., lifestyle, the family), including the elements that make up that domain and processes that link the elements. Each domain contains at least one prototype, or best exemplar, of the domain. While all cultural models will be conditioned by individual biography, it is the sharing of cultural models that makes all social life possible.

Cultural models vary in the degree to which they are shared. The sharing of a cultural model can be verified and quantified using the cultural consensus model (Romney et al. 1986; Weller 2007). The cultural consensus model examines the degree to which the similarity in individuals' responses to a standardized set of questions about a domain (e.g., "How important is it to own a house in order to live a good life"? This question is repeated for multiple items populating the domain of lifestyle.) can be estimated by positing an underlying shared model of "culturally correct" responses. Note that the investigator does not know what is culturally correct; rather, what is culturally correct is estimated from the degree to which individuals agree among themselves in their responses.

Using a factor analysis of the similarities in response among individuals across a given knowledge base, cultural consensus analysis generates three estimates: (1) the overall degree of sharing, calculated from the ratio of the first-to-second eigenvalue of a factor analysis of persons (or Q-factor analysis); (2) the degree to which each individual shares in the knowledge base, referred to as *cultural competence*, estimated by the individual's loading on the first unrotated factor; and (3) the estimated culturally correct responses, calculated as the weighted average of the responses of individuals, giving higher weight to individuals who are agreed with more strongly by others.

A cognitive theory of culture, operationalized using the cultural consensus model, provides a theoretically and methodologically satisfying way of systematically identifying for a group of people features of life and living " . . . which are customary, or are at least widely encouraged or approved, in the societies to which they belong" (Townsend 1979:31).

As Bourdieu (1984) has repeatedly reminded us, however, people do not merely think things, they do things as well. This is the importance of the concept of cultural consonance, defined as the degree to which individuals approximate, in their own beliefs and behaviors, the prototypes for belief and behavior encoded in shared cultural models. Using a measure of cultural consonance, the degree to which individuals are able to put into practice their shared understanding within a cultural domain can be evaluated. Why would people not be culturally consonant? The first and most obvious answer is that they choose to be different. This is probably more rare than it might seem, especially for a cultural domain in which there is wide agreement.

The second reason that individuals will have low cultural consonance in a domain is that "life chances," to borrow Weber's term, are stacked against them. They do not have the resources—principally economic, but also including racial and gender inequalities—to put into motion the understanding of how life is to be lived that they share with their neighbors.

Individuals with low cultural consonance suffer a relative deprivation, when cultural consonance is measured in terms of broadly shared life goals. A rough sketch of how socioeconomic health disparities are mediated by cultural consonance is as follows: (1) there are widely shared cultural domains that define "goals in life," ways of living to which individuals aspire across the lifespan; (2) being able to achieve cultural consonance within a domain requires a variety of personal resources, especially socioeconomic resources; (3) when these resources are lacking, individuals are unable to achieve cultural consonance; (4) they see themselves, and are seen by others, not to have achieved widely shared life goals; (5) this results in a low sense of coherence, or the feeling that life has not worked out the way it is supposed to; (6) this also leads to unsatisfying mundane social interactions in which low cultural consonance individuals are treated with a lack of respect because they embody this status; (7) repeated arousal of the hypothalamus–pituitary–adrenal axis and the sympathetic nervous system, as a result of unsatisfying social interaction and a low sense of coherence, lead to higher allostatic load; and (8) higher allostatic load over a lifetime results in poor health.

We have examined this process in research in urban Brazil over the past 20 years, testing key parts of this hypothesized causal chain. Furthermore, combining data from two time periods (1991 and 2001), we can examine the association of cultural consonance with health outcomes (blood pressure and perceived stress), relative to the socioeconomic gradient and relative to income inequality.

CULTURAL CONSONANCE AND HEALTH IN URBAN BRAZIL

We have carried out research in the city of Ribeirão Preto, Brazil, over nearly 30 years, with the past 20 years focusing on cultural consonance and health. Specifically, we collected data in 1991 (Dressler et al. 1997, 1998), in 2001 (Dressler, Balieiro et al. 2005; Dressler et al. 2007a), and we are currently collecting data in a study initiated in 2011 (Dressler et al. 2015). Research on cultural consonance requires a two-stage method in which the cultural models for domains in which cultural consonance is to be measured are investigated first using ethnographic methods, and then social survey research is carried out using measures of cultural consonance derived from the first stage. Both stages were carried out in 1991 and 2001; in the 2011 study, we have completed the cultural modeling stage and are engaged in collecting social survey data.

The Research Site

Ribeirão Preto is a city of 600,000 people in the north of the state of São Paulo. Located in a rich agricultural region, it is a center for light manufacturing and financial services related to the cultivation of sugar, coffee, citrus, and soy. It is also a regional leader in education and health care. It is known as unusually affluent. Despite, or because of, its affluence, Ribeirão Preto exhibits the differences between rich and poor that characterize all Brazilian communities. In the 1990s the Gini coefficient for Brazil exceeded 0.60, ranking it as one of the most unequal advanced industrial nations. Since then, the Gini coefficient has declined to nearly 0.50. This diminishing inequality is a function of a variety of factors, including both the stabilization of the currency under the government of Fernando Henrique Cardoso, and aggressive programs to deal with poverty under the governments of Luiz Inácio Lula da Silva and Dilma Rouseff.

All research in Brazil must take social inequality into account. In our research we have done this in two ways. When collecting ethnographic data, care has been taken to interview respondents distributed by educational level as a proxy for social class. For our survey data, we collected random samples stratified by neighborhood. Four neighborhoods were selected to represent socioeconomic differences in Ribeirão Preto. The first began its life as a classic *favela*, or squatter settlement. In late 1992, the municipality built a small *conjunto* (housing area or subdivision) of two-room cinder block houses and residents of the *favela* were moved there. *Favelados* paid rent to the municipality on a rent-to-own basis. Many *favelados*, due to their unstable employment, were unable to maintain these payments and left for other *favelas* in the area. This enabled persons of slightly higher means, who could amass the capital to purchase these abandoned houses from the city, to move into this neighborhood. Today, it is a lower-class area of the city, with fewer than half the residents from the original *favela*. Residents tend to work as unskilled laborers and domestic servants.

The second neighborhood is a classic *conjunto habitacional*. These are subdivisions that are built in partnership between the municipality and a contractor. The neighborhood started as uniform four-room cinder-block houses, but quickly transformed as residents added rooms, garden walls, and even second stories. Over the years it has developed its own commercial district with a supermarket, pharmacies, retail stores, and bars. Residents are employed in varied occupations, including school teachers, nurses aids, store clerks, and other lower-level professions (e.g., computer technician).

The third neighborhood is an old, traditional, middle-class area that dates to the founding of Ribeirão Preto. Built in a European style, houses present seamless walls to cobbled streets. Older residents remember the time when families would spend the evenings sitting outside on the sidewalk, exchanging news and gossip with neighbors. The neighborhood boasts its own central *praça* or "plaza" fronting the Catholic Church, and there is a large and vibrant business section that rivals the city center. Residents tend to work as lower-level professionals (teachers, nurses), to own their own small businesses, or to work as managers in local businesses.

The fourth neighborhood is a housing area adjacent to a university. Many residents are university professors, but many are also in the professions (physicians, attorneys) or the owners of large businesses and factories. The homes in the neighborhood tend to be quite large and spacious, with large and well-tended gardens.

Cultural Models and Cultural Consensus

Our research has evolved over the years in the study of cultural models and cultural consensus. In the 1991 study, we used cultural consensus principally to confirm the shared ideas around the cultural domains of lifestyle and social support that had been selected for study because of their theoretical importance as predictors of health status (Dressler et al. 1996, 1997; Dressler and Santos 2000). In 2001, we used systematic techniques of cultural domain analysis (Borgatti 1994) to identify and explore four cultural domains: lifestyle, social support, family life, and national identity (Dressler, Borges et al. 2005). In our recent study, begun in 2011, we have examined the same four domains from 2001, specifically to determine how cultural consensus changes or remains stable (Dressler et al. 2015).

The domain of lifestyle refers to material goods (such as owning a home, a car, having Internet access) and leisure activities (being with friends, joining a sports club, shopping) that are seen as necessary for living a good life. Social support is the ability to call on specific sources of support (family, friends, coworkers, church members, specialists) in times of

TABLE 1. Cultural Consensus in Various Cultural Domains in Three Studies

	Year of Study		
Cultural Domain	1991	2001	2011
Lifestyle			
Eigenvalue ratio	5.55	6.59	7.70
Mean competence	0.65 (±.15)	.71 (±.12)	.72 (± .11)
Social Support			
Eigenvalue ratio	3.11	6.53	5.21
Mean competence	.61 (±.10)	.67 (± .14)	.65 (±.16)
Family Life			
Eigenvalue ratio	–	7.42	9.62
Mean competence		.82 (±.09)	.84 (±.09)
National Identity			
Eigenvalue ratio	–	3.97	3.50
Mean competence		.57 (±.19)	.61 (±.16)

felt need (common problems ranging from needing a ride to psychological difficulties). Family life refers to the characteristics, including both structure and emotional bonds, that define a good Brazilian family. And, national identity organizes the characteristics that make Brazilians, Brazilian (see Dressler et al. 2004; Dressler, Balieiro, et al. 2005, 2007a, b; Dressler, Borges et al. 2005 for more detailed descriptions of these domains).

For each domain, we focused on a single dimension of value or importance to test for cultural consensus; that is, do people rank elements of each domain as more or less important in ways consistent enough to infer that they are drawing on a shared cultural model in making their assessments? Table 1 summarizes data on cultural consensus for all three of these studies. In each study, in each domain, there is a broad cultural consensus that organizes people's thinking. The level of cultural consensus varies by domain, but nevertheless, there is broad agreement within the community, through time, and based on different samples, of the importance of these elements within these domains. Furthermore, the cultural consensus displayed in Table 1 does not vary by socioeconomic status. The importance assigned to elements of each domain is equivalent across socioeconomic groups (Dressler et al. 2015; Dressler, Borges et al. 2005).

The cultural domains that we have examined here can be grouped together under a larger meta-domain we have labeled "goals in life." That is, these overlapping cultural domains describe ends to which individuals aspire as they pass through life stages.

Cultural Consonance

How effectively can people act on these shared understandings? This is the question of cultural consonance. As we have shown elsewhere, the degree to which individuals, in their own lives, actually match the profile of beliefs and behaviors that are collectively regarded as important in each domain can be measured in each domain (Dressler 1996, 2005; Dressler, Borges et al. 2005). And, we have found that low cultural consonance is associated with higher blood pressure (Dressler et al. 1997, 1998, 2005), higher body mass (Dressler et al. 2008, 2012), immune system challenge (Dressler 2006), and higher psychological distress (Dressler et al. 2007a, b). Some outcomes are associated with cultural consonance in specific domains; most, however, are associated with generalized cultural consonance. This refers to the tendency for individuals to be consonant across multiple domains (Dressler et al. 2007a).

The dilemma posed by low cultural consonance can be illustrated in Figure 1. In the graph in Panel A, cultural competence, averaged across four cultural domains, is shown in relation to educational attainment; there is no difference among the groups in average cultural competence (i.e., cultural *knowledge*). In Panel B, generalized cultural consonance is shown in relation to education level. These differences are highly significant. In other words, many people live in an environment of meaning in which they know what is valued and desired in life, but they are unable to achieve it in their own behaviors.

Cultural Consonance, Economic Inequality, and Health

With the data we have from Brazil, we can examine how cultural consonance mediates and moderates the association of economic inequality and health. Throughout this article, we have oscillated in the discussion of socioeconomic health disparities between the social gradient and conditions of income inequality. Using our 1991 and 2001 data together, we can examine the association of both these types of inequality and health, relative to cultural consonance. At the outset it should be emphasized that this is best regarded as an illustrative exercise rather than a definitive test of any hypotheses. While the data collection was guided by a single theoretical orientation, from one study to the next we were more concerned with refining and extending our theory and methods than with precise replication; however, we do have some data in common between studies that can serve for at least an exercise. Obviously, age (in years) and gender (coded as women = 0 and men = 1) are comparable, as is the body mass index (BMI), calculated from height (in meters) and weight (in kilograms). For a measure of socioeconomic status, we can use family income, collected in both studies as the number of minimum salaries coming into the household, and then converted to constant 2001 *reais* (the Brazilian currency). The study itself (coded as 1991 = 0 and 2001 = 1) can serve as a measure of changing income inequality, since the Gini coefficient for Brazil declined from about 0.60 in 1991 to 0.55 in 2001.

There are data available to roughly measure cultural consonance in one cultural domain: lifestyle. In 1991, to assess cultural competence, we asked people to rate the importance of items as defining one as "a success in life." In 2001, respondents rated items in terms of their importance "for having a good life." There are 14 items in common between these two inventories. Furthermore, the two sets of ratings are correlated at $r = .81$. This justifies combining them as a measure of cultural consonance. To do so, we weighted each item by its 1991 rating of importance, and summed these for each individual. The higher the value of this scale, the more an individual approaches in his or her own life a lifestyle that is collectively valued.

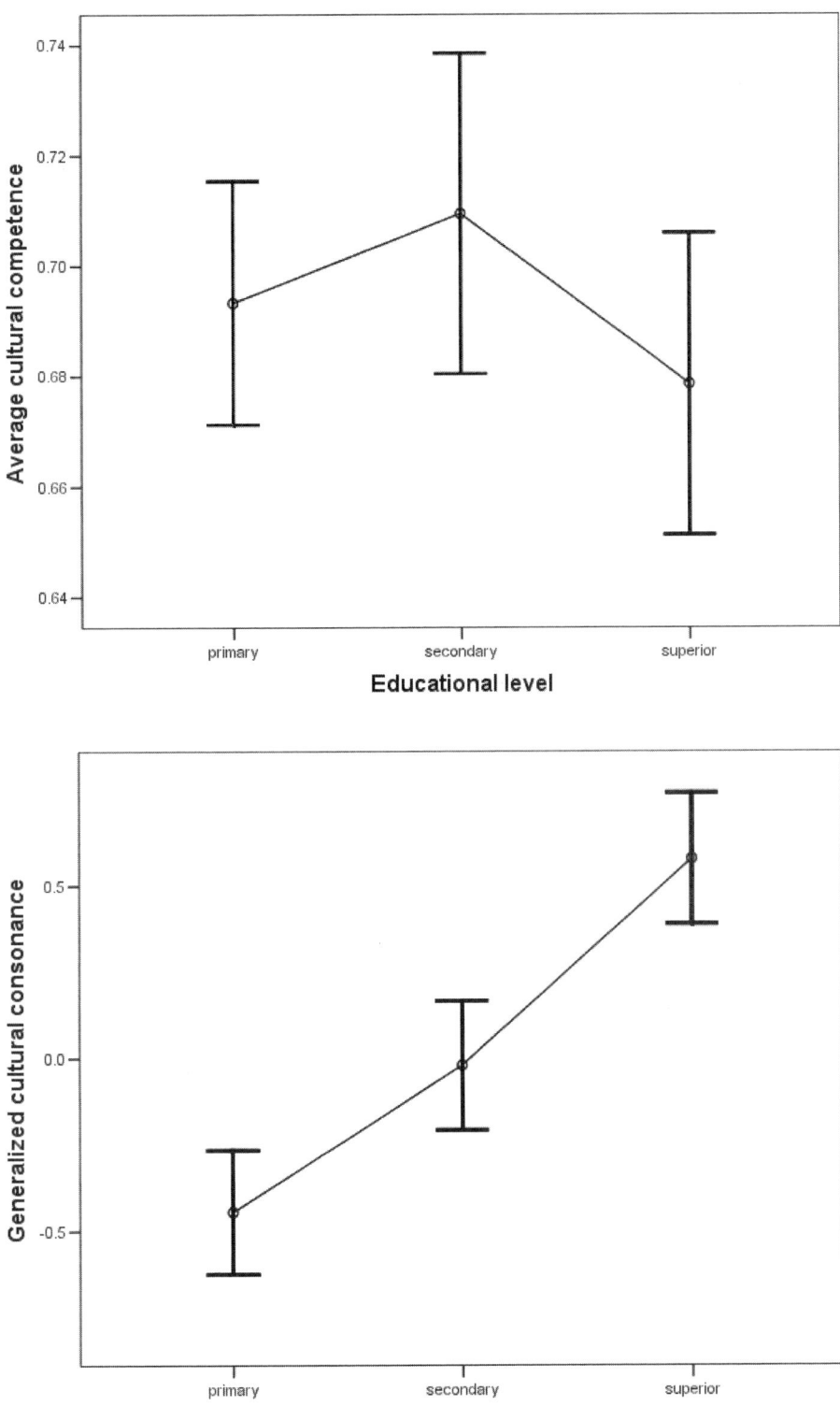

FIGURE 1. Association of educational level with cultural consensus (Panel A) and cultural consonance (Panel B).

TABLE 2. Descriptive Statistics

	1991 (n = 304)	2001 (n = 271)	Total sample (n = 575)
Age[*]	38.5 (± 12.4)	40.9 (± 11.6)	39.6 (± 12.1)
Sex (percentage of male)	40.5	39.1	39.8
BMI	24.5 (± 4.8)	25.2 (± 5.2)	24.8 (± 5.0)
Family income	1,309.8 (± 650.5)	1,381.1 (± 596.3)	1,343.3 (± 626.0)
Cultural consonance[**]	10.4 (± 3.4)	12.6 (± 2.5)	11.5 (± 3.2)
Perceived stress[**]	11.1 (± 6.9)	9.3 (± 5.7)	10.2 (± 6.5)
Systolic blood pressure	123.1 (± 17.7)	122.9 (± 16.4)	123.0 (± 16.9)

Tests of differences between studies.

[*]$p < .01$, [**]$p < .001$.

Finally, with respect to health outcomes, we collected Cohen's Perceived Stress Scale (Cohen et al. 1983) in 1991 and 2001. This is a ten-item scale of globally perceived stress that is widely used and assesses the degree to which individuals feel their lives are in control and predictable. It has acceptable internal consistency reliability in both studies (Cronbach's $\alpha = .80$ and .79, respectively). Also, we have blood pressure, measured using a DINAMAP Vital Signs Monitor 845XT. This is an automated blood pressure monitor that essentially removes observer error. In each study, it was regularly calibrated against a standard mercury sphygmomanometer. For ease of presentation, we will only use systolic blood pressure as an outcome measure.

Descriptive data on these variables, for each study separately and the studies pooled, are shown in Table 2. The sample from 2001 is slightly older than 1991. There is no overall change in family income, although the group comparison obscures the fact that income increased significantly in the two lowest SES neighborhoods, leveled off in the third, and increased slightly in the fourth. Overall, cultural consonance in lifestyle increased from 1991 to 2001, and perceived stress decreased. There was no change in blood pressure, BMI, or gender distribution.

Tables 3 and 4 present hierarchical multiple regression models for each dependent variable. In each analysis, age, sex, and family income (and BMI for blood pressure) are entered into the equation first. For both perceived stress and blood pressure, family income has an inverse association with the outcomes, confirming the social gradient. Next, study is entered into the equation as a dichotomous variable. The significant regression coefficient in Table 4 shows that perceived stress declined over the ten years between studies, while blood pressure did not. Next, cultural consonance in lifestyle is entered. There is an inverse association between cultural consonance and each outcome; furthermore, when cultural consonance is entered and controlled, the inverse effect of family income disappears. Finally, a term for the interaction between cultural consonance and study is entered. For blood pressure this is nonsignificant. For perceived stress it is significant, indicating that in the 2001 study, the size of the association between cultural consonance and perceived stress was smaller than in the 1991 study.

TABLE 3. Regression of Systolic Blood Pressure on Covariates, Cultural Consonance, Year of Study, and Interaction of Cultural Consonance × Year of Study (Standardized Regression Coefficients)

Variables	Model 1	Model 2	Model 3	Model 4
Age	.353[*]	.357[*]	.359[*]	.359[*]
Sex	.257[*]	.256[*]	.251[*]	.251[*]
BMI	.238[*]	.241[*]	.248[*]	.253[*]
Family income	−.165[*]	−.162[*]	−.051	−.019
Study		−.051	.014	.007
Cultural consonance			−.223[*]	−.255[*]
Cultural consonance × study				.058
Multiple R	.555[*]	.557[*]	.577[*]	.579[*]
Multiple R^2	.308	.310	.333	.335

[*]$p < .001$.

TABLE 4. Regression of Perceived Stress on Covariates, Cultural Consonance, Year of Study, and Interaction of Cultural Consonance × Year of Study (Standardized Regression Coefficients)

Variables	Model 1	Model 2	Model 3	Model 4
Age	−.123[*]	−.110[*]	−.107[*]	−.106[*]
Sex	−.199[**]	−.202[**]	−.210[**]	−.211[**]
Family income	−.178[**]	−.172[**]	.010	−.022
Study		−.124[*]	−.041	−.062
Cultural consonance			−.276[**]	−.349[**]
Cultural consonance × study				.145[*]
Multiple R	.310[**]	.333[**]	.381[**]	.398[**]
Multiple R^2	.096	.111	.145	.158

[*]$p < .01$, [**]$p < .001$.

DISCUSSION

Our aim in this article has been to explore the utility of a biocultural approach to the study of health disparities. Specifically, we have examined cultural consonance as a measure of relative deprivation in Townsend's (1979) terms. Socioeconomic disparities were conceptualized and measured as a socioeconomic gradient of individuals and as time periods varying in level of income inequality. Results from our research in Brazil suggest that cultural consonance mediates the social gradient and is moderated by income inequality.

The most straightforward results here come from the analysis of blood pressure. There is an inverse association between family income and systolic blood pressure; when cultural consonance is entered into the analysis, it absorbs all of the explanatory variance of family income. This is consistent with a simple linear path model:

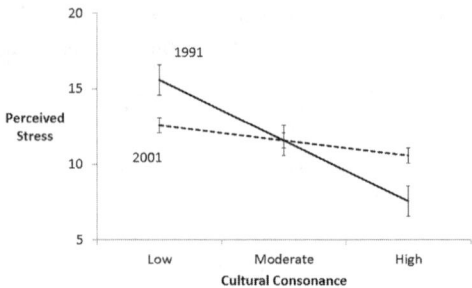

FIGURE 2. Perceived stress by year of study and cultural consonance.

Family income → Cultural consonance → Blood pressure.

Borrowing a term from a statistical technique—path analysis—for testing causal models, family income is an *exogenous variable*. It stands at the beginning of the causal sequence and is, itself, causally unaccounted for. Through a variety of means (family of origin, educational opportunities, employment opportunities, inheritance, marriage) an individual is able to attain a particular income level. This in turn represents the resources that he or she can draw on and invest in achieving the widely shared life goals defined by a cultural consensus within the domains organizing those life goals and operationalized by the measure of cultural consonance. Again, borrowing from path analysis, cultural consonance is an *endogenous variable*, because it is causally accounted for by the exogenous variable, family income. Then, higher cultural consonance leads to lower blood pressure. Cultural consonance mediates the inverse relationship between position in the socioeconomic gradient and blood pressure.

This description of the results is true also for perceived stress, except that the impact of cultural consonance on perceived stress is moderated by overall conditions of income inequality. As the overall level of inequality declines, the effect of cultural consonance on perceived stress weakens. The pattern of these results is shown in Figure 2.

These results may indicate the differing effects that cultural consonance has for a variable that does not depend on the conscious reporting of some state by the respondent—blood pressure—versus an outcome that depends on that conscious reporting—perceived stress. As we argued earlier, the chronic stress associated with low cultural consonance ultimately involves pathways via the hypothalamic-pituitary-adrenal axis and sympathetic nervous system arousal. The allostatic load associated with repeated arousals of these systems can lead directly to a coarsening of the smooth muscle tissue surrounding arterioles and, ultimately, sustained higher blood pressure. The source of that chronic stress must of course be meaningful to the individual, and we are arguing that it is the collective meaning attached to these cultural domains that is important.

In the case of perceived stress, all of the same processes are at work *plus* the conscious awareness and reporting of felt distress. It may be that under conditions of declining income inequality the experience of lower cultural consonance is less distressing because there is, at least, a sense of the potential for life to improve. In the case of Brazil specifically, this may have been enhanced in 2001 by the election of Luis Inácio Lula da Silva, or, as he was popularly known, "Lula." (We date the study as 2001, but survey research actually extended over the period of 2001–03, which encompasses Lula's campaign for and election to the Brazilian presidency.) Lula represented the *Partida dos Trabalhadores* or Worker's Party (abbreviated as PT). The PT campaign specifically focused on the need to help alleviate the suffering of the poorest segments of the Brazilian population, ultimately implementing programs such as *Fome Zero* (Zero Hunger) and *Bolsa Família* (Family Allowance). These programs provided various forms of direct and indirect assistance to poor families, often consolidating and adding to programs that had been initiated by previous administrations.

The actual effectiveness of these social programs is not really the issue here; rather, Lula's election and the promise of these programs, coupled with the measureable reduction in income inequality (certainly initiated by the *Plano Real*, or currency stabilization program under the earlier administration of Fernando Henrique Cardoso), may have provided a different ethos for the poorer members of Brazilian society such that the conscious strain associated with low cultural consonance was less likely to be reported.

There is, however, an alternative explanation for the moderating effect of lower income inequality. The measure of cultural consonance we are using here may not be sufficiently sensitive to assess this variable in 2001. With reduced inequality, achieving what is, in essence, a 1991 level of cultural consonance may, in 2001, be easy enough to restrict the range of variation of cultural consonance in 2001. This could spuriously produce the observed moderating effect.

This is, nevertheless, an example of a useful approach to the study of socioeconomic health disparities in anthropology. Anthropologists have been strangely silent in the empirical study of the health effects of economic inequality, despite their vocal advocacy for the poor (Dressler 2010). We argue that a biocultural theory, explicitly derived from the integration of perspectives in cultural and biological anthropology, provides a productive avenue for better understanding socioeconomic health disparities. While the actual results must be interpreted with a certain caution, given that the data were not truly designed to test these hypotheses, the theory and method of cultural consonance appears to provide a means for refining our grasp of processes that generate socioeconomic health inequalities. Future research may profit from adopting the approach explicitly.

NOTE

Acknowledgments. Research reported here was supported by the following grants from the National Science Foundation: BNS-9020786, BCS-0091903, and BCS-1026429. Jason DeCaro and Kathryn S. Oths offered helpful comments on earlier drafts of the paper.

REFERENCES CITED

Belk, Russell W.
   1988   Possessions and the Extended Self. Journal of Consumer Research 15(2):139–168.
Bell, Carolyn S.
   1995   What Is Poverty? The American Journal of Economics and Sociology, 54(2):161–162.

Black, Douglas and Peter Townsend
    1982   Inequalities in Health: The Black Report. Harmondsworth: Penguin.
Borgatti, Stephen P.
    1994   Cultural Domain Analysis. Journal of Quantitative Anthropology 4(4):261–278.
Bourdieu, Pierre
    1984   Distinction: A Social Critique of the Judgement of Taste. Cambridge: Harvard University Press.
Cohen, Sheldon, Tom Karmack, and Robin Mermelstein
    1983   A Global Measure of Perceived Stress. Journal of Health and Social Behavior 24:385–396.
Douglas, Mary and Baron Isherwood.
    1979   The World of Goods: Towards an Anthropology of Consumption. New York: Basic Books.
D'Andrade, Roy
    1984   Cultural Meaning Systems. In Culture Theory: Essays on Mind, Self, and Emotion. Richard A. Shweder, ed. Pp. 88–122. Cambridge: Cambridge University Press.
    1995   The Development of Cognitive Anthropology. Cambridge: Cambridge University Press.
Dressler, William W.
    1996   Culture and Blood Pressure: Using Consensus Analysis to Create a Measurement. Cultural Anthropology Methods 8(3):6–8.
    2006   Cultural consonance and C-reactive protein in urban Brazil. Abstracts of the 105th Annual Meeting of the American Anthropological Association, November 15–19, San Jose, CA.
    2005   What's Cultural about Biocultural Research? Ethos 33(1):20–45.
    2010   Social Inequality and Health: A Commentary. Medical Anthropology Quarterly 24(4):549–554.
Dressler, William W., Mauro C. Balieiro, and José Ernesto dos Santos
    1997   The Cultural Construction of Social Support in Brazil: Associations with Health Outcomes. Culture, Medicine, and Psychiatry 21(3):303–335.
    1998   Culture, Socioeconomic Status, and Physical and Mental Health in Brazil. Medical Anthropology Quarterly 12(4):424–446.
    2015   Finding Culture in the Second Factor: Stability and Change in Cultural Consensus and Residual Agreement. Field Methods 27:22–38.
Dressler, William W., Mauro C. Balieiro, Rosane P. Ribeiro, and José Ernesto Dos Santos
    2005   Cultural Consonance and Arterial Blood Pressure in Urban Brazil. Social Science and Medicine 61(3):527–540.
    2007a   Cultural Consonance and Psychological Distress: Examining the Associations in Multiple Cultural Domains. Culture, Medicine, and Psychiatry 31(2):195–224.
    2007b   A Prospective Study of Cultural Consonance and Depressive Symptoms in Urban Brazil. Social Science and Medicine 65(10): 2058–2069.
Dressler, William W., Camila D. Borges, Mauro C. Balieiro, and José Ernesto dos Santos
    2005   Measuring Cultural Consonance: Examples with Special Reference to Measurement Theory in Anthropology. Field Methods 17(4):331–355.
Dressler, William W., and José Ernesto dos Santos
    2000   Social and Cultural Dimensions of Hypertension in Brazil: A Review. Cadernos de Saúde Pública 16(2): 303–315.
Dressler, William W., José Ernesto dos Santos, and Mauro C. Balieiro
    1996   Studying Diversity and Sharing in Culture: An Example of Lifestyle in Brazil. Journal of Anthropological Research 52(3):331–353.
Dressler, William W., Kathryn S. Oths, Mauro C. Balieiro, Rosane P. Ribeiro, and José Ernesto Dos Santos
    2012   How Culture Shapes the Body: Cultural Consonance and Body Mass in Urban Brazil. American Journal of Human Biology 24(3):325–331.
Dressler, William W., Kathryn S. Oths, Rosane P. Ribeiro, Mauro C. Balieiro, and José Ernesto Dos Santos
    2004   Eating, Drinking and Being Depressed: The Social, Cultural and Psychological Context of Alcohol Consumption and Nutrition in a Brazilian Community. Social Science and Medicine 59(4): 709–720.
    2008   Cultural Consonance and Adult Body Composition in Urban Brazil. American Journal of Human Biology 20(1):15–22.

Engels, Friedrich
    1958 [1845] The Condition of the Working Class in England. New York: Macmillan.
Goodenough, Ward
    1996 Culture. In Encyclopedia of Cultural Anthropology, vol II. David Levinson and Melvin Ember, eds.
        Pp. 291–299. New York: Henry Holt & Co.
Hallerod, Bjorn
    1996 Deprivation and Poverty: A Comparative Analysis of Sweden and Great Britain. Acta Sociologica
        39(2):141–168.
Healthy People 2020
        N.d. Disparities. http://www.healthypeople.gov/2020/about/DisparitiesAbout.aspx, accessed July 1,
        2013.
Kawachi, Ichiro, and Bruce P. Kennedy
    1999 Income Inequality and Health: Pathways and Mechanisms. Health Services Research 34(1 Pt 2):215–
        227.
Mack, Joanna, and Stewart Lansley
    1985 Poor Britain. London: George Allen and Unwin.
Marmot, Michael G.
    2004 The Status Syndrome: How Social Standing Affects Our Health and Longevity. New York: Henry
        Holt & Co.
McCracken, Grant D.
    1988 Culture and Consumption: New Approaches to Symbolic Character of Consumer Goods and Activ-
        ities. Bloomington, IN: Indiana University Press.
Romney, A. Kimball, Susan C. Weller, and William H. Batchelder
    1986 Culture as Consensus: A Theory of Culture and Informant Accuracy. American Anthropologist 88(2):
        313–338.
Shore, Bradd
    1991 Twice-Born, Once Conceived: Meaning Construction and Cultural Cognition. American Anthro-
        pologist 93:9–27.
Townsend, Peter
    1979 Poverty in the United Kingdom: A Survey of Household Resources and Standards of Living. Berkeley:
        University of California Press.
Veblen, Thorstein
    1918 The Theory of the Leisure Class: An Economic Study of Institutions. New edition. New York: B. W.
        Huebsch.
Weinberg, Daniel H.
    1995 Measuring Poverty: Issues and Approaches. In Race, Poverty, and Domestic Policy. C. Michael Henry,
        ed. Pp. 99–116. Washington, DC: U.S. Bureau of the Census.
Weller, Susan C.
    2007 Cultural Consensus Theory: Applications and Frequently Asked Questions. Field Methods 19(4):339–
        368.
Wilkinson, Richard D.
    1994 The Epidemiologic Transition—From Material Scarcity to Social Disadvantage. Daedalus 123(4):
        61–77.
Wilkinson, Richard G., and Kate E. Pickett
    2006 Income Inequality and Population Health: A Review and Explanation of the Evidence. Social Science
        and Medicine 62(7): 1768–1784.
    2007 The Problems of Relative Deprivation: Why Some Societies Do Better than Others. Social Science
        and Medicine 65(9):1965–1978.
    2011 The Spirit Level: Why Greater Equality Makes Societies Stronger. New York: Bloomsbury Press.

USING A BIOCULTURAL APPROACH TO EXAMINE FOOD INSECURITY IN THE CONTEXT OF ECONOMIC TRANSFORMATIONS IN RURAL COSTA RICA

Ernesto Ruiz
University of South Florida

David A. Himmelgreen
University of South Florida

Nancy Romero Daza
University of South Florida

Jenny Peña
Monteverde Institute

This article outlines a biocultural approach that employs a mixed-methods research design to the study of food insecurity in the context of economic transformations in the Monteverde Zone (MVZ), Costa Rica. Using structured survey data related to household (n = 200) and individual level variables as well as on anthropometric measurements, linear regression analyses were run in order to try to predict food insecurity based on biological and cultural data. Additionally, 100 in-depth, qualitative interviews were carried out with heads of households in order to situate the quantitative findings ethnographically. A multiple linear regression model accounting for 36 percent of the variation in food insecurity was constructed with two predictors: an aggregate index of reported illness symptoms and a categorical variable concerning the strategies employed for the purchase of basic grocery items. Data on reported illness frequency and purchasing strategies predict a sizeable proportion of the variation of food insecurity in the study sample. This highlights the complex, biocultural nature of food insecurity processes. [food insecurity, ecotourism, economic transformations, biocultural research, Latin America]

Social, economic, and environmental disadvantages are attributed to health disparities or differences in the health among two or more groups of people (www.healthypeople.gov 2020). Because of these disadvantages, structural barriers emerge, including limited access to quality nutrition and adequate health care, which facilitate widening gaps in health outcomes over time. Though health disparities are often examined in the context of ethnicity and race, other intersecting social determinants including gender, sexual orientation, mental health, and socioeconomic status are also considered important (Dean et al. 2013). Much of the research on health disparities has been done in the United States, yet with the rise of global capitalism and growing economic inequalities

ANNALS OF ANTHROPOLOGICAL PRACTICE 38.2, pp. 232–249. ISSN: 2153-957X. © 2015 by the American Anthropological Association. DOI:10.1111/napa.12054

worldwide, it is worthwhile to examine the relationship between globalization induced economic disadvantages and health disparities in lower and middle-income countries, particularly in places where there has been rapid economic transformation.

In this article, we draw on data from a National Science Foundation supported three-year study (BSN0753017: Himmelgreen, PI) that examines how the transition from an agricultural economy to a mixed economy of tourism and agriculture has impacted food security status and nutritional health in the Monteverde Zone (MVZ), Costa Rica. In particular, we will examine how rapid and far reaching alterations in the local economy and growing economic insecurity are affecting household food security status, health status, and food beliefs and purchasing strategies.

Food insecurity has been defined as the lack of access to safe, sufficient, and nutritious food at all times to maintain a healthy and active life (FAO, IFAD and WFP 2013) and is associated with social and economic disadvantages, and is ultimately tied to health disparities. A critical biocultural perspective is employed here to examine the role that food security may have on practice, body composition, and health. This theory incorporates the understanding that nutritional health becomes transformed socially (Goodman and Leatherman 1998; Leatherman and Goodman 2005) through political economic processes, and that social and economic disadvantages can become embodied in human biology (Himmelgreen 2014). Researchers employing critical biocultural approaches also examine the interaction between semiotics, practice, and the embodiment of identity, with the aim of trying to draw out the implications that symbolically bound identities have on the internalization of rank, status, and distinction, through ethnographic thick description and cultural theorization (Ruiz 2014).

All societies are constrained by the manner in which resources are produced, consumed, and reproduced in systemic and cyclical fashion. Under a materialist hierarchy of constraints—construed as a "negative determinism," food acquisition stands at the top of priorities for social practice. Thus, in this rapidly globalizing world, food studies hold a privileged position for a critically minded analysis of social change and development strategies.

STUDY AREA: LOCAL CONTEXT, GLOBAL SIGNIFICANCE

Once an area dedicated mostly to dairy and subsistence-level agricultural production, the MVZ has undergone rapid economic alterations in the past 30 years, shifting toward a heavy reliance on ecotourism as an economic strategy (Himmelgreen et al. 2006, 2013b; Ruiz 2014). Thus, an examination of how this transition may be impacting people's access to food is timely

Research during the past decades has consistently documented the links between the shift toward a tourist-based economy and a reduction in the dietary diversity in many areas of the underdeveloped world, as a result of larger political-economic forces (Daltabuit and Leatherman 1998; Leatherman and Goodman 2005; Maxwell 1999; Popkin 2006). Generally speaking, research in this vein links increasing economic inequality resulting from neoliberal policies (Peña and Bacallao 2002) as well as the economic incentives and production power of economies of scale that have come to characterize the production of calories in an ever-globalizing world economy (Drewnowski and Specter 2004; Popkin 2006) with poor nutritional health outcomes (Popkin 2006). These nutritional and economic trends are evident in the recent and contemporary history of Central America, with tourism development as a particularly marked form of neoliberal development.

Since the late 1980s, rates for tourism in Central America were the fastest growing for all of the world (Tardanico 2003); the increase in tourist influx is attributed to the end of violent conflicts as well as to the macro-political-economic restructuring entailed the Structural Adjustment Programs (Stonich 1988). These programs diverted public spending from educational, social, and health programs, reinvesting them in infrastructural development related to tourism (Leatherman and Goodman 2005) and the export of natural resources (Laurell 2000). These structural rearrangement resulted in drastic declines in industrial and agricultural jobs (Vivanco 2006). What was once an inward oriented economy, shifted toward the opening up to the global market place, resulting in the creation of Export Processing Zones (Rodriguez-Clare 2001). The early 1980s witnessed an increase of the composition of the nonskilled wage labor force, with more women entering the job market than previously. This change in the labor force, in turn, contributed to decreases in the participation and completion of schooling, which resulted in depressed wages and greater income inequality during the 1990s (Gindling and Trejos 2005). Furthermore, the composition of the public sector labor force changed drastically. Tardanico (2003) notes that while the overall national employment accounted for by the state decreased from 28.3 to 23.4 percent during the 1980–91 period, the constitution of the public sector was affected differently depending on educational status: whereas it decreased by 31.8 percent for workers with primary schooling only, it grew by 8.5 percent for those with secondary education. Neoliberal policies thus exasperated preexisting socioeconomic inequalities.

The MVZ is located in the Northwestern Tilarán Mountains province in Puntarenas (see Figure 1) along the Continental Divide at altitude of 1,200–1,400 m above sea level. The uppermost region of the zone is characterized by the collision of warm, humid Caribbean air currents that with dryer, cool Pacific winds. Some areas receive in excess of 251 cm of rain annually, experience temperatures that range from the mid-50s to the upper-70s Fahrenheit, and have strong seasonal winds (Guswa and Rhodes 2007). The uppermost region of the zone is home to the Monteverde Cloud Forest Preserve, one of the world's most threatened ecosystems (Vivanco 2006). Given the diverse topography and microclimates, there is wide array of flora and fauna in the zone, which attracts an increasing number of tourists. Today, the MVZ is the second most popular tourist destination in Costa Rica with more than 250,000 visitors annually (ICT 2009; Monahan 2004).

The political-economic forces just described, and their nutritional correlates are quite evident today in the MVZ. For the past three decades, this area has been experiencing a drastic transformation as a result of a shifting economic base. Although the people of this region have historically been mostly devoted to dairy farming and other

FIGURE 1. Map of Costa Rica with Monteverde Zone (MVZ).

agricultural pursuits, today they are rapidly becoming involved in the ecotourist economy (Himmelgreen 2014; Himmelgreen et al. 2006; Vivanco 2006).

In a recent exploratory study, Himmelgreen and colleagues found food insecurity rates of 67–73 percent in the towns of Santa Elena and San Rafael, in the MVZ. The authors found that not being a member of a food cooperative, not having a working stove, and having an elevated body mass index (BMI) predicted food insecurity in these two towns (Himmelgreen et al. 2006). A more recent study in the MVZ found food insecurity rates of roughly 30 percent (Ruiz 2014).

Himmelgreen and colleagues' (2006) findings are consistent with what Leatherman and Goodman, as well as other researchers, have found in studies that examined the impact that integrating into a market-based economy can have on food systems of people in rural areas of the world (Maxwell 1999). These findings also shaped the research project from which the data presented here are drawn.

RESEARCH DESIGN AND METHODOLOGY

The data for this article come from the first year of a three-year, NSF-funded (#BCS 0753017) research project examining the causes and consequences of food insecurity in

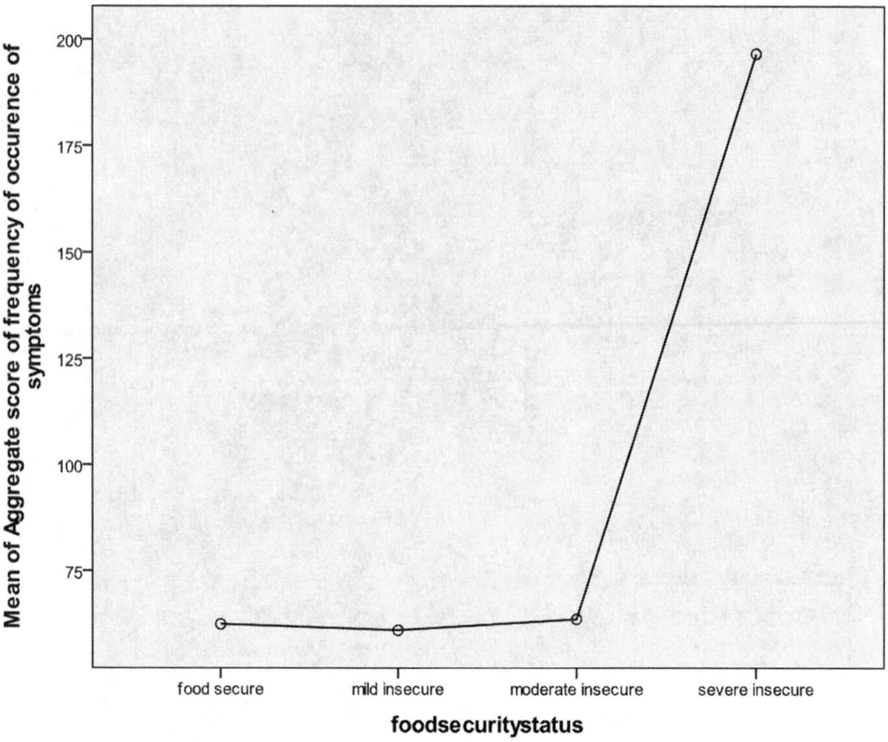

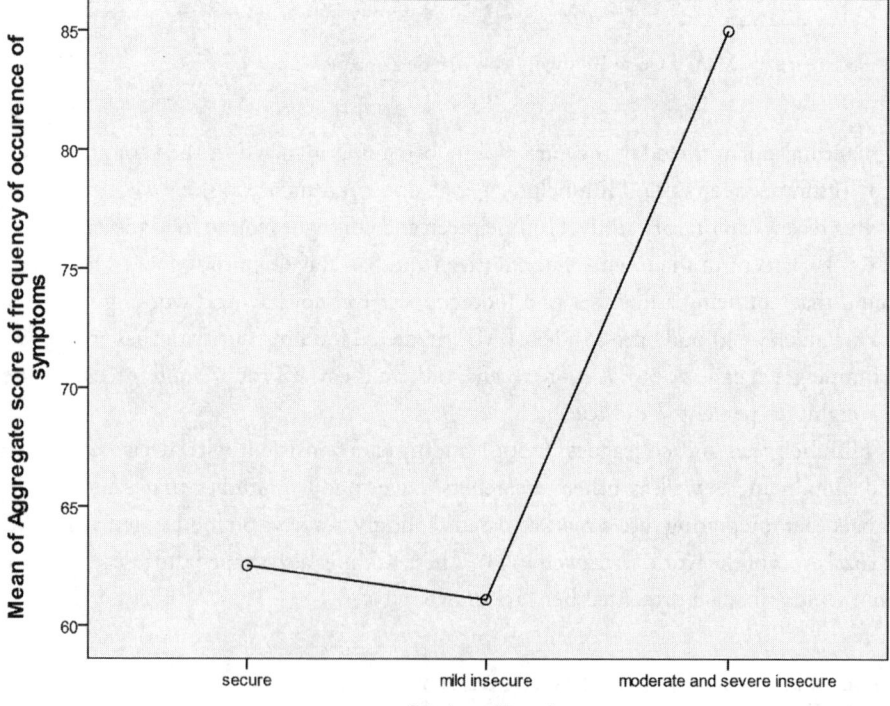

FIGURE 2. Means of aggregate illness symptom index by food security status.

Monteverde, Costa Rica. Analytically, the project examines three distinct but interrelated levels: communities, households, and individuals. The three respective levels consist of two communities, 200 households, and 215 individuals between the ages of 18 and 65 years. The sample was obtained from two distinct communities because of the different degrees to which ecotourism is developed in each one. The first community, representing the primary hub of ecotourism is a conglomeration of various neighborhoods and the town of Santa Elena. This includes Monteverde, Cerro Plano, Los Llanos, Cañitas, La Plaza, and Perro Negro. The second community, San Luis, lies approximately five miles down the Pacific slope of the continental divide from Monteverde. San Luis has a greatly reduced population density in relation to the first community, much less developed infrastructure (there is no supermarket; in Santa Elena there are two larger ones and various smaller ones), and more people involved in agriculture. Tourism is much less developed in San Luis, and the majority of tourist options available in San Luis are agro-touristic (for instance, organic coffee farm tours). This is not to say that people in San Luis are not involved in the ecotourism sector. In many ways, the residents of San Luis are dependent on the larger, more ecotourist, and infrastructurally developed community. This dependence ranges from employment, to the procurement of food and household necessities and medical care, and for postprimary education.

Various structured questionnaires that addressed sociodemographics, food security status (the Household Food Insecurity Access Scale (HFIAS)), food frequency consumption, employment, a 30-day retrospective illness recall, food procurement, social support, and involvement in agricultural activities were administered to the heads of households ($n = 200$). For study purposes, a head of household was defined as an individual within the household who self-reported as responsible for food procurement and preparation. Individuals were defined as belonging to a household if they ate and slept there for at least four months out of the year.

All questionnaires were devised and pretested with the aid of local informants to insure their cultural appropriateness. Versions of our sociodemographic and food frequency questionnaire were used in this same community previously by Himmelgreen and colleagues (2006). The HFIAS, in turn, has been successfully administered throughout the globe and has been shown to be a good indicator of food insecurity (Coates et al. 2007). This instrument asks respondents nine questions related to the experience of worry or anxiety over food quality or quantity or actual material reductions in the quality or quantity of food consumed within a household. These nine questions are followed by a frequency of occurrence question, and the responses are coded in a way that households that experience more events related to food insecurity, at greater frequencies, will score higher on the HFIAS scale (ranging from 0 to 27). The majority of responses came from female heads of households, since, generally speaking, women in this area are in charge of food- and child-related tasks. In addition, women were more likely to be at their house at the time the research team paid its visits. On several occasions, women stopped answering questions when their husbands or partners arrived. Statements such as "he knows best" characterized the typical unfolding of this dynamic. During these situations, the researchers continued administering the questionnaires, receiving either responses solely from the men or responses initiated by the women, with confirmation or elaboration offered by their male partners. This brings up potential limitations concerning the consistency of the data collected during these situations. The authors stress, however, that these instances were exceptions to the rule. In fact, in most cases the male heads of households would flat out say that they knew little about what we were asking and that their partners were the experts.

A snowball sampling strategy was employed to enroll participating households. Relying on key informants, members of the data collection team, and the local partner institution for the project (The Monteverde Institute), households were first approached to explain the purposes of the study and to outline what would be required of participating households. During this initial visit, copies of the informed consent document were left with the adults of the household so they could read about the study. Households that expressed interest in the study were contacted either by phone or visit approximately a week later to confirm their participation.

Additionally, following standard procedures (Gibson 1993), the research team has collected the following anthropometric measurements on all willing individuals within the household between the ages of 18 and 65 years ($n = 215$): heights (Seca Hammer Steindam 9–25, Hamburg, Germany), weights (Tanita BWB-800, Tokyo, Japan), triceps and subscapular skin folds (Harpenden Calipers), and waist, hip, and mid-upper arm circumferences (using Seca measuring tapes). Additionally, two blood pressure readings (Omron, Tokyo, Japan) were taken five minutes apart. Lastly, bioelectrical impedance analysis (BIA) (Biodynamics, BIA 450, Shoreline, WA) was conducted on all participants who were not pregnant or did not have any heart conditions. BIA provided data on the amount of lean and fat tissue (in kilograms and as a percentage of total body weight).

Finally, in-depth qualitative interviews were conducted with the heads of 100 households from the study sample in order to allow for the contextualization and elucidation of the quantitative patterns. Themes explored in the interviews included changes in the economic and nutritional landscape during the interviewees' lifetime, food procurement choices, and pros and cons of tourist development. Transcripts of the interviews were coded for similar themes. Insights gained from these interviews are employed throughout the Discussion section of this chapter, again to aid in the interpretation of the quantitative results. The research goals and procedures of this project were reviewed and approved by the Institutional Review Board of the University of South Florida.

ANALYSIS

General descriptive and univariate statistics were run on the data in order to create representative tables and instructive plots. Multiple linear regression models were run in order to predict food security outcomes (based on the 0–27 score assigned to households from the HFIAS; a score of 0 indicates no occurrence of food insecurity events/worries) with anthropometric, sociodemographic, illness recall, and employment variables as predictors, using the stepwise entry procedure. The stepwise function ensures that the

TABLE 1. Descriptive Statistics for the Study Population

		N	Percentage	Mean
Community	Monteverde, Cerro Plano, Los Llanos, Cañitas, Sta Elena, La Plaza, Perro Negro	135	62.8	
	San Luis	80	37.2	
	Total	215	100	
Sex	Female	187	87.0	
	Male	28	13.0	
	Total	215	100	
Age (years)		215		40.15
BMI		215		27.59

most significant predictors are introduced into the regression model, removing those that do not contribute meaningfully to the explanation of the dependent variable's behavior. From the illness recall data, an aggregate index of the frequency of times respondents reported illness symptoms was constructed and used as a predictor. Various transformations were carried out on our predictors in order to improve the linear fit with the dependent variable. Similarly, the dependent variable (HFIAS score) was squared and used in the models. Diagnostic tests for homoscedasticity, linearity, colinearity, and a full residual analysis were carried out. Nonparametric tests of mean ranks were also run on predictor variables (illness recall) by aggregated food insecure status levels (combining moderate and severe food insecure households into one category due to small cell sizes). The procedures were carried out using PASW (SPSS) 18. The statistical results presented below are contextualized with data acquired from more than 36 months of participant observation carried out by several of the authors, as well as from 100 in-depth qualitative interviews carried out with study participants.

RESULTS

Table 1 presents descriptive information about the study sample. As mentioned previously, most of our respondents were women, with the majority coming from the ecotourism hub (62.8 vs. 37.2 percent). The study sample is of relatively young age (mean of 40.15), and with a mean BMI of 27.59 (i.e., overweight). Alarmingly, food insecurity rates in this study sample are very high, with 50.9 percent of households experiencing some form of food insecurity.

The linear regression analysis yielded one interesting model. This model includes two predictors: an aggregate index of the number of times that respondents said they experienced symptoms from the retrospective illness recall (raised to the 4th power) and whether or not respondents purchased their basic groceries twice a month. It is important to note that none of the anthropometric variables made it into the regression model. The second predictor stemmed from the sociodemographic questionnaire, in which respondents were asked how frequently they purchased their basic grocery items

TABLE 2. Linear Regression Model

	Dependent	Predictor 1	Predictor 2
	HFIAS score-squared	Aggregate occurrence of illness symptoms raised to the 4th power	Purchase basic grocery items twice a month
Coefficients		0.0005	20.053

TABLE 3. Monthly Purchase Strategy by Food Security Status

		Purchase basics once a month				
		No	Percentage	Yes	Percentage	Total
Food secure	No	54	50.9	52	49.1	106
	Yes	54	49.5	55	50.5	109
Total		108	50.2	107	49.8	215

(Pearson chi-square = 0.042, $p = .837$)

TABLE 4. Bimonthly Purchase Strategy by Food Security Status

		Purchase basics twice a month				
		No	Percentage	Yes	Percentage	Total
Food insecure aggregate	No	83	78.3	23	21.6	106
	Yes	76	69.7	33	30.3	109
Total		159	73.9	56	26.1	215

(Pearson chi-square = 2.052, $p = .152$)

(once or twice a month, once weekly, etc). The model has an adjusted R-square of .36 and no issues of multicolinearity (tolerance = .999 and VIF = 1.001, for both predictors; $F = 56.64, p = .000$).

Table 2 presents information on the coefficients for each predictor in the model. This indicates that for each increase in the aggregate scale of illness symptoms (to the 4th), the value of HFIAS squared will increase by a factor of 0.0005, holding the other predictor constant. That is, greater frequency of reported illness episodes results in an elevated predicted score for the HFIAS. Similarly, households that purchase their basic food items twice a month will have an increase in the HFIAS-squared value of 19.097, holding the other predictor constant. In this case, households with this pattern of purchasing their basic items will have an increase in their squared HFIAS score of 20.053 points. Tables 3 and 4 show descriptive statistics for informants' purchasing strategies, stratified by food security status (in this case, all three levels of food insecurity [i.e., mild, moderate, and severe] are lumped into one category for the sake of brevity). As can be seen from the tables, no significant differences between purchasing strategy and food security status were detected by means of Pearson chi-square tests.

The first plot of Figure 1 shows a means plots for the mean aggregate occurrence of reported symptom index by food security status with the disaggregated insecure categories. Figure 2 shows the same means plots but with a combined category for moderate and severe food insecure households (since only eight households were classified as severely insecure). Given the small cell size for severely insecure households ($n = 8$), a Kruskal–Wallis test for differences in mean ranks was run, confirming the significant results found from our multiple linear regression models (chi-square $= 12.85$, df $= 3$, $p = .005$).

DISCUSSION

The multivariate linear regression model discussed above highlights the multilayered and biocultural nature of food insecurity experiences. In essence, this model has captured dynamics related to two distinct but interrelated levels: physiological and sociobehavioral/economic.

Symptom Recall and Food Insecurity

The positive relationship between reported illness symptoms and the HFIAS score suggests two possible things: individuals from food insecure households are more likely to be ill than those from food secure households; and individuals who are more frequently ill have greater chances of becoming food insecure. From the regression model, it is not possible to infer causality, since all of the measures were collected during the same time. And yet, uncovering the exact steps by which these two processes unfold may not be necessary, since a narrowed focus on the immediate causality of either frequency of illness or food insecurity might obscure the complex and systemic relations that govern both of these processes. Recent theoretical trends in human biology have emphasized the dialectical nature of human adaptability, with particular attention being paid to the ways in which a series of biobehavioral adjustments or accommodations to a given stressor, in turn, initiate a whole new cycle with new stressors and coping strategies involved (Crooks et al. 2007; Thomas 1998). Drawing from the theoretical work in evolutionary biology of Levins and Lewontin (1985), biocultural researchers now pay more attention to the role that individual agency has in the shaping of the environment and stressors that humans face. Furthermore, drawing on insights from critical medical anthropology (Singer 1998), human biological diversity is now understood as being intimately related to political economic forces, such as the distribution of resources essential for the reproduction of biocultural systems.

The systemic relationship between food insecurity and immune function is probably best documented in the context of the HIV and AIDS pandemic in Africa. Singer has coined the term "syndemic" (2009) to refer to the complex feedback loop of multiple diseases, poverty, and unequal access to resources that underpins the reproduction of negative health outcomes among vulnerable populations. This syndemic perspective is now widely recognized as being a useful conceptual framework for the development of research and policy strategies having to do with both negative health outcomes and food insecurity issues (Himmelgreen et al. 2009). The intimate connections between food insecurity and illness are not surprising, given what is known about the relationship between nutritional status and immune function.

Complications associated with general malnutrition include greater permeability of the intestinal lining, leading to heightened secretion of ions and fluids, dehydration, and decreased absorption of nutrients necessary for metabolic processes (Ferraris and Carey 2000). Further, malnourishment results in lower conversion rates of riboflavin into its cofactors (Capo-chichi et al. 2000), growth retardation, suppressed thymic functions, T-lymphocyte development, decreased red blood cell circulation, among other harmful consequences (Koury and Ponka 2004). Researchers have begun to suggest potential epigenetic mechanisms that alter organismal developmental trajectories stemming from nutritional stress—and resulting in negative health outcomes—pointing to altered DNA methylation rates (Burdge and Lillycrop 2010; Delage and Dashwood 2008). These epigenetic mechanisms are posited to explain the rapidly increasing relationship seen today between under- and overnutrition, resulting in populations with decreased height-for-age *and* increased weight-for-height (Frisancho 2003).

Food insecure households have been consistently found to have overweight and obese individuals, in areas with increasing reliance on ecotourist economies (Daltabuit and Leatherman 1998; Himmelgreen et al. 2006, 2012; Leatherman and Goodman 2005), and elsewhere (Casey et al. 2001, 2006; Drewnowski et al. 2009; Jyoti et al. 2005; Kaiser et al. 2004; Oh 2003). Furthermore, it is now well documented that overweight and obesity are linked to an increased risk for cardiovascular disease, diabetes, sleep apnea, asthma, and gastroesophageal reflux (Mokdad et al. 2004).

As mentioned previously, no anthropometric variable was found to be an important predictor of food security status in this sample. This is an interesting finding given the trend just discussed in which food insecure people tend to be heavier than their food secure counterparts. Several factors probably contribute to this lack of body composition difference between our study's food secure and insecure individuals. From the descriptive data presented previously, it can be seen that the average BMI for the sample is in the obese range (29.5). Recall also that women represent the bulk of study participants. As is discussed in the next section, dietary habits in the MVZ during the recent years have tended to include an increase of processed foods. The authors suggest that overall, the nutritional environment in the MVZ is one that fosters negative nutritional outcomes regardless of a household's access to socially acceptable food, through socially acceptable means. To put it differently, food security—understood as a relational concept of societal structural integration (Ruiz 2014)—necessarily entails that people have access to a particular food system. If greater integration through greater access to this system entails a less than optimal diet, then the outcomes on the anthropometric front will concomitantly be less than optimal. Analytically, this situation raises interesting questions about the limitations of a household level variable (food security status) when dealing with an extra-household level phenomena such as food systems. It may behoove anthropologists to begin to think about food secure communities in addition to households and individuals.

Economic Transformation, Food Beliefs, and Food Insecurity

This combination of under- and overnutrition for an individual is more likely to be found among individuals from food insecure households, as they are more likely to be subject to seasonal fluctuations of caloric intake (especially in areas with highly seasonal economies, like that of the MVZ and other tourist locales. Furthermore, as is the case for the study participants, many communities undergoing economic transformations as they become more involved in market-based economies, also experience changes in the kinds of foods they are likely to consume. This often leads to more reliance on processed foods high in refined sugars and fats and low in complex carbohydrates (Popkin 2006). It is worth restating that while the connection between overweight and obesity and food security status was not found in the sample, the health concerns discussed in this section nevertheless apply to the majority of study participants.

In the MVZ, the transition from an agricultural and dairy farming to a mostly ecotourist economy has brought with it changes in the patterns of consumption, and therefore, nutritional status of the people in the area (Himmelgreen et al. 2006, 2012). Leatherman and Goodman (2005:838) coined the term "coca-colonization" to refer to the process of dietary delocalization and commercialization of food systems that accompany the processes of globalization, specifically the penetration of the market economy in underdeveloped areas of the world. The process of coca-colonization entails two mutually enforcing processes: (1) a material alteration in the economic conditions of a population following the penetration of the capitalist market economy, and (2) an ideological and symbolic shift in the conceptualization of food as a commodity and status symbol. Himmelgreen et al. (2006) documented an economic alteration in the food productive and consumptive process in which income and cash flows varied dramatically with the advent of the low tourist season, while prices for food and goods remained high year round.

As mentioned above, in-depth ethnographic research was conducted alongside the structured data collection of this study. Through this mixed approach, the authors have found that certain changes in the conceptualization of food items have come about with the introduction of ecotourism in the area. Responses from 100 in-depth, qualitative interviews carried out indicate that there are two general ways of conceptualizing the changes that have and are taking place in the area as the reliance on ecotourism as an economic strategy continues to supplant the previous reliance on agricultural and dairy production. In response to a question asking the interviewees to discuss changes they have seen in relation to dietary habits as a result of the introduction of ecotourism in the area, common themes included an increased knowledge concerning healthy diets. Respondents listed alfalfa sprouts, basil, whole wheat bread, and hummus, among other items, that they associated with tourists and listed as healthy. Emphasis on eating less red meats and pork and on removing the fat from these meats were additional changes cited as resulting from interactions with tourists (many households host North American students and said they learned about healthy eating from the students).

Another common theme in the interviewee responses revolved around the negative aspects that have stemmed from the adoption of tourism in the area. Many respondents mentioned the increased reliance on foods produced outside the MVZ and expressed concern over the quality and cleanliness of the foods being imported to the area. A vast majority of the interviewees stated that they were raised growing most of what they consumed, or at least knowing where the food was grown and by whom, and repeatedly stated that with the current state of dietary delocalization, they could not know whether the food had more chemicals nowadays. Furthermore, the actual process of bringing the food up to the MVZ was cited as a cause for concern, since exhaust from the trucks was thought as a likely source of contamination to the food. Importing food into the area, it should be noted, has also drastically increased food prices. Parallel to concerns about the provenance and price of food were worries about the growing presence of fast foods and drugs that research participants saw as accompanying the influx of tourists. Many respondents expressed concern that their children were learning to eat junk food through a combination of advertising and by witnessing tourists consuming these same items.

Thus, in the context of shifting conceptualization concerning food items, another potential source for the greater number of reported illness symptoms among food insecure households may stem from lifestyle incongruence and psychosocial stress. A large corpus of research has shown status incongruity can result in negative physiological manifestations (Dressler 2005; Dressler and Bindon 2000; Dressler et al. 1998, 1999). The inability to obtain food in a socially acceptable way or the inability to eat foods of a culturally acceptable quality and quantity could theoretically contribute to psychosocial stress. A review article by Weaver and Hadley (2009) lends empirical support to the assertion that food insecurity and mental stressors are positively associated with each other. The authors note that despite various limitations from the studies they reviewed, consistent results from publications dealing with food insecurity and psychological factors indicate that the experience of food insecurity can negatively affect mental health. More recently, Amador (2014) found high rates of psychosocial stress and depression among food insecure individuals in Florida. Thus, there are ample empirical and theoretical explanations for why food insecure individuals from our sample are reporting more illness symptoms than their food secure counterparts.

Food Purchasing Strategies

Through informal and in-depth qualitative interviews and participant observation, the authors have found that the prevailing strategy for the purchasing of basic food items in the MVZ used to be one of buying on a monthly basis. The purchases made on a month-to-month basis are referred to as *el diario* (the daily) to represent the items consumed or used on a day-to-day basis. They are constituted by grains, legumes, and vegetables that preserve well (such as onions, tubers), coffee, soap, etc. Due either to economic constraints or the inability to maintain the freshness of certain items (such as meats), the diario is supplemented with small purchases (or slaughters/harvests) throughout the month. Reasons for this pattern of food acquisition include the fact that most people grew or raised a substantial portion of what they consumed, making frequent trips to stores unnecessary. Furthermore, given the mountainous terrain and amount of precipitation in the area, travelling to Santa Elena to visit the supermarket can be a daunting and expensive task. As recently as two or three generations ago, the diario was purchased by making a trek to either Puntarenas (the capital port city of the province Puntarenas, of which Monteverde is a part) or to Las Juntas de Abangares, in the province of Guanacaste. Either destination entailed at least an entire day of travel, with added expenses of meals, bus passes, and potentially overnight lodging. Men in their sixties and seventies today recount walking up the mountain from Sardinal to Monterverde or San Luis, with 100 kilograms worth of rice on their soldiers (a hike of approximately 35 kilometers, lasting six to ten hours).

While people have greater local options to purchase food and goods today, access still presents very real and very steep challenges to many families in the area. Several study participants reported that they preferred to walk up to three hours each way (from San Luis to Santa Elena), rather than pay a taxi fare of around US$20–30 each way; walking translates into approximately 30 percent more groceries. For these people, it also translates into most of the work day spent on the road and at the store. For one informant, in particular, it meant added strain on his back, hips, and knees, which could result in an extra day missed from work as he recovers from the previous day's walk. This informant gained close to 700 milliseconds in altitude in his hike from his house to Santa Elena. With these considerations in mind, it is not surprising that most respondents prefer to purchase the basic grocery items on a monthly basis. The downside to a month-to-month pattern of purchasing is, of course, greater economic investment at a given time. It therefore would make sense for food insecure households to try to lessen the economic investment in groceries, even though they may incur other costs by doing so in the long run. Interview responses support the preceding discussion, as respondents consistently stated that they made more frequent visits to the store because they were less certain about their income, preferring to spend it in a more measured way. Therefore, the higher HFIAS-squared score for individuals from households that purchase their basic items twice a month can be seen as a reflection of the anxieties and worries experienced by these households when it comes to planning expenses related to basic and necessary goods.

CONCLUSION

In this article, we have presented a multiple linear regression model that accounts for over a third of the variation in food insecurity measures (through the squared score of the HFIAS). Two theoretically and ethnographically relevant predictors were found: an aggregate index of reported illness symptoms and a purchasing strategy where the basic groceries are bought twice a month. Our analyses highlight that food insecurity is indeed a complex process, with manifestations in biological and sociocultural realms. Unfortunately, the findings presented in this article conform to patterns seen in many different locations across the world. As is the case elsewhere, people with uncertain or limited access to essential resources are forced to engage in behavioral responses that may potentially mitigate stressors in an immediate sense, but re-produce them in the long term. Furthermore, exposure to food insecurity stressors—whether anxiety and worry, or reductions in the quality and quantity of food consumed—might be seen to contribute to greater frequency of illness episodes. The analysis presented here is limited by the fact that biological measures of immune activation or cell-mediated immunity status (such as C-reactive protein, or Epstein Barr Virus, respectively) were not collected. Future studies on food insecurity should examine these same issues with biological measures as well as self-reported symptom recalls. Despite this limitation, this study contributes to advancement of theoretical models related to the distribution of human cultural and biological variation. By linking macrosociological processes to specific instances of stress and coping, this study further highlights the important role that a holistic anthropology can play in documenting and critiquing certain forms of social arrangements—in this case, an unmeasured and unplanned reliance on market-based strategies, through ecotourism. The study's finding also calls into question the need to explicitly situate the *access* component of food security vis-à-vis the larger food productive system. If the implications of "coca-colonization" are correct, then we should expect communities undergoing commodification of their food systems to develop unhealthy palates fueled by industrial food production and consumerism. If such is the case, a food secure household might be one that has socially acceptable access to food in desirable quantity and quality, but that may lead to deleterious biological outcomes. Biocultural anthropologists possess great tool kits to contextualize the food environment within a larger societal structure. This entails attention to political economy and shared cultural norms about food and lifestyle more broadly (Ruiz 2014). Researchers dealing with food security issues should also begin to think about analytical units beyond the household as being potentially food (in)secure. In a theoretical sense, this entails a return to anthropological structuralism.

NOTE

Acknowledgments. This study was sponsored by National Science Foundation (BSN 0753017).

1. During the time between this initial study, and the one being reported on in here, the presence and impact of cooperatives has decreased dramatically. The Monteverde Cheese Factory—an enterprise started by Quaker settlers from the United States, turned Costa Rican Cooperative—has been bought out by Mexican investors. Coffee cooperatives still are active in the San Rafael area, but as a general rule, they have become almost inexistent in the area, being replaced by eco-agro-tourist outfits.

REFERENCES CITED

Amador, Edgar
    2014 Can Anyone with Low Income Be Food Secure? Mitigating Food Insecurity among Low Income Households with Children in the Tampa Bay Area. Doctoral dissertation. University of South Florida.
Burdge, Graham C., and Karen A. Lillycrop
    2010 Nutrition, Epigenetics, and Developmental Plasticity: Implications for Understanding Human Disease. Annual Review of Nutrition 30(7):315–339.

Capo-chichi, Callinice D., François Feillet, Jean-Louis Guéant, Kou'Santa Amouzou, Noël Zonon, Ambaliou Sanni, Emmanuelle Lefebvre, Kossi Assimadi, and Michel Vidailhet
  2000 Concentrations of Riboflavin and Related Organic Acids in Children with Protein-Energy Malnutrition. American Journal of Clinical Nutrition 71(4):978–986.
Casey, Patrick H., Kitty Szeto, Shelly Lensing, Margaret Bogle, and Judy Weber
  2001 Children in Food-Insufficient, Low-Income Families: Prevalence, Health, and Nutrition Status. Archives of Pediatrics & Adolescent Medicine 155(4):508–514.
Casey, Patrick H., Pippa M. Simpson, Jeffrey M. Gossett, Margaret L. Bogle, Catherine M. Champagne, Carol Connell, David Harsha, Beverly McCabe-Sellers, James M. Robbins, and Janice E. Stuff
  2006 The Association of Child and Household Food Insecurity with Childhood Overweight Status. Pediatrics 118(5):e1406–1413.
Coates, Jennifer, Anne Swindale, and Paula Bilinsky
  2007 Household Food Insecurity Access Scale (HFIAS) for Measurement of Household Food Access: Indicator Guide (v. 3). Washington, DC: Food and Nutrition Technical Assistance Project, Academy for Educational Development.
Crooks, Deborah L., Lisa Cligget, and Steven M. Cole
  2007 Child Growth as a Measure of Livelihood Security: The Case of Gwembe Tonga. American Journal of Human Biology 19(5):669–675.
Daltabuit, Magalí, and Thomas L. Leatherman
  1998 The Biocultural Impact of Tourism on Mayan Communities. In Building a New Biocultural Synthesis: Political Economic Perspectives on Human Biology. Alan H. Goodman and Thomas L. Leatherman, eds. Pp. 317–338. Ann Arbor, MI: University of Michigan Press.
Dean, Hazel D., Kim M. Williams, and Kevin A. Fenton
  2013 From Theory to Action: Applying Social Detriments of Health to Public Health Practice. Public Health Reports 3(128): 1–128.
Delage, Barbara, and Roderick H. Dashwood
  2008 Dietary Manipulation of Histone Structure and Function. Annual Review of Nutrition 28(1):347–366.
Dressler, William W.
  2005 What's Cultural About Biocultural Research? Ethos 33(1):20–45.
Dressler, William W., and James R. Bindon
  2000 The Health Consequences of Cultural Consonance: Cultural Dimensions of Lifestyle, Social Support and Arterial Blood Pressure in an African American Community. American Anthropologist 102(2):244–260.
Dressler, William W., Mauro Campos Balieiro, and Jose Ernesto Dos Santos
  1998 Culture, Socioeconomic Status and Physical and Mental Health in Brazil. Medical Anthropology Quarterly 12(4):424–446.
  1999 Culture, Skin Color, and Arterial Blood Pressure in Brazil. American Journal of Human Biology 11(1):49–59.
Drewnowski, Adam, Colin Rehm, and Harold Goldstein
  2009 Poverty and Childhood Overweight in California Assembly Districts. Health & Place 15(2):631–635.
Drewnowski, Adam, and S. E. Specter
  2004 Poverty and Obesity: The Role of Energy Density and Energy Costs. The American Journal of Clinical Nutrition 43(9):6–16.
FAO, IFAD, and WPF
  2013 The Sate of Food Security in the World 2013. The Multiple Dimensions of Food Security. Rome: FAO.
Ferraris, Ronaldo P., and Hannah V. Carey
  2000 Intestinal Transport during Fasting and Malnutrition. Annual Review of Nutrition 20(1):195–219.
Frisancho, A. Roberto
  2003 Reduced Rate of Fat Oxidation: A Metabolic Pathway to Obesity in the Developing Nations. American Journal of Human Biology 15(4):522–532.

Gibson, Rosalind S.
  1993 Nutritional Assessment: A Laboratory Manual. New York: Oxford University Press.
Gindling, T. H., and Juan Diego, Trejos
  2005 Accounting for Changing Inequality in Costa Rica: 1980–99. Journal of Development Studies 41(5):898–926.
Goodman Alan H., and Thomas L. Leatherman, eds.
  1998 Building a New Biocultural Synthesis: Political-Economic Perspectives on Human Biology. Ann Arbor: The University of Michigan Press.
Guswa, Andrew J., and Amy L. Rhodes
  2007 Meterology of Monteverde, Costa Rica 2007: Technical Report Submitted to the Monteverde Institute. Northhampton, MA: Smith College. http://www.science.smith.edu/˜aguswa/papers/MetReport2007.pdf, accessed September 28, 2014.
Himmelgreen, David
  2014 Food Insecurity, Early Environment Adversity, and Long-Term Health: Using Critical Biocultural Approaches and the Life Course Perspective to Find Solutions. Anthropology News 55(3):8–9.
Himmelgreen, David A., Nancy Romero-Daza, Edgar Amador, and Cindy Pace
  2012 Tourism, Economic Insecurity, and Nutritional Health in Rural Costa Rica: Using Syndemic Theory to Understand the Impact of the Globalizing Economy at the Local Level. Annals of Anthropological Practice 36(2):346–364.
Himmelgreen, David, Nancy Romero-Daza, David Turkon, Sharon Watson, Ipolto Okello-Uma, and Daniel Sellen
  2009 Addressing the HIV/AIDS—Food Insecurity Syndemic in Sub-Saharan Africa. African Journal of AIDS Research 8(4):2–12.
Himmelgreen, David, Nancy Romero-Daza, and Maribel Vega
  2006 "The Tourist Season Goes Down But Not the Prices." Tourism and Food Insecurity in Rural Costa Rica. Ecology of Food and Nutrition 45(4):295–321.
ICT (Instituto Costarricense de Turismo)
  2009 Anuario Estadístico de Turismo. San José, Costa Rica. http://desarrolloturistico.gob.ar/estadistica/anuarios-estadisticos, accessed September 28, 2014.
Jyoti, Diana F, Frongillo, Edward A, and Jones, Sonya J.
  2005 Food Insecurity Affects School Children's Academic Performance, Weight Gain, and Social Skills. The Journal of Nutrition 135(12):2831–2839.
Kaiser, Lucia L., Marilyn S. Townsend, Hugo R. Melgar-Quiñonez, Mary L. Fujii, and Patricia B. Crawford
  2004 Choice of Instrument Influences Relations Between Food Insecurity and Obesity in Latino Women. American Journal of Clinical Nutrition 80(5):1372–1378.
Koury, Mark J., and Prem Ponka
  2004 New Insights into Erythropoiesis: The Roles of Folate, Vitamin B12, and Iron. Annual Review of Nutrition 24(1):105–131.
Laurell, Asa Cristina
  2000 Structural Adjustment and the Globalization of Social Policy in Latin America. International Sociology 15(2):306–325.
Leatherman, Thomas L., and Alan H. Goodman
  2005 Coca-colonization of Diets in the Yucatan. Social Science & Medicine 61(4):833–846.
Levins, Richard, and Richard Lewontin
  1985 The Dialectical Biologist. Cambridge: Harvard University Press.
Maxwell, Daniel
  1999 The Political Economy of Urban Food Security in Sub-Saharan Africa. World Development 27(11):1939–1953.
Mokdad Ali H., James S. Marks, Donna F. Stroup, and Julie L. Gerberding
  2004 Actual Causes of Death in the United States, 2000. Journal of the American Medical Association 291(10):1238–1245.

Monahan, Jane

    2004 Unique Costa Rica Rainforest at Risk. BBC News World Edition [online]. http://news.bbc.co.uk/2/hi/americas/4061833.stm, accessed September 28, 2014.

Oh, Se-Young, and M. J. Hong

    2003 Food Insecurity is Associated with Dietary Intake and Body Size of Korean Children from Low-Income Families in Urban Areas. European Journal of Clinical Nutrition 57(12):1598–1604.

Peña, Manuel, and Jorge Bacallao

    2002 Malnutrition and Poverty. Annual Review of Nutrition 22(1):241–253.

Popkin, Barry M.

    2006 Global Nutrition Dynamics: The World Is Shifting Rapidly toward a Diet Linked with Noncommunicable Diseases. American Journal of Clinical Nutrition 84(2):289–298.

Rodríguez-Clare, A.

    2001 Costa Rica's Development Strategy Based on Human Capital and Technology: How it Got There, the Impact of Intel, and Lessons for Other Countries. Journal of Human Development 2(2):311–324.

Ruiz, Ernesto

    2014 Growing Children: The Relationship Between Food Insecurity and Child Growth and Development. Doctoral dissertation. University of South Florida.

Singer, Merrill

    1998 The Development of Critical Medical Anthropology: Implications for Biological Anthropology. Building a New Biocultural Synthesis: Politicaleconomic Perspectives on Human Biology. AH Goodman and TL Leatherman, eds. Pp. 93–123. Ann Arbor, MI: University of Michigan Press.

    2009 Introduction to Syndemics: A Critical Systems Approach to Public and Community Health. San Francisco, CA: John Wiley & Sons.

Stonich, Susan

    1988 Political Ecology of Tourism. Environmentally Sound Tourism in the Caribbean Annals of Tourism Research 25(1):25–54.

Thomas, R. Brooke

    1998 The Evolution of Human Adaptability Paradigms: Toward a Biology of Poverty. *In* Building a New Biocultural Synthesis: Political Economic Perspectives on Human Biology. Alan H. Goodman and Thomas L. Leatherman, eds. Pp. 43–74. Ann Arbor, MI: University of Michigan Press.

Tardanico, Richard

    2003 Employment Transformations and Social Inequality: A Comparison of Costa Rica, Guatemala and the Dominican Republic. Social and Economic Studies 52(3):119–141.

Vivanco, Luis A.

    2006 Green Encounters. Shaping and Contesting Environmentalism in Rural Costa Rica. New York: Berghan Books.

Weaver, L. J., and Craig Hadley

    2009 Moving Beyond Hunger and Nutrition: A Systemic Review of the Evidence Linking Food Insecurity and Mental Health in Developing Countries. Ecology of Food and Nutrition 48(4):263–284.

EXPLORING THE ROLE OF CULTURE IN THE LINK BETWEEN MENTAL HEALTH AND FOOD INSECURITY: A CASE STUDY FROM BRAZIL

LESLEY JO WEAVER
Emory University

DAVID MEEK
University of Georgia

CRAIG HADLEY
Emory University

Food insecurity has traditionally been characterized as a driver of health disparities because of its potential impacts on nutritional status. Food, however, has important social and cultural valences that make it much more than a nutritional vehicle. Recent research that is sensitive to the social meanings of food has drawn attention to the complex and far-reaching mental and social health effects of food insecurity. In this article, we outline several theoretical pathways linking food insecurity to reduced physical and mental well-being, and then present results of a preliminary study in rural Brazil designed to test the relative importance of each of these pathways. Our results tentatively suggest that in this context, food insecurity is closely related to both mental and physical health disparities, but the pathways connecting food insecurity and mental health remain somewhat unclear. We present lessons learned and propose a set of research steps to further address the relationships between the social meaning of food and mental health. [food insecurity, mental health, biocultural, Brazil]

INTRODUCTION

Food insecurity occurs whenever an individual is unable to reliably access food in sufficient quality and quantity to maintain an active and healthy lifestyle (Frongillo 1999). There is currently no metric to directly estimate the global distribution of food insecurity, although there are several widely used proxy measures (e.g., the Global Hunger Index; von Grebmer et al. 2012) that begin to reveal the extent of the problem globally and the considerable disparities across nations. For example, since 2008, the Gallup Organization has been asking a large sample of individuals in 169 countries if, in the past 12 months, they did not have enough money to buy food for their family (Gallup-Healthways 2014). Results of that study show that the global distribution of food insecurity is highly disparate, centered in Africa, and closely linked with country-level indicators of economic productivity (Figure 1). In higher income countries, the average level of food insecurity was around 10 percent (e.g., Belgium, Australia), but was 29 percent in middle-income

ANNALS OF ANTHROPOLOGICAL PRACTICE 38.2, pp. 250–268. ISSN: 2153-957X. © 2015 by the American Anthropological Association. DOI:10.1111/napa.12055

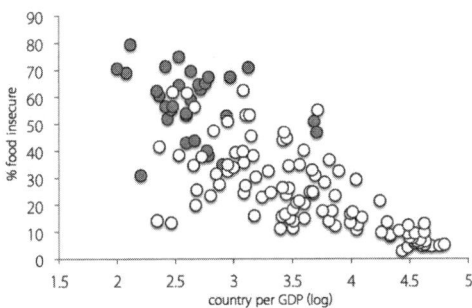

FIGURE 1. Prevalence of food insecurity by country and log of country GDP. *y*-axis is prevalence of food insecurity and *x*-axis is log of country GDP. Data from Headey (2011) and World Bank (2013). Countries in red are in Africa.

countries (e.g., Venezuela, Albania), and 46 percent in low-income countries (e.g., Ghana, Burundi; reported in Headey 2011). These country-level indicators provide important insights about the unequal distribution of food insecurity. But they obscure considerable within-country variation and are rarely able to consider the consequences of food insecurity for health and well-being.

Anthropologists have devoted considerable attention to understanding the experiences, inequalities, causes, and consequences of food insecurity with communities and households, often with an emphasis on periods of scarcity (Himmelgreen and Kedia 2010). Much of the anthropological writing on food insecurity has explored how populations cope with uncertainty in food supplies, and focused on the nutritional consequences of food insecurity (Campbell 1990; de Garine and Harrison 1988). For humans, as nutritional anthropologists and others have long pointed out, food has cultural, as well as biological, value, and thus insecure access to food has impacts that extend beyond physical well-being and into the realm of mental health (Weaver and Hadley 2009).

In this article, we review existing theory and research linking food insecurity to nutritional outcomes, and nonnutritional outcomes, such as mental health. We then draw on our original research in Brazil to explore possible reasons why food insecurity is linked with high levels of depression. We conclude by addressing the broad implications of food insecurity for population health disparities, and outline a novel research program that seeks to unite the biological and cultural aspects of food insecurity.

Food as a Biocultural Vehicle

We take as our starting point the position that for humans, food is of fundamental biological *and* social importance. In biological terms, humans require approximately 2,000 kilocalories per day to fuel biological and social activities. The form that these calories come in and the manner by which they enter the body, however, matter deeply to humans. Unlike other animals, we have elaborate cultural systems that define how food should be obtained, when it should be consumed, what types of foods should be consumed at each meal, who should be present at meals, how the food should be put into the mouth, the posture and stance of consumers while eating, the order in which items should be consumed, how important the foods are that others are eating, and what items should be consumed together (Farb and Armelagos 1980). Insecure access to food is rarely solely an issue of inadequate quantity or quality of food.

Despite this fact, a focus on the biological and nutritional importance of food insecurity has typically dominated research on the topic. Many scholars have used anthropometric measures as proxy variables for food insecurity, with the implicit assumption that food insecurity will impact dietary quality and quantity, and will ultimately manifest as reduced weight and/or height for age. Specifically, food insecurity is often theorized as a *managed process* that begins with anxiety and then leads to downward shifts in dietary quality (Radimer et al. 1992). Although the details vary somewhat by context, studies typically find that households first exhibit anxiety over their food supply, then begin to alter the *type* of food (the quality of food) that they consume, and then reduce the *amount* of food (the quantity), and finally experience outright hunger (Coates et al. 2006).

Consistent with this nutritional model, in lower income countries, poorer nutritional status is frequently associated with household and child food insecurity, although the effects are often small and occasionally disappear when other measures of socioeconomic status (SES) are statistically controlled (Hadley and Crooks 2012). In other cases, however, individuals in food-insecure households *do not* show evidence of lower weight or height for age. In higher income settings, a growing number of studies are demonstrating that children and adults (especially women) can be overweight in food-insecure households (Casey et al. 2006; Dinour et al. 2007; Townsend et al. 2001). Thus, the presumed link between nutritional status and food insecurity may not be as straightforward as we once thought.

Linking Food Insecurity and Mental Well-Being in the United States and Abroad

While the data linking food insecurity to nutritional status are somewhat equivocal, a growing body of evidence has linked food insecurity and various indicators of mental well-being. A number of studies from the United States and elsewhere have explored the relationship between insecure access to food and various measures of common mental disorders, such as anxiety and depressive disorders. In an early effort, Alaimo et al. (2001) used a single measure of food insufficiency to explore the consequences of food insufficiency on well-being for young people in the United States. Even after controlling for income effects, youth living in food-insufficient households had higher rates of suicidal ideation and were more likely to be dysthymic. This study was followed up by two others that focused on mothers in the United States, both of which confirmed that, even after statistically controlling for a range of covariates, food insecurity was associated with mental health (Casey et al. 2006; Whitaker et al. 2006). Casey et al.'s study, for instance, found that food-insecure women had 2.7 times the odds of returning a positive depression screen than food-secure women.

A wave of studies on food insecurity and mental health in sub-Saharan Africa followed, demonstrating largely similar results. Hadley and Patil (2006) found that among Tanzanian women there was a significant link between food insecurity and depressive symptoms. This association remained even across diverse ethnic groups and subsistence economies, suggesting that the link between insecure access to food and lower mental well-being were not likely group-specific. Subsequent work from Ethiopia showed that food insecurity was associated with nearly three times greater odds of high symptoms of anxiety and depression (Hadley et al. 2008; see also Maes et al. 2010 and Cole and Tembo 2011). The level of social support to which women have access appears to be an important modifier of the relationship between food insecurity and poor mental health, as demonstrated by Tsai et al. (2012) in rural Uganda, and by Kollannoor-Samuel et al. (2011) among Latino women in the United States. Although the studies differ in their design and the tools used to measure mental health, there is a clear pattern that food insecurity is linked globally to poorer mental health or poorer well-being (Weaver and Hadley 2009).

Why Is Being Food Insecure So Harmful to Mental Well-Being?

Anthropologists agree that food holds both intrinsic nutritional qualities and extrinsic social value. Mary Douglas (1972) refers to food as "code" and asks, "Where is the pre-coded message"? The message, of course, is held in the collective minds of a group of people; in other words, in the shared knowledge that constitutes culture (Dressler et al. 2005). Barthes (1997:24) also observes that food "is not only a collection of products that can be used for statistical or nutritional studies. It is also, at the same time, a system of communication, a body of images, a protocol of usages, situations, and behavior." Barthes goes on to say that when someone consumes a food, that food "signifies" and "transmits information." Douglas and Barthes describe food as a vehicle that reliably transmits social information (see also Caplan 2002).

This theoretical emphasis on the meaning of food, rather than its nutritional content, corresponds closely with observations of how people think about food. Shepard et al. (2006), for instance, systematically reviewed the evidence for why young people preferred unhealthy foods, and argued that such foods held meanings that included "friends, pleasure, and relaxation." Stead et al. (2011) followed up on this study using semistructured interviews and found that, among 13- to 15-year olds in England, specific foods, brands, and even modes of consumption (e.g., using a spoon: "You look stupid getting a big metal spoon out of your bag" [Stead et al. 2011:1135]) were rich with meaning. The cultural meaning of food is so salient that families are often willing to pay more to meet cultural goals of their diets; an empirical study on French diets showed that consuming foods that aligned with "mainstream French diets ... sharply increased food plan costs, without improving nutritional value" (Maillot et al. 2010:1178). Veblen's (2009[1899]) discussion of conspicuous consumption famously addresses the signaling power of various modes of consumption (not only food). Even writings on meat hunting and sharing among hunter gatherers often attribute the choice of hunting meat less to its nutritive qualities, and more to the prestige that meat can confer on the hunter (Bliege Bird et al. 2001).

An emphasis on the social meaning of food potentially transforms our understanding of the consequences of food insecurity for health and well-being, and we can posit that there are clear social and cultural dimensions to food insecurity. Qualitative studies

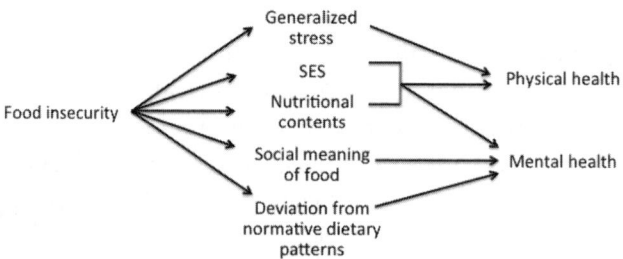

FIGURE 2. Pathways through which food insecurity might impact mental and physical health.

nearly always reveal that respondents view the shifts in dietary intake that occur during periods of food insecurity as consumption of "low-income food," and children especially "felt ashamed about having to eat it" (Hoisington et al. 2002). Food-insecure families routinely mention their constrained options, limited choices, and shame from how foods were acquired, prepared, or consumed. These patterns have been reported from New York (Radimer 1990), Quebec (Hamelin et al. 2002), Burkina Faso (Nanama and Frongillo 2012), and Ethiopia (Hadley et al. 2012). Importantly, some studies from the United States suggest that there is no difference in caloric intakes between food-secure and food-insecure households (Zizza et al. 2008). Food-insecure people tend to consume nonpreferred foods. Up to a point, these are not likely to have a negative impact on nutritional outcomes, but may very well influence mental well-being.

Thus, when viewed from a biocultural perspective, foods that are consumed during periods of food insecurity may or may not have lower biological value, but often occupy low status positions within the cultural domain of edible foods. Consumption of these foods, which are laden with meaning as well as nutrients, may negatively impact people's psychosocial well-being before affecting their nutritional status. There are various reasons why this may be stressful, but one is because the act of consuming foods that are considered "low quality" or "poor people's foods" may render visible poverty, which might have otherwise been an invisible condition. In a sense, people literally consume the negative social meaning of the food; not unlike a meaning response associated with the placebo effect (Moerman and Jonas 2002). This stigma may be particularly acute among children for whom outward symbols of social status are widely shared and deeply entrenched (Stead et al. 2011; Sweet 2010) and among parents, for whom the inability to provide "high quality" foods may be seen as an indictment of their parenting abilities (see also Brewis and Gartin 2006 and Crooks 1999).

Under this alternative perspective, we anticipate that families experiencing food insecurity may shift the foods they are consuming to include more foods of lower social status. These foods may or may not also be of lower nutritional value. The shifts not only in the nutrient value of the foods, but also in the *meaning* of the foods they are consuming may impact mental well-being. Food insecurity may therefore impact nutritional well-being through one pathway, and mental health through other pathways (Figure 2).

The evidence we have reviewed up to this point suggests that food insecurity can generate health disparities through various routes. It may impact nutritional status via dietary quality and quantity, and can potentially impact mental well-being via two pathways: by creating stress about the everyday lack of food (Hammen 2005), or by constraining individuals to interact with food in ways that are nonnormative or stigmatized. A third potential option is that the dietary shifts associated with food insecurity lead to nutrient deficiencies, which in turn impact mental health (Bodnar and Wisner 2005). All of these potential pathways are illustrated in the conceptual model above (Figure 2).

Toward a Research Agenda Exploring the Biocultural Causes and Consequences of Food Insecurity

How might we assess the hypothesis that food insecurity impacts mental well-being through the social meaning of food? A study exploring the biocultural influences of food insecurity on health should assess the outcome measure of health, both physical and mental, in several ways. Second, it would include a robust assessment of food insecurity, of which there are now several (Radimer et al. 1992, Swindale and Bilinsky 2006). Third, to measure the shared social value of food, a study should collect information on foods that are widely consumed and then rank those in terms of prestige or status, which speaks to the importance of ethnography. To ensure that these ranks are *shared* within a community, such a study could then conduct various assessments of the degree of agreement between respondents (Weller 2007). Then, in another sample, respondents could describe how often they consume each food; the hypothesis here being that food-insecure individuals would consume more foods with negative social valence, and that this would mediate the relationship between food insecurity and mental health. With complementary food frequency data, a study could then assess the multiple pathways hypothesized in the review section of this article to link food insecurity and well-being (Figure 2). The hypothesis that the social value of food explains—or in statistical parlance, mediates—the link between food insecurity and mental health could be assessed by entering the measure of consumption of social foods into a statistical model (Frazier et al. 2004). Comparing the relationships between food insecurity and mental health before and after inclusion of the social value of food variable would serve as a test of the extent of mediation.

Below, we briefly describe a study conducted in rural Brazil that attempted to follow this research agenda. We then present some preliminary results. We conclude by discussing implications, lessons learned, and next steps.

THE BRAZIL MENTAL HEALTH AND FOOD INSECURITY STUDY

Research Setting

This project took place in a small (approximately 600-household) farming community in rural southern Pará state, Brazil. In the early 1970s, this area experienced an influx of migrants fleeing a severe drought in the northeast, which led to the then-president Medici's claim that the Amazon region would become a "land for men, for men without land" (Mahar 1979). Subsequent federal development organizations, such as the National Institute of Colonization and Agrarian Reform (INCRA), put forth projects that further encouraged migration to the Amazon to increase the region's agricultural production (Foweraker 1981; Hecht and Cockburn 1989). Southern Pará has been described as part of the Amazon's infamous "arc of deforestation" (Brandão and Souza 2006), and its smallholders are at the center of a debate about the role of subsistence agriculture in land use and landscape change (Arima and Uhl 1997; Cattaneo 2008; Nepstad et al. 2006; Pacheco 2009). This is an area, then, that has historically embodied the complex relationships between agricultural production, social justice, food sovereignty, and environmental degradation.

The community took root as an agrarian reform settlement of the *Movimento dos Trabalhadores Rurais Sem Terra* (MST, or Landless Workers' Movement). Established 18 years ago, the community's original purpose was to provide land for landless peasants to engage in subsistence and small-scale commercial farming. It now consists of a small town center surrounded by 50-hectare (124-acre) tracts of land for farming, which residents own or have sold to others. While the community once produced a wide range of crops, today most farming activity is centered around cattle ranching, a more prestigious occupation (Hoelle 2011). As a result, the once food-sovereign community now relies on commerce to obtain basic foodstuffs, such as rice, beans, and vegetables. At the time of research, there were three small general stores in town where most residents bought the vast majority of their basic foodstuffs. Diets in the community are largely homogeneous, with socioeconomic variation being reflected in the *quality* of the foodstuffs consumed, rather than in their type. Breakfast is small, and usually consists of sweet coffee and cheese rolls, or corn porridge. Lunch and dinner are usually the same foods, consisting of store-bought white rice accompanied by one of two bean dishes: either a small quantity of locally grown climbing beans, or a bean soup made with store-bought pinto or black beans. The beans are flavored with onions, garlic, and a mixture of green onions and cilantro, all of which are purchased locally, or less frequently grown in home gardens. At least once a day, those who can afford it purchase beef, pork, chicken, or fish from the local shops to accompany the beans and rice. Once a week, or more frequently if they are wealthy, most families have a salad consisting of cabbage and tomatoes purchased from outside the community. The penetration of a commercial economy has also brought many processed foods to the town, which people consume between meals, such as salty snacks, candy, sodas, and condiments such as mayonnaise and ketchup, as well as lifestyle changes associated with the introduction of electricity and television in the early 2000s. Himmelgreen et al. (2006) have suggested that the influx of condiments may shift ideas about the social status of food with consequences for food insecurity. Although diabetes and heart disease are presently uncommon, hypertension has become endemic. The impending municipal incorporation of the community promises to bring larger-scale industry and increasing development.

Methods

This preliminary study involved a three-stage data collection process. All interviews were conducted by the first author and a local research assistant in Portuguese. Interviews for all stages took between 15 and 30 minutes and were conducted in respondents' homes. Oral informed consent was obtained prior to participation, and all study procedures were preapproved by the Institutional Review Board of Emory University.

The first stage consisted of free-list interviews (Borgatti 1998) with a sample of adults purposively chosen to capture a range of ages, genders, and socioeconomic status. Participants were asked to name as many prestigious foods as they could think of, then to name nonprestigious foods. The majority of participants were female, as women are typically at home during daytime hours caring for the household and children. Additional interviews were conducted until no new items were obtained; the final sample size was 15 individuals. Items mentioned more than three times were retained for further use, as were items mentioned only once or twice but considered theoretically important, such as reheated food, which is highly stigmatized in this community and was expected to associate strongly with low prestige. The final list contained 28 prestigious and nonprestigious foods (see Table 1). Some respondents interpreted *prestigious* foods as those most integral to local diets (e.g., rice and beans or second-grade beef), while others interpreted *prestigious* foods as those that are difficult to afford on a regular basis (e.g., pork, ice cream, first-grade beef, and salad vegetables). Vegetables, sausage, and various meats tended to have high prestige rankings, while tripe, reheated food, and climbing beans were rated low.

The second stage involved asking a sample of 30 purposively selected individuals to rank each of the 28 food items in order from most prestigious to least prestigious. The initial sample contained a majority of women to match the gender ratios obtained during free listing, and we eventually eliminated the ten male individuals from the sample to leave an all-female sample of 20 individuals. Based on a consensus analysis, we were then able to assign each food item a "prestige score."

The third stage involved a questionnaire with 55 household heads randomly selected from the four quadrants of town, again, of which most were female. Households with no children or adolescents were excluded from the study. The questionnaire included demographics, a simple assessment of socioeconomic status based on household assets, self-reported physical health, frequency of consumption of the 28 key food items (obtained from free listing) in the past week, and validated Brazilian Portuguese versions of the USDA Food Insecurity Module (Peréz-Escamilla et al. 2004) and the CES-D (Center for Epidemiological Studies Depression Measure) for depression (Silveira and Jorge 1998). The food insecurity and depression measures were modified slightly to include only "yes" or "no" responses, and one item was eliminated from the CES-D because it made respondents and the research assistant uncomfortable ("I thought my life has been a failure"). Individuals who scored between 0 and 4 affirmative responses on the food insecurity scale were recoded as food secure, and all others were categorized as food insecure (Table 2). We also measured participants' hemoglobin, mid–upper arm

TABLE 1. The 28 Food Items Identified by Community Members, Listed in Order from Most to Least Prestigious

Eggs
Bread
Sausage
Fish (fished)
Fish (purchased)
First-grade rice
Ice cream
Boney beef
Pork
Cheese
Cornmeal porridge
Cabbage
Salty snacks
Second-grade rice
Second-grade beef
Desserts
First-grade beef
Vegetables
Southern beans
Fruits (purchased)
Chocolate/bonbons
Tomatoes
Chicken
Lard for cooking
Carbonated beverages
Climbing beans
Tripe, head, or liver
Reheated food

TABLE 2. Results of Backward Stepwise Regressions Models for Score on the Modified CES-D (Center for Epidemiological Studies Depression Measure) and Upper Arm Fat Area ($n = 56$)

Variable	Mental Health Score			Upper Arm Fat Area		
	β	SE	p	β	SE	p
Intercept	−0.67			31.21		
SES (higher is wealthier)						
Food insecurity score	0.64	0.14	<.001	−1.37	0.67	.04
Female				12.98	5.6	.02
Age, years						
Education, any						

circumference, and triceps skinfold thickness to assess physical health and nutritional status. Using the skinfold and mid–upper arm circumference data, we calculated each person's mid–upper arm fat area (Frisancho 1990) that provides a better indicator of the amount of fat or stored energy. We also collected market prices for 25 of the 28 food items from the three local general stores.

To assess whether respondents agreed in their ranking of the 28 foods, we relied on cultural consensus analysis (Weller 2007). Raw data were entered in UCINET, and we calculated the model based on interval-level data. Consensus was initially low. We therefore reduced the sample to include only women. Using only the female sample, it was clear that there was high variability around the ranking of cheese; we then removed this item from the analysis. With these changes, we were able to reach consensus. One reason for the lack of initial consensus might be the varied interpretations of *prestige* mentioned above.

Depression and socioeconomic status summary scores were calculated for each individual and treated as continuous outcomes in analysis, while food insecurity was treated as both dichotomous and continuous. Using weights obtained from the ranking exercises in the second stage, we calculated a "food prestige score" for each household based on the number and frequency of consumption of prestigious and nonprestigious items in the past week. This score links the social value of food with actual consumption patterns. We also calculated a food price score for each respondent by multiplying the reported times each food was consumed by the market price of each food. Univariate, bivariate, and multivariate statistics on the questionnaire data were calculated in SPSS.

Results

Eighty-two percent of the 55-person questionnaire sample was female, and the mean age was 44 years (range 21–74 years). Most respondents had some primary education, but only 27 percent had received any secondary or higher education. The average household size was 4.4 individuals (range 2 to 10), with average 2.4 children (range 1 to 8).

The food item ranking data did not reveal any outright consensus, but when we eliminated males from the ranking sample and removed one food item (cheese) whose status was inconsistently rated between individuals, a consensus emerged with a ratio between the first and second eigenvalues of 3.03, which is indicative of fairly low levels of agreement but just over the conventional cutoff for consensus of 3.0 (Weller 2007). While low, this ratio suggests that respondents hold a shared understanding of food prestige that leads them to rank the 27 food items in a similar manner, with minimal variation resulting from individual idiosyncrasies rather than different underlying models of food prestige.

We then took the culturally correct answers generated from the cultural consensus analysis for each food and multiplied the number of times a food was consumed by that value; higher scores indicate greater consumption of prestigious items. We hypothesized that food-insecure households would have lower food prestige scores. Summing across the consumption of all foods weighted by their prestige score in the food frequency portion of the questionnaire revealed that food-insecure households had an average food prestige score of 537 compared with a score of 685 among food-secure households ($p =$ .04), which is consistent with the prediction. Further analysis showed that food-insecure households scored higher on four foods that were generally ranked with intermediate prestige: fish (caught, not purchased), second-grade rice, climbing beans (a locally grown alternative to popular but expensive southern beans), and bread. Removing these items from the calculation led to a much larger difference in prestige scores between food-secure and food-insecure households (578 vs. 379 points; $p = .005$). The composite measure of household socioeconomic status was also associated with household food insecurity, as expected ($\beta = -1.23, p < .001$).

We also took the unit price of each food (except caught fish, tripe, pork, and lard, for which prices were not available) and multiplied the unit price (in USD) by the amount of each item reportedly consumed by the household. Food-insecure households' total cost of consumed food was significantly lower than food-secure households (US\$98 vs. US\$132, $p = .002$). This result remained significant in a regression model controlling for total amount of food consumed, demonstrating that food-secure households were consuming higher priced food, on average. The food prestige score was also associated positively with food cost score ($r = .8, p < .01$), even when total food consumed was controlled. Together this suggests that food-secure households consumed more food, consumed more prestigious foods, and consumed more expensive foods.

Next, we tested for an association between food insecurity and two measures of well-being: depression symptoms and upper arm fat area. These measures were intended to capture mental and physical (nutritional) health status, respectively. Individuals living in food-secure households scored an average of 0.08 on the modified CES-D, whereas the average among food-insecure respondents was 3.5 ($p < .001$). This finding is consistent with the studies reviewed above, which have shown that food insecurity is strongly related to depression, and with the theoretical assumption that insecure access to food is harmful to mental well-being because it is extremely stressful. Respondents in food-insecure households also had less mid–upper arm fat, and this difference was more pronounced once respondent gender was statistically controlled. Food-insecure respondents had mid–upper arm fat values that were about 10 units smaller than those in food-secure households ($p = 0.02$). This finding is consistent with the dietary model of food insecurity outlined in the introduction, which suggests that food insecurity is harmful to physical well-being because it can lead to undernutrition.

Next, we explored whether simple measures of socioeconomic status and human capital reduced the association between food insecurity and mental health symptoms, but they did not. Results of these backward stepwise regression models are shown in Table 1. As is clear in the models, the standard measures of SES and human capital (specifically, age, gender, education level, and our composite measure of SES) did not predict mental health symptomology, but food insecurity did. Similarly, the measure of food insecurity predicted upper arm fat area, but the SES measure did not. The upper arm fat area result is important because it shows that a self-report measure (i.e., food insecurity) predicts a biomarker. Similarly, in preliminary analyses, food insecurity was inconclusively associated with lower hemoglobin levels ($p < 0.10$), although it did not predict frank anemia.

These analyses suggest that both physical outcomes of food insecurity and mental consequences of food insecurity are linked to well-being; that is, food insecurity harms well-being by creating the conditions for undernutrition and by creating high levels of distress. This distress is likely due at least partially to the direct stress of uncertain access to a basic resource, but it might also be related to the social stigma surrounding consumption of foods that are deemed by the community to be low status, a pattern that food-insecure families often adopt.

The key remaining question is whether the food insecurity variable's predictive power (as demonstrated in Table 1) is reduced by including the measure of food prestige in the regression model. If the social meaning of food matters for the link between mental health and food insecurity, then the food prestige variable should be a significant predictor of depression symptoms; but if other factors are more important, then the prestige variable should be nonsignificant.

Contrary to our expectations, and despite greater insecurity being associated with consumption of lower prestige foods, the prestige score of food did not predict depression score ($r = -0.05$; $p = 0.69$). Further, food insecurity's association with greater depression symptomatology was not mediated by the food prestige score. As an alternative measure of prestige, we also tested whether the average cost of food (calculated as the total food cost divided by the total food reportedly consumed) was associated with depression scores, once food insecurity was controlled. A comparison of the raw values suggests that the highest depression burden was among food-insecure individuals who consumed highly prestigious foods, but statistical analysis showed that this was not significantly different from the depression scores among those who were food insecure and consumed mostly lower prestige foods. This is a topic to explore in future research.

DISCUSSION

In this article, we have outlined a model that links the experience of food insecurity to physical health through nutritional status and to mental health through two pathways: a direct-stress pathway and a cultural pathway operating through the shared social meaning of food (Figure 2). We then used preliminary data from a study in rural Brazil to explore these alternative pathways. We predicted that at least a portion of the association between food insecurity and mental health would be accounted for by the consumption of low-prestige foods. Food insecurity was associated with a measure of physical health (upper arm fat area) and mental health (depression symptomatology). Food-insecure households also reported consuming less food overall, less prestigious food, and less expensive food. Yet, contrary to our hypothesis, the measure of household food prestige was *not* associated with mental or physical health, nor was the effect of food insecurity on mental health mediated by the prestige score. We also found that neither of our measures of nutritional status (upper arm fat area and anemia) predicted mental health or mediated the relationship between food insecurity and mental health, as would be suggested by a model that links food insecurity to poor mental health through a dietary pathway.

Food is undoubtedly much more than a means for supporting biological function because it has clear social meaning. So why were our results inconsistent with our theoretical model? One possibility is that our measure of prestige was ineffective; certainly this is consistent with the low agreement between respondents evidenced by the small difference between the first and second eigenvalues in the cultural consensus model. This may be due to a lack of shared cultural model about the prestige of various foods, although ethnographic observations from the community suggest this is unlikely. For instance, there are clearly foods that are reserved for special occasions, such as cakes and other desserts, *churrasco* (grilled first-grade beef), and *feijoada*, a dish typically prepared on Sundays that consists of black beans and pork. More likely, the low level of consensus is a result of the difficulty that some respondents had differentiating foods that were *prestigious* from those that were *important* in the community's regular diet. We asked participants to name foods that they considered most *chique* (chic) and which had the most *reputação* or *prestígio* (repute, prestige) in the community, and those they considered least *chique* and which had least *reputação* or *prestígio*. The terms *reputação* and *prestígio* have connotations both of prestige, and of importance. To partially address this confusion, we suggest that future work to test the social hypothesis should rely on a pairwise comparison task rather than a ranking task (Weller and Romney 1988).

We also could have measured individuals' own thoughts on the prestige of the foods they were consuming; for instance, Isabella might feel that bony beef is a very low quality food, so the fact that she eats it every day might be quite distressing, whereas Fátima might feel it is a high prestige food, and thus eating it every day is a sign of success. This could be tested by first conducting a 24-hour dietary recall and then asking the respondent how they think each food would be viewed by others in their community. One potential advantage of this approach is that it would capture nuanced differences in combination dishes, such as eating cereal with water rather than milk in the United States, or in Brazil preparing *Maria-Isabel* (a combination beans-and-rice dish) with only a few beans, which might be impossible to identify in a food frequency questionnaire.

A third possibility is that more important than the shift in the social value of consumed foods, is a shift in the *ways*—or the context—they are being consumed, how they are accessed, and the meaning attached to each of those processes (the deviation from normative dietary practices in Figure 2). Nanama and Frongillo (2012) find ample evidence of this in their case study of food insecurity in rural Burkina Faso. The most common experience of food insecurity reported by respondents was not having "enough food for needs," which at first glance appears as an incredibly obvious result. However, as Nanama and Frongillo describe, in this context, "food to meet one's needs" extends beyond individual and familial consumption. In Burkina Faso, food is used to help those in need, fulfill religious obligations, cement and reinforce kin ties, and fuel wedding parties and name ceremonies. For several men in their study, an inability to give to charity placed them in conflict with their religious obligations, and consequently they often took from their wives' food stores to make amends with their religion (but this generated tension with their wives). In extreme cases, men reported having to ask others for food, which led to feelings of shame and loss of social status. Women reported feeling shame when their children went to eat at other, more food-secure households. Food insecurity led to concerns about having enough food to meet both nutritional and social requirements. Similar results were reported in a qualitative study of food insecurity in Quebec (Hamelin et al. 2002). In that study, several themes emerged that related to the ability to exercise freedom of choice (i.e., to consume what one wants to consume) and the capacity to assume social responsibilities and participate in food-related rituals. This led to feelings of social alienation, and food insecurity overall lead to perturbations within the household, very similar to what was described in Burkina Faso. And in a study of urban food insecurity in Ethiopia (Hadley et al. 2012), food insecurity appeared to be a primary stressor not because of the nutritional content of the foods that people were constrained to eat, but because of the social and cultural implications of food insecurity. Food-insecure respondents noted that they were often unable to participate in food-based rituals, such as bringing food to a funeral, and expressed concern about their neighbors knowing that they were hungry. This too led to feelings of shame and alienation. Ethnography in the Brazil setting suggested that severely food-insecure individuals felt the same way, and often concealed their need, to such an extent that non-food-insecure individuals were completely unaware of the presence of food insecurity in the community.

These cases suggest that the social dimension of food insecurity might have less to do with the cultural value of the foods being consumed, and more to do with the act(s) of eating, and specifically the extent to which food insecurity constrains options and denies individuals and families the ability to participate in normative food behaviors. Taking this view, future biocultural studies of food insecurity should focus on more precisely measuring the prestige associated with various foods, measure those foods in a more nuanced manner, and, most importantly, focus on individuals' or families' inability to enact normative behaviors around eating (i.e., inviting guests over). Based on the findings of this study, we hypothesize that these social aspects of consumption may be the key mediators between food insecurity and poor mental well-being. One could test this by asking respondents to free-list aspects of the experience of food insecurity; this may lead to comments such as, "I've had to invite myself to another home because I did not have enough to eat" or "We close our doors so that our neighbors cannot see what we are eating" or "I would like to invite friends to dine but we do not have enough food." Future research could build a checklist like this from the ground up (Borgatti 1998), and then, in another sample, assess the extent to which these items explain the association between food insecurity and mental health. This would effectively link existing research programs on cultural consonance (cf. Dressler and colleagues' article in this volume) with the nutritional literature on food insecurity.

LIMITATIONS

As with any research study, readers should keep in mind the limitations of the research presented here. First, the relatively small sample size means that its results may lack statistical power. Second, its cross-sectional nature obviates the possibility of drawing conclusions about the directions of the statistical associations observed. Finally, although qualitative discussions with community members suggested that there would be a clear consensus regarding the relative prestige of food items, finding statistical consensus in the pile sort data was not straightforward. Consensus was reached by manipulating the ranking sample to include only women and removing one highly contested item.

An additional limitation has to do with the relatively narrow dietary diversity in the study community. Food prestige score differences were presumably limited in this context by the fact that the food ecology is also limited; most people purchase their foods from the three existing stores. A community with more diverse food ecology would likely demonstrate stronger links between the social status of food and well-being because food prestige scores would span a wider range. Communities in the United States, for example, where over 21,000 new food and beverage products were introduced in 2010 (USDA Economic Research Service 2013), might be especially vulnerable to the effects of food prestige on well-being because the range of possible consumption patterns is so much broader and because the attributes of food are so much more heavily advertised.

CONCLUSIONS

Our goal throughout this article has been to establish theoretical and methodological approaches for exploring the physical, mental, and social consequences of food insecurity in tandem. Although food insecurity studies have historically focused on the nutritional outcomes associated with uncertain access to food, an equally important concern for health disparities research is the social consequences associated with being food insecure. Our literature review and previous research suggest that the social value of food makes the experience of food insecurity extraordinarily stressful, and therefore makes it a potent generator of both physical and mental health disparities. Food is social in that there are shared cultural meanings about various foods, and food can be used in building and maintaining social relationships (e.g., commensal eating). Future work should focus on the social aspect of eating; for when one lacks the resources to engage in appropriate social interactions surrounding food, shame, stigma, and interrupted social relationships can add another layer of stress to the already stressful experience of lacking a basic resource for health maintenance.

We have shown that mental health and food insecurity are linked in a rural community in Pará, Brazil, but the consumption of low-prestige foods is not necessarily a key link between lower mental health and higher food insecurity in this context. We have suggested methodological and theoretical reasons why this might be, as well as future directions for research.

Although our results are context-specific, they have important implications for similar studies in other settings. First, they suggest that the relationship between food insecurity and mental health might be stronger in communities with broader food ecologies. Second, they suggest that food prestige ranking exercises must be phrased carefully to avoid respondent confusion, and that a pairwise comparison task might be more appropriate than a ranking exercise. Third, from a policy perspective, they suggest that the mental health impacts of food insecurity may extend well beyond simple stress related to lack of resources. If this is true, food insecurity may have further-reaching effects on mental health than was once thought.

The biocultural research agenda set forth in this article asserts that the physical, mental, and social health effects of food insecurity must be examined together in order to fully grasp the contribution of food insecurity to global health disparities. While past work has established the deleterious effects of food insecurity on physical health, present and future work is revealing its more insidious effects on mental well-being.

REFERENCES CITED

Alaimo, Katherine, Christine M. Olson, and Edward A. Frongillo
    2001 Food Insufficiency and American School-Aged Children's Cognitive, Academic, and Psychosocial Development. Pediatrics 108(1):44–53.
Arima, Eugenio Y., and Christopher Uhl
    1997 Ranching in the Brazilian Amazon in a National Context: Economics, Policy, and Practice. Society and Natural Resources 10(5):433–451.
Barthes, Roland
    1997 Toward a Psychosociology of Contemporary Food Consumption. *In* Food and Culture: A Reader. Carole M. Counihan and Penny Van Sterik, eds. Pp. 20–27. London: Routledge.
Bliege Bird, Rebecca, Eric Smith, and Douglas W. Bird
    2001 The Hunting Handicap: Costly Signaling in Human Foraging Strategies. Behavioral Ecology and Sociobiology 50(1):9–19.
Bodnar, Lisa M., and Katherine L. Wisner
    2005 Nutrition and Depression: Implications for Improving Mental Health among Childbearing-Aged Women. Biological Psychiatry 58(9):679–685.
Borgatti, Stephen P
    1998 Elicitation Techniques for Cultural Domain Analysis. *In* Ethnographer's Toolkit, Vol. 3. Margaret D. LeCompte, Jean J. Schensul, Bonnie K. Nastasi, and Stephen P. Borgatti, eds. Pp. 115–149. Newbury Park, CA: Sage.
Brandão, Amintas, and Carlos Souza
    2006 Deforestation in Land Reform Settlements in the Amazon. Imazon 7:1–4.
Brewis, Alexandra, and Meredith Gartin
    2006 Biocultural Construction of Obesogenic Ecologies of Childhood: Parent-Feeding versus Child-Eating Strategies. American Journal of Human Biology 18(2):203–213.
Campbell, David J.
    1990 Strategies for Coping with Severe Food Deficits in Rural Africa: A Review of the Literature. Food and Foodways 4(2):143–162.
Caplan, Pat, ed.
    2002 Food, Health and Identity. London: Routledge.
Casey, Patrick H., Pippa M. Simpson, Jeffrey M. Gossett, Margaret L. Bogle, Catherine M. Champagne, Carol Connell, David Harsha, Beverly McCabe-Sellers, James M. Robbins, Janice E. Stuff, and Judith Weber
    2006 The Association of Child and Household Food Insecurity with Childhood Overweight Status. Pediatrics 118(5):e1406–e1413.
Cattaneo, Andrea
    2008 Regional Comparative Advantage, Location of Agriculture, and Deforestation in Brazil. Journal of Sustainable Forestry 27(1/2):25–42.
Coates, Jennifer, Edward A. Frongillo, Beatrice Lorge Rogers, Patrick Webb, Parke E. Wilde, and Robert Houser
    2006 Commonalities in the Experience of Household Food Insecurity across Cultures: What Are Measures Missing? Journal of Nutrition 136(5):1438S–1485S.

Cole, Steven M. and Gelson Tembo

2011 The Effect of Food Insecurity on Mental Health: Panel Evidence from Rural Zambia. Social Science and Medicine 73(7):1071–1079.

Crooks, Deborah L.

1999 Child Growth and Nutritional Status in a High-Poverty Community in Eastern Kentucky. American Journal of Physical Anthropology 109(1):129–142.

de Garine, Igor, and Geoffrey A. Harrison

1988 Coping with Uncertainty in Food Supply. Oxford: Clarendon Press.

Dinour, Lauren M., Dara Bergen, and Ming-Chin Yeh

2007 The Food Insecurity-Obesity Paradox: A Review of the Literature and the Role Food Stamps May Play. Journal of the American Dietetic Association 107(11):1952–1961.

Douglas, Mary

1972 Deciphering a Meal. Daedalus 101(1):61–81.

Dressler, William W., Camila D. Borges, Mauro C. Balieiro, and José Ernesto dos Santos

2005 Measuring Cultural Consonance: Examples with Special Reference to Measurement Theory in Anthropology. Field Methods 17(4):331–355.

Farb, Peter and George Armelagos

1980 Consuming Passions: The Anthropology of Eating. New York: Houghton Mifflin.

Foweraker, Joe

1981 The Struggle for Land: A Political Economy of the Pioneer Frontier in Brazil from 1930 to the Present Day. New York: Cambridge University Press.

Frazier, Patricia A., Andrew P. Tix, and Kenneth E. Barron

2004 Testing Moderator and Mediator Effects in Counseling Psychology Research. Journal of Counseling Psychology 51(1):115–134.

Frisancho, A. Roberto

1990 Anthropometric Standards for the Assessment of Growth and Nutritional Status. Ann Arbor, MI: University of Michigan Press.

Frongillo, Edward A.

1999 Validation of Measures of Food Insecurity and Hunger. Journal of Nutrition 129(2): 506S–509S.

Gallup-Healthways

2014 State of Global Wellbeing: Results of the Gallup-Healthways Global Well-Being Index™. http://info.healthways.com/hs-fs/hub/162029/file-1634508606-pdf/WBI2013/Gallup-Healthways_State_of_Global_Well-Being_vFINAL.pdf, accessed November 14, 2104.

Hadley, Craig, and Deborah L. Crooks

2012 Coping and the Biosocial Consequences of Food Insecurity in the 21st Century. American Journal of Physical Anthropology 149(Suppl. 55):72–94.

Hadley, Craig, and Crystal L. Patil

2006 Food Insecurity in Rural Tanzania Is Associated with Maternal Anxiety and Depression. American Journal of Human Biology 18(3):359–368.

Hadley, Craig, Edward G. J. Stevenson, Yemesrach Tadesse, and Tefera Belachew

2012 Rapidly Rising Food Prices and the Experience of Food Insecurity in Urban Ethiopia: Impacts on Health and Wellbeing. Social Science and Medicine 75(12):2412–2419.

Hadley, Craig, Ayalew Tegegn, Fasil Tessema, John A. Cowan, Makonnen Asefa, and Sandro Galea

2008 Food Insecurity, Stressful Life Events and Symptoms of Anxiety and Depression in East Africa: Evidence from the Gilgel Gibe Growth and Development Study. Journal of Epidemiology and Community Health 62(11):980–986.

Hamelin, Anne-Marie, Micheline Beaudry, and Jean-Pierre Habicht

2002 Characterization of Household Food Insecurity in Quebec: Food and Feelings. Social Science and Medicine 54(1):119–132.

Hammen, Constance

2005 Stress and Depression. Annual Review of Clinical Psychology 1:293–319.

Headey, Derek

    2011 Was the Global Food Crisis Really a Crisis? Simulations Versus Self-Reporting. International Conference on Applied Economics—ICOAE. http://kastoria.teikoz.gr/icoae2/wordpress/wp-content/uploads/2011/10/024.pdf, accessed September 29, 2014.

Hecht, Susannah B., and Alexander Cockburn

    1989 The Fate of the Forest: Developers, Destroyers and Defenders of the Amazon. Chicago, IL: University of Chicago Press.

Himmelgreen, David, and Satish Kedia, eds.

    2010 The Global Food Crisis: New Insights into an Age-Old Problem. NAPA Bulletin 32. New York: John Wiley & Sons.

Himmelgreen, David A., Nancy Romero Daza, Maribel Vega, Humberto Brenes Cambronero, and Edgar Amador

    2006 "The Tourist Season Goes Down But Not the Prices." Tourism and Food Insecurity in Rural Costa Rica. Ecology of Food and Nutrition 45(4):295–321.

Hoelle, Jeffrey

    2011 Convergence on Cattle: Political Ecology, Social Group Perceptions, and Socioeconomic Relationships in Acre, Brazil. Culture, Agriculture, Food, and Environment 33(2):95–106.

Hoisington, Anne, Jill Armstrong Shultz, and Sue Butkus

    2002 Coping Strategies and Nutrition Education Needs among Food Pantry Users. Journal of Nutrition Education and Behavior 34(6):326–333.

Kollannoor-Samuel, Grace, Julie Wagner, Grace Damio, Sofia Segura-Pérez, Jyoti Chhabra, Sonia Vega-López, and Rafael Pérez-Escamilla

    2011 Social Support Modifies the Association between Household Food Insecurity and Depression among Latinos with Uncontrolled Type 2 Diabetes. Journal of Immigrant and Minority Health 13(6):982–989.

Maes, Kenneth C., Craig Hadley, Fikru Tesfaye, and Selamawit Shifferaw

    2010 Food Insecurity and Mental Health: Surprising Trends among Community Health Volunteers in Addis Ababa, Ethiopia During the 2008 Food Crisis. Social Science and Medicine 70(9):1450–1457.

Mahar, Dennis J.

    1979 Frontier Development Policy in Brazil: A Study of Amazonia. New York: Praeger.

Maillot, Matthieu, Nicole Darmon, and Adam Drewnowski

    2010 Are the Lowest-Cost Healthful Food Plans Culturally and Socially Acceptable? Public Health Nutrition 13(8):1178–1185.

Moerman, Daniel E., and Wayne B. Jonas

    2002 Deconstructing the Placebo Effect and Finding the Meaning Response. Annals of Internal Medicine 136(6):471–476.

Nanama, Siméon, and Edward A. Frongillo

    2012 Altered Social Cohesion and Adverse Psychological Experiences with Chronic Food Insecurity in the Non-Market Economy and Complex Households of Burkina Faso. Social Science and Medicine 74(3):444–451.

Nepstad, Daniel C., Claudia M. Stickler, and Oriana T. Almeida

    2006 Globalization of the Amazon Soy and Beef Industries: Opportunities for Conservation. Conservation Biology 20(6):1595–1603.

Pacheco, Pablo

    2009 Smallholder Livelihoods, Wealth and Deforestation in the Eastern Amazon. Human Ecology: An Interdisciplinary Journal 37(1):27–41.

Peréz-Escamilla, Rafael, Ana Maria Segall-Corrêa, Lucia Kurdian Maranha, Maria de Fátima Archanjo Sampaio, Leticia Marín-León, and Giseli Panigassi

    2004 An Adapted Version of the U.S. Department of Agriculture Food Insecurity Module Is a Valid Tool for Assessing Household Food Insecurity in Campinas, Brazil. Journal of Nutrition 134(8):1923–1928.

Radimer, Kathy L.

    1990 Understanding Hunger and Developing Indicators to Assess It. Ph.D. dissertation, Cornell University, Ithaca, NY.

Radimer, Kathy L., Christine M Olson, Jennifer C Greene, Cathy C. Campbell, and Jean-Pierre Habicht
  1992 Understanding Hunger and Developing Indicators to Assess It in Women and Children. Journal of Nutrition Education 24(1):36S–44S.
Shepherd, J., A. Harden, R. Rees, G. Brunton, J. Garcia, S. Oliver, and A. Oakley
  2006 Young People and Healthy Eating: A Systematic Review of Research on Barriers and Facilitators. Health Education Research 21(2):239–257.
Silveira, Dartiu Xavier, and Miguel Roberto Jorge
  1998 Propriedades Psicométricas da Escala de Rastreamento Populacional para Depressão CES-D em Populações Clínica e Não Clínica de Adolescentes e Adultos Jovens. Revista de Psiquiatria Clínica 25(5):251–261.
Stead, Martine, Laura McDermott, Anne Marie MacKintosh, and Ashley Adamson
  2011 Why Healthy Eating Is Bad for Young People's Health: Identity, Belonging and Food. Social Science and Medicine 72(2):1131–1139.
Sweet, Elizabeth
  2010 "If Your Shoes Are Raggedy You Get Talked About": Symbolic and Material Dimensions of Adolescent Social Status and Health. Social Science and Medicine 70(12):2029–2035.
Swindale, Anne, and Paula Bilinsky
  2006 Development of a Universally Applicable Household Food Insecurity Measurement Tool: Process, Current Status, and Outstanding Issues. Journal of Nutrition 136(5):1449S–1452S.
Townsend, Marilyn S., Janet Peerson, Bradley Love, Cheryl Achterberg, and Suzanne P. Murphy
  2001 Food Insecurity Is Positively Related to Overweight in Women. Journal of Nutrition 131(6):1738–1745.
Tsai, Alexander C., David R. Bangsberg, Edward A. Frongillo, Peter W. Hunt, Conrad Muzoora, Jeffrey N. Martin, and Sheri D. Weisner
  2012 Food Insecurity, Depression and the Modifying Role of Social Support among People Living with HIV/AIDS in Rural Uganda. Social Science and Medicine 74(12):2012–2019.
USDA Economic Research Service
  2013 New Product Introductions of Consumer Packaged Goods. http://www.ers.usda.gov/topics/food-markets-prices/processing-marketing/new-products.aspx#.UfHIXKwwbs0, accessed July 25, 2013.
Veblen, Thorstein
  2009 [1899] The Theory of the Leisure Class: An Economic Study of Institutions. New York: Oxford University Press.
von Grebmer, Klaus, Claudia Ringler, Mark W. Rosegrant, Tolulope Olofinbiyi, Doris Wiesmann, Heidi Fritschel, Ousmane Badiane, Maximo Torero, Yisehac Yohannes, Jennifer Thompson, Constanze von Oppeln, and Joseph Rahall
  2012 Global Hunger Index: The Challenge of Hunger: Ensuring Sustainable Food Security under Land Water and Energy Stresses. Bonn: Welthungerhilfe and Green Scenery, IFPRI, and Concern World Wide.
Weaver, Lesley Jo, and Craig Hadley
  2009 Moving beyond Hunger and Nutrition: A Systematic Review of the Evidence Linking Food Insecurity and Mental Health in Developing Countries. Ecology of Food and Nutrition 48(4):263–284.
Weller, Susan C.
  2007 Cultural Consensus Theory: Applications and Frequently Asked Questions. Field Methods 19(4):339–368.
Weller, Susan C., and A. Kimball Romney, eds.
  1988 Systematic Data Collection. London: Sage Publications.
Whitaker, Robert C., Shannon M. Phillips, and Sean M. Orzol
  2006 Food Insecurity and the Risks of Depression and Anxiety in Mothers and Behavior Problems in their Preschool-Aged Children. Pediatrics 118(3):e859–e868.
World Bank
  2013 Data Indicators. http://data.worldbank.org/indicator, accessed August 1, 2013.
Zizza, Claire A., Patricia A. Duffy, and Shirley A. Gerrior
  2008 Food Insecurity Is Not Associated with Lower Energy Intakes. Obesity 16(8):1908–1913.

A WORLD OF SUFFERING? BIOCULTURAL APPROACHES TO FAT STIGMA IN THE GLOBAL CONTEXTS OF THE OBESITY EPIDEMIC

ALEXANDRA A. BREWIS
Arizona State University

AMBER WUTICH
Arizona State University

Even as obesity rates rise, weight-related stigma remains widespread in the United States and leads to many documented social, economic, and health disparities. These include lower wages, less academic achievement, social exclusion as early as childhood, psychosocial stress, depression, and additional weight gain. Recent research documents the proliferation of antifat beliefs across the globe, but we know little about how this fat stigma varies across cultures. A clearer empirical and theoretical understanding of fat stigma in cultural context is essential to gauging its likely biocultural impacts across populations. Using data from Paraguay, Bolivia, India, and students and Muslim women in the United States (N = 414 women), we show that psychometric scales suggest high levels of stated or expressed fat stigma in all these samples, capturing globalizing anti-fat norms. However, when we assess what people think implicitly through reaction-time implicit association tests, we find marked variation across sites in the degree to which people are internalizing these stigmatized ideas around obesity. In India and among U.S. university students, women tend to internalize the idea of "fat" negatively. Paraguay women present, on average, fat-neutral internalized views. In Bolivia and among Muslim women in the United States, average assessments suggest fat-positive internalized views. This indicates fat stigmatizing norms are not always internalized, even as explicit fat stigma otherwise appears to be globalizing. Our findings indicate that the proposed biocultural relationships between fat stigma and health disparities may be complex and very context specific. [obesity, stigma, body image]

One of the most striking human biological trends of recent decades has been massive globalization of overweight and obesity. Two-thirds of all people live in countries where overnutrition kills more people than undernutrition (World Health Organization [WHO] 2013). Substantive scientific evidence points to the critical role of interrelated structural factors such as poverty, food systems, work patterns, and the built environment in explaining why so many people are gaining so much weight and have such difficulty losing it. Yet, the dominant cultural model in both clinical treatment and public health discourse around obesity remains one focused on the role of individual responsibility and failure (Brewis 2011). The core moral stigmatizing messages that equate *fat* with *bad*

ANNALS OF ANTHROPOLOGICAL PRACTICE 38.2, pp. 269–283. ISSN: 2153-957X. © 2015 by the American Anthropological Association. DOI:10.1111/napa.12056

(e.g., laziness, lack of willpower, lack of effort) in this way are pervasive, powerful, and shape national and local policy, public health strategies, the whole approach to clinical care of overweight patients, and the billion dollar weight loss industry. Importantly, this widespread pattern of weight-blaming undermines individual weight loss efforts because it tends to disincentivize healthier behaviors (Vartanian and Smyth 2013; Wott and Carels 2010).

In the United States (where most of the existing research has been conducted), we do know that the experience of being stigmatized and discriminated against because of weight (hereafter glossed as "fat stigma") negatively impacts almost every area of everyday life. By early childhood, weight-related teasing and bullying is common. As people move into adulthood, high body weight becomes a strong negative predictor of worse academic, romantic, and career opportunity and success. Obesity is also associated with worse treatment in health-care settings (see Puhl and Heuer 2009 and Puhl 2010 for reviews). One of the reasons the emotional suffering around fat stigma can be so profound is because the body can trump all other aspects of self in identify formation (Bordo 1993; Carryer 1997). These beliefs are so deeply internalized that heavier people can have strong negative moral reactions to obesity: for example, one recent study showed that obese patients are more likely to feel stigmatized when being treated by an obese primary care physician (Bleich et al. 2013).

Within a critical framework, the fervent public discourse around the "obesity epidemic" has been posited by some as moral panic (Campos et al. 2006). Others similarly point to the neo-liberalization of the obesity debates whereby "human worth is reduced to market worth . . . for marginalizing people who are obese on the basis of their apparent economic liability" (Townend 2009). Also of great concern, obesity is increasingly associated with poverty and income inequality in the United States and elsewhere—and intersects with other such risks for socioeconomic exclusion as minority ethnicity and female gender (Caprio et al. 2008; Levine 2011). This suggests that fat stigma may become a powerful force for structural violence (following Farmer 1999, 2005) and hence an underlying factor in the creation of economic and health disparities generally.

When viewed beyond the political economic context to incorporate a biocultural model, the likely connections between weight-related stigma and obesity-related health disparities become even clearer. As we have argued elsewhere, there are at least five basic pathways by which fat stigma can promote additional weight gain or reinforce weight maintenance (Brewis 2014). One example is that fat stigma amplifies exposures to psychosocial stress, which is linked in longitudinal studies to gains in adipose tissue. Another example is that, by forcing people into downwardly mobile economic pathways, the stigma may make them more likely to live in obesogenic environments with restricted opportunities for exercising and eating healthy foods. As with the case of economic discrimination mentioned above, fat stigma often layers with the effects of other stigmas (such as those of poverty, residence location, or immigrant status) to lead to even greater reinforcement of disparities in obesity-related health status and health-care availability (Hatzenbuehler et al. 2013; Wutich et al. 2014).

Most of the research on obesity and intersectional disparities is set in the United States. When we look to the global contexts of obesity, our understanding of how fat stigma might intersect with other vulnerabilities to elevate health disparities becomes less clear. Recent studies show that judgmental, blaming, stigmatizing ideas about "fat" that map onto this focus on individual blame appear to be proliferating in developing countries where poverty is more common, even as a more adipose body becomes the new physical norm in most of the world. For example, Brewis et al. (2011) show that some of the highest recorded levels of expressed fat stigma have been observed in supposedly traditionally fat-positive settings such as American Samoa, Puerto Rico, and Paraguay. This is in stark contrast to the traditional renderings of the anthropological record, which suggested substantial variation in the meanings applied to body fat across the ethnographic spectrum with a preponderance of societies seeing plumpness as beautiful, valuable, and desired (Anderson-Fye 2004; Brown and Konner 1987; Brown and Sweeney 2009; Popenoe 2004; Sobo 1994). Yet, the stigma around obesity is very little studied, and the personal suffering fat stigma creates for millions is barely recognized, let alone understood, especially outside of the Anglosphere.

These more recent findings raise important questions related to how the current global obesity "epidemic" intersects with these changing ideas (norms) about bodies, and how that may be shaping and expanding peoples' emotional suffering related to weight. For example, how do these changing (increasingly antifat) norms intersect with changing body sizes? Why would fat stigma become more profound if more people are obese— are these trends intimately related? Even as anti-fat norms have become widespread, do some cultural or structural contexts amplify people's vulnerability to internalizing and hence feeling the effects of fat stigma? One of the challenges in addressing critically the globalization of anti-fat norms is the lack of much direct evidence to inform even the most preliminary theory building. For example, there is almost no understanding even in the U.S. case of why one person may demonstrate less or more anti-fat bias than another (Carels and Musher-Eizenman 2010).

There are, however, clues we can glean from several detailed ethnographic studies that link the biological (weight) and the cultural (weight-related norms) in ways that would reflect the physical embodiment of weight bias and that suggest articulation with dynamic global processes of change. First, the ethnographies suggest media may be important. The long-term ethnographic study of Fijian women by Becker (1995, 2004) has concluded that media and technology (especially television) are driving the adoption of new (pro-slim) norms among younger women. Second, in both Becker's Fijian work and Sobo's study of Jamaican women (1994) conducted in the 1980–90s, we see that the anchoring of individual identity in community versus self is seemingly protective against various forms of body distress.

Third, some dynamic combination of wealth, poverty, income inequality, and upward mobility appear to be important. Based on participant observation and surveys of university students in the United Arab Emirates, Trainer (2012) found that concerns around socioeconomic upward mobility (marriage and education) drive fat-fear and pathological eating in ways that make it more difficult for young women to regulate their weight.

Based on long-term ethnographic work in Belize (2004, 2009), Anderson-Fye proposes that participation in a transnational economy, drive for success in that new economy, and changing dietary options have introduced eating disturbance and awareness of body size and control among youth (both male and female, although more so for women). In *Pretty Modern*, Edmonds (2011) uses the case of the emergence of socially acceptable and widely sought plastic surgery (including liposuction) in Brazil to suggest that body displays and beauty are a unique realm in which social inequalities are differently displayed and negotiated, realigning the traditional symbolic values of material class markers. As such, he argues "the cult of young and health" provides a mechanism that allows young and poor individuals to transcend traditional class structures and have opportunities for upward mobility. By adding surgical enhancements, he suggests, people are able to convert symbolic body capital into harder forms of wealth and power, so that for girls, especially, body replaces the mind as the "basis for identity as well as a source of power" (Edmonds 2011:251). In such a world as he describes, being labeled as *fat* essentially destroys the means of women's upward mobility.

PILOTING A BIOCULTURAL APPROACH TO UNDERSTANDING GLOBALIZING OBESITY STIGMA

In summer 2011 we piloted a biocultural approach that would allow us to develop better rudimentary theory relating these proposed aspects of weight and weight stigma across diverse socioecological settings, using these suggestions from the ethnographies as a starting point. Our preliminary hypotheses were focused on the notion that individual levels of implicit (internalized) fat stigma would minimally be a function of the interactions of explicit (stated) fat norms with such factors as one's own weight status, socioeconomic status, sense of self in community, and media exposure. We thus importantly distinguished between explicit (what people say) and implicit (what people think) stigma, as suggested by Krieger et al.'s recent work (2010) on racism. We focused our pilot study on women only; women are more at risk of obesity in most parts of the world, and historically the pattern in the industrialized nations has been that women's concerns around weight have been greater than men's (see review in Brewis 2011).

We collected five diverse purposive convenience samples. Given the vast majority of studies done on body image to date have been with U.S. student populations, we included a 48 U.S. student sample in our study. We collected data with $N = 201$ urban women in Paraguay (100 percent Mestizo), a site previously measured as having very high rates of stated fat stigma (Brewis et al. 2011). We also collected data for 101 women in urban Bolivia (87 percent Quechua), where overweight rates have been increasing rapidly (Perez-Cueto et al. 2009). This was supplemented with small samples of women in Chennai, India ($N = 41$). A small sample of Muslim women in the United States ($N = 23$) was also included as a contrast to U.S. university students.

Body mass index (BMI) was estimated from height and weight measures, collected using standard anthropometric procedures. Media exposure was captured in interviews based on reports of types and frequency of media use in a typical week. Here, exposure to media was measured as number of hours in a normal week spent reading newspapers or magazines or watching television. Sense of self in community was measured using an adaptation of Aron's "inclusion of other in self" (IOS) scale (Aron et al. 1992). This tool is a single-item pictorial measure of closeness intended to tap into people's sense of personal connection. Respondents select from a set of seven Venn-like diagrams with different levels of overlap between two circles. Participants are asked to identify which of the seven different circle sets best described the relationship between themselves and their community. Number of years of formal schooling was our (crude) measure of socioeconomic status.

To capture *explicit* fat stigma, what people will consciously acknowledge, we used the widely applied Attitudes to Obese People (ATOP) 20-item scale and the Beliefs About Obese People (BAOP) 8-item scales. It is reasonable to assume that scales such as the ATOP capture socially constructed and environmentally mediated norms whereas implicit attitude tests capture the internalization of social norms as personal beliefs (Vartanian et al. 2005). These are both 6-point Likert-type scales (from "I strongly agree" to "I strongly disagree") that have shown good reliability in prior studies (Allison et al. 1991). Statements are both positive and negative, and include "Most non-obese people would not want to marry anyone who is obese" or "Most obese people are not dissatisfied with themselves". A higher score is suggestive of less antifat attitudes (i.e., lower score = more explicit fat stigma). We have previously validated these tools cross-cultural use (Brewis and Wutich 2012).

To capture implicit fat stigma, we used cognitive testing in the forms of *implicit* association tests (IATs). By *implicit*, we mean what people might otherwise be unwilling or unable to report, and may actually even lie outside their explicit awareness (Schwartz et al. 2006). In the United States, previous studies have shown that some people may be unwilling to express extreme fat stigma on standard scales such as the ATOP, but high levels of prejudice can nonetheless be captured on IATs (similar to the patterns observed in relation to deep-seated racial biases in the contexts of political correctness). IAT scores also appear to better predict actual discriminatory behaviors, such as how closely someone will sit to an obese person (Bessenoff and Sherman 2000). This suggests that a more potentially damaging set of beliefs, either in terms of negative prejudicial judgments of self or of others, is captured by the IAT than the reports people give on the scales such as the ATOP.

In administering the IAT, each participant is presented with lists containing opposing categories: fat and slim, and good and bad. They are asked to classify synonyms for these words correctly as fast as they can in 20 seconds (see Table 1). Essentially, the IAT is a timed-reaction text that is based on the idea that if someone is accustomed to making an association they will be able to do so more quickly. Thus, if people can make more fat-negative associations than fat-positive ones in a 20-second block, then this is taken as a measure of greater anti-fat bias. This test can be done both with a computer interface and with pen and paper, but we selected the latter because in some sites people are not used to using computers. For more details on how the pen-and-paper IAT was scored, see Brewis and Wutich (2012). In prior studies (mostly with U.S. samples), respondents

TABLE 1. Example of the Implicit Association Test (IAT) Format Using Categorization of Fat Versus Thin and Good Versus Bad

Fat People Good		Thin People Bad
✓	Obese	
	Horrible	✓
	Slim	✓
✓	Excellent	
✓	Large	
	Nasty	✓
✓	Fat	
✓	Joyful	
	Thin	✓
✓	Wonderful	
	Skinny	✓
	Terrible	✓

In this example, "fat people" are associated with "good" words; "thin people" are associated with "bad" words. Correct responses are shown with checks.

have been found consistently to associate fat with bad and thin with good more strongly than their reverse pairings (Schwartz et al. 2003; Teachman and Brownell 2001).

For the purposes of this study, we also wanted some way to identify the level to which people would *personally* be motivated to avoid being obese, since these other tools are capturing how people feel about others as much as themselves. We used interview questions related to trade offs they would be willing to make. This tool was adapted from Schwartz et al. (2006). Respondents were asked to state if they would "absolutely yes," "probably yes," "probably no," or "absolutely no" rather be _____ than obese. The six options people had were as follows: divorced, unable to have children, lose a limb, severely depressed, alcoholic, or blind. A higher score indicates there are more conditions the person would be possibly willing to trade off to avoid being obese (i.e., higher score = higher stigma). We also asked people how many years of their life they would be willing to give up to avoid being obese as a single summary measure of their willingness to trade personally to avoid being obese.

Thus, through the triangulation of these three different ways to capture fat stigma, we can then start to articulate multiple different profiles of how women recognize, understand, and internalize fat stigma in relation to their own body size: for example, among obese women you can distinguish those who do or do not recognize social norms that view fat negatively and ascribe individual blame for being fat (high vs. low fat stigma on the ATOP and BAOP), who do or do not believe that fat people are of less value than others (high negative fat stigma on the IAT vs. neutral or positive score), and personally care a lot or do not care at all about this in relation to their own status (high willingness to trade other awful outcomes to avoid being fat, vs. no desire to trade). An obese woman

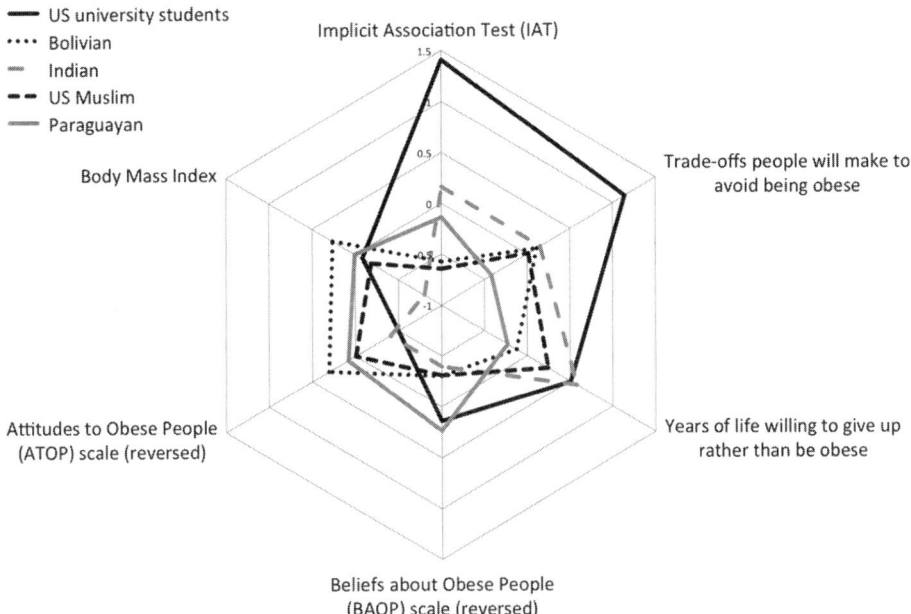

FIGURE 1. Radar graph illustrates sample differences in key measures related to fat stigma. Each sample (U.S. student, Bolivian, Indian, U.S. Muslim, Paraguayan) is depicted with a different line. Each measure (IAT, trade-offs, BAOP, ATOP, BMI) occupies a distinct spoke on the radar. For all the stigma measures shown here, a larger positive number indicates a higher level of stigma. For the purposes of ease of reading the scale, variables have each been standardized as *z*-scores, and some scales have been reversed.

who scores high on all of these would be expected to be more vulnerable in general to the felt effects of fat stigma.

GLOBALIZING WEIGHT AND WEIGHT STIGMA: SOME SUGGESTIVE FINDINGS

Table 1 provides the mean scores for key variables alongside sample characteristics by site. Figure 1 shows visually the variation across the different measures of fat stigma, converted to standardized scores. We observe much greater variation in the levels of implicit stigma (measured by the IAT) than levels of explicit stigma (measured in the ATOP). ATOP results of *all* the samples present very stigmatizing mean scores. The BAOP scores—concerned with the level of blame people place on the individual—show more variability, with Paraguyans (least educated sample) and the U.S. students (most educated sample) displaying the lowest means (most blaming; Table 2).

By comparison, there is highly significant variation across groups in the level of implicit stigma expressed on the IAT (Figure 2). The average IAT score for the U.S. students is much higher (more stigmatizing) than in the other groups; on average, Paraguayan women sit around zero (neutral score), and Bolivia and U.S. Muslim women are below zero, indicating they associated fat with good more than with bad. Indian women are less

TABLE 2. Demographics and Mean Scores for Key Variables by Sample (Standard Deviations Are Shown in Parentheses)

Population	Sample Size	Mean BMI	Mean Age	Mean Community Inclusion Scores 1–7 Scale	Percent Completing High School	Mean Hours of Media Per Week	Beliefs about Obese People (BAOP) Scale. HIGHER Score, Less "Blaming"	Attitudes to Obese People (ATOP) Scale. HIGHER Score, Less Fat Stigmatizing	Mean Score of Number Conditions They Would Trade. LOWER Score, More Fat Avoiding	Mean Number of Years of Life Would You Be Willing to Give Up Rather Than Be Obese	IAT Score. HIGHER Score, More Fat Prejudiced
U.S. undergraduate students, Phoenix, Arizona	48	23.50 (5.6)	21.8 (4.2)	3.5 (1.4)	100%	4.9 (5.2)	16.4 (19.4)	64.6 (18.9)	19.8 (3.8)	4.8 (6.2)	12 (6.8)
U.S. Muslim women, Phoenix, Arizona	23	23.09 (3.2)	30.4 (9.7)	5.2 (0.85)	96%	9.2 (9.7)	19.5 (4.7)	56.9 (15.4)	22.8 (2.6)	3.1 (10.8)	6.2 (4.8)
Chennai, India	41	20.45 (3.6)	20.9 (2.2)	5.0 (1.7)	98%	10.1 (7.0)	20.1 (6.7)	63.1 (11.1)	22.4 (2.9)	5.3 (16.0)	2.6 (3.5)
San Lorenzo, Paraguay	200	23.88 (4.3)	38.9 (13.4)	6.7 (0.91)	80%	9.0 (5.6)	15.7 (7.9)	55.6 (14.7)	23.9 (0.39)	0.1 (0.3)	0.03 (1.9)
Ascension, Bolivia	101	24.98 (3.2)	34.4 (9.5)	4.0 (1.6)	7%	7.2 (7.5)	19.5 (4.1)	52.1 (14.3)	22.4 (2.3)	0.8 (1.9)	5.4 (5.2)

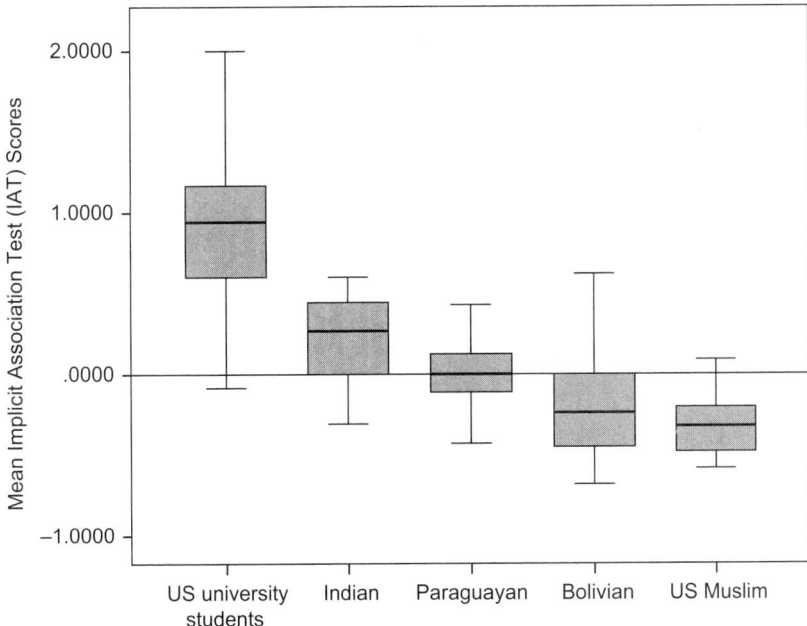

FIGURE 2. Box-plot showing mean implicit association test (IAT) scores for women from five cross-cultural samples. Scores are based on the ratio of time taken by subjects to match fat = bad and fat = good. A positive score (>0) indicates a person reacts more quickly to pairing fat with bad than with good, and indicative of higher levels of implicit fat stigma.

negative than the United States by a large margin, but still on the whole are fat negative rather than neutral or positive. That is, the variation we observe is some groups have more clearly internalized the idea that fat = bad and others that fat = good.

We also see large across-sample variation in how women were willing to personally trade to avoid being obese, either as compared to other stigmatized condition or years of life. This measure is much higher in the U.S. students than all other samples. By contrast, all Paraguayan women (bar one, who wished to be divorced) said they would trade neither years of life nor any other stigmatizing conditions to avoid being obese (see Table 1).

To identify suggestive patterns across the population samples, we used a logistic regression model, with U.S. students as a reference category. Once all the other factors are taken into account (age, BMI, media exposure, education level, community inclusion), we find that IAT scores were 14.2 times more likely to be high in U.S. students than women in Bolivia and 5.9 times more likely than Muslim women in the United States (both $p < .05$). This is not the case with the ATOP, where the odds were not predicted to be significantly different by country once the other factors such as body weight were taken into account. In examining the ATOP scale, Bolivia ($p < .05$) was significantly different from U.S. students, with the odds being 1/.205 greater that a U.S. student would rate as less stigmatizing on the ATOP. This was also the case for Paraguay (odds ratio = 1/.216, $p = .026$). In terms of the BAOP scale, all except Bolivia had significantly lower odds of

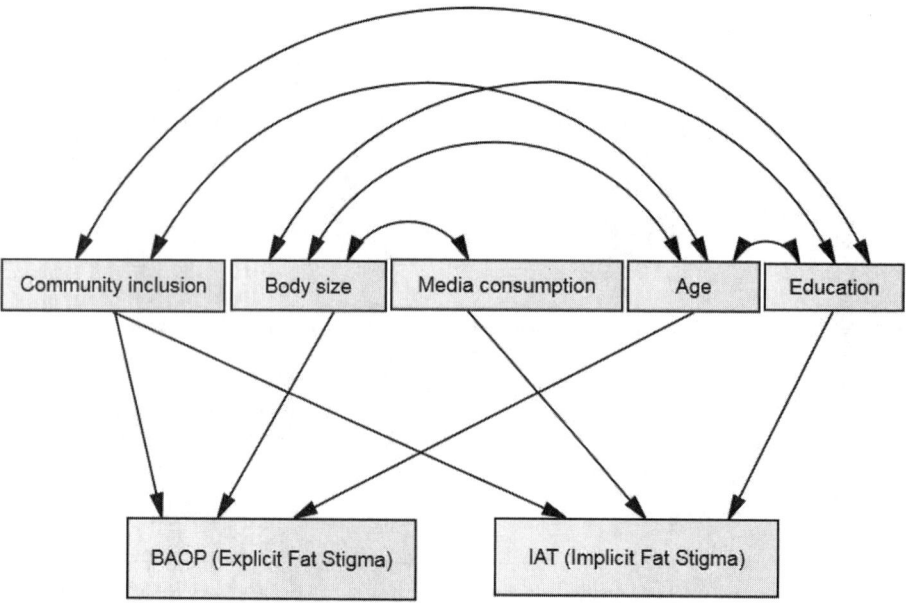

FIGURE 3. Final model showing significant relationships between key social and demographic variables and implicit and explicit stigma scores. Model building and analysis was done in SPSS AMOS 19. Only significant relationships ($p < .05$) are indicated. Significant covariates are shown by double arrows, although all potential covariates were tested in the initial model.

scoring high in terms of "blame" for fat compared to the U.S. students (India: Odds Ratio [OR] = .087, p = .000; Muslim women: OR = .125, p = .003; Paraguay: OR = .084, p = .001).

Following the suggestions derived from the key ethnographies that media, anchoring of self, and socioeconomic context may be key explanatory factors related to the adoption of anti-fat norms, we then used AMOS to develop a basic model. The key predictive variables in the total model included age, body size, media consumption, level of community inclusion, and level of education (our indirect measure of wealth). Figure 3 shows the basic model predicting implicit fat stigma (the IAT) and one measure of explicit fat stigma (the BAOP).

In terms of implicit stigma (the IAT), more community inclusion (Beta = −0.249), more media (Beta = −0.252), and more education (Beta = −0.279) all have a negative effect on IAT scores, meaning that participants are predicted to have *lower* levels of implicit fat stigma if they are *more* community connected, spend more hours consuming standard media (TV, magazines, newspapers), and completed high school.

We then ran additional models separately for Bolivia and Paraguay, having sufficient subsample sizes in those two cases. In both these single cases, we also find that more community inclusion and more media consumption predict lower (less-stigmatizing) IAT scores (Beta = −0.183 for Bolivia and −0.231 for Paraguay for community inclusion and −0.291 for Bolivia and −0.152 for Paraguay for media).

In terms of BAOP (blaming) score, community inclusion had a positive effect (Beta = 2.84). Note that, reverse of the IAT, a higher BAOP suggests less explicit stigma. Thus, the relationship with media is similar for both the implicit and explicit measures in that more media exposure is associated with less-measured stigma.

Importantly, BMI did not prove significant in predicting either outcome variable, meaning people's weight is not a good explanation for why people's levels of either explicit or implicit stigma differ. We hypothesized that BMI would influence the degree to which people internalized fat norms as revealed in the IAT, but the finding here suggests this is not so. Rather, greater community inclusion seems protective against internalizing stigmatizing ideas. We also find that more use of standard media, and having more education (our proxy for wealth) are also protective.

DISCUSSION

Based on the analysis provided here of five pilot case studies, we can provide several key observations that can guide broader biocultural theorizing and practical interventions around the current global landscape of obesity-related stigma.

First, explicit anti-fat norms are widely expressed across an array of socioecological contexts at a consistently high level, but the variation in the IAT (implicit stigma) results suggest that the emotional costs of "being fat" may be very different from place to place. For women in places such as Paraguay where they may "talk fat-as-bad" but do not "think fat-as-bad" and are unwilling to make any personal trades against being obese, it would be expected that the emotional costs of being socially labeled as "fat" would be less—even if stated anti-fat norms (such as seen in the ATOP) otherwise appear to be highly stigmatizing.

As global public health campaigns gear up to take on the growing challenge of obesity in non-Western and lower income nations, basic knowledge about the sociocultural bases of fat stigma will be vital to their success. Such public health campaigns should be informed by an understanding of when and how fat stigma helps or hurts people—both in terms of economic and biocultural impacts. Additionally, it is essential for health providers to determine when fat stigma triggers or undermines the critical behavior change desired in clinical and public health interventions. Because fat stigma carries a clear and well-documented risk of harming those struggling with their weight, we urge extreme caution in the use of fat stigma (both planned and unintentional) in clinical and public health settings.

Second, high anti-fat norms as expressed by items on standard scales such as the ATOP do not necessarily reflect underlying internalization of those norms as personally salient beliefs, as represented on the IAT. Furthermore, we find the ATOP and IAT scores do not correlate, and explicit and implicit fat stigma need to be considered as separate phenomena. This is very important because it is the implicitly, not the explicitly, prejudicial ideas that likely most affect discriminatory behavior toward others and one's own levels of psychosocial stress. It also nicely matches Krieger et al.'s (2010) finding that explicit and implicit measures of racial discrimination are only weakly correlated in the United States.

Third, media matters—but not in the ways we predicted. We observe a counterintuitive pattern of media influence, whereby higher stigma levels are predicted by less media consumption. When we examine our findings in the context of Becker's Fijian work, we can suggest that media may be extremely important when exposure to thin ideals is a new phenomenon. Our findings should be interpreted with caution because we adopted a classic measure of media consumption in our study; this measure does not assess social media use (e.g., blogs, Facebook). The rapid and recent growth in social media use likely explains why average media use estimates are lower in the U.S. student sample than the others, reflecting that students in the United States are getting more of their media from social media sources. Thus, our measures of greater use of television and magazines could represent a distancing from current pop culture messaging, rather than greater intimacy with it.

Fourth, findings regarding education level (our rather crude proxy for wealth) did not predict meaningfully or consistently any variation in either the expression or internalization of fat stigma in these samples of women. On the basis of this analysis, we cannot conclude much about the role of wealth except to say that better measures will be needed in future studies.

Fifth, our finding regarding the importance of one's own community identification advances our understandings of how globalization, weight gain, and weight stigma might be mediated. Ethnographically, studies such as Becker's in Fiji have suggested that incursion of Western media such as television may be the key to understanding why increasingly people prefer thin and dislike fat (Becker 1995). In the Fiji case, she has clearly demonstrated through narrative analysis that shift of identity from community to a sense of self-anchored in careful body presentation (such as thinness) happens as new external ideas about bodies are introduced. Studies that can test which underlying factors best mediate these changes are an important and often different perspective on a very complex and slow process. The finding here, for example, suggests that even as media exposure, changing body sizes, and changing sense of self in the context of community increasingly converge, we can better specify that is the changing sense of self that is most influential in shaping changes in how people adopt—and perhaps more importantly internalize—new body norms.

CONCLUSION

In the context of the global obesity rise, fat stigma appears to be driving social, economic, and health disparities in ways that are little understood. Fat-blaming ideas continue to frame much of the current medical, public health, and policy approaches to obesity, leading to discriminatory practices and creating barriers that lead to worse health care (Bombak 2014; Foster 2003; Harvey and Hill 2001; Puhl et al. 2013). But how does fat stigma operate beyond the clinic? A clearer empirical and theoretical understanding of fat stigma in cultural context is essential to gauging its likely biocultural impacts across populations. Using data from Paraguay, Bolivia, India, and university students and Muslim women in the United States ($N = 414$ women), we show that psychometric scales suggest high levels of stated or expressed fat stigma in all these samples, capturing globalizing anti-fat norms.

However, when we assess what people think implicitly through reaction-time IATs, we find marked variation across sites in the degree to which people are internalizing these stigmatized ideas around obesity. In India and among U.S. university students, women tend to internalize the idea of *fat* negatively. In Paraguay, women present, on average, fat-neutral internalized views. In Bolivia and among Muslim women in the United States, average assessments suggest fat-positive internalized views. This indicates fat-stigmatizing norms are not always internalized, even as explicit fat stigma otherwise appears to be globalizing. Our findings indicate that the proposed biocultural relationships between fat stigma and health disparities may be complex and very context specific.

These results suggest it may be easier to prevent or undo the structural effects of fat stigma in places such as Bolivia and Paraguay where stated anti-fat norms have not (yet) become internalized beliefs. Critical biomedical approaches, concerned with how political economic processes "get under our skin" (Leatherman and Goodman 2011:30), are most often focused on understanding how structures affect vulnerabilities on the ground. These findings suggest the means to use empirical analysis of human cultural and biological variation to flip that perspective, allowing the possibility to "look upward" to consider how differences in people's vulnerabilities might be leveraged to find the best localized strategies to tackle structural factors with the goal to create better health.

REFERENCES CITED

Allison, David B., Vicent C. Basile, and Harold E. Yuker
 1991 The Measurement of Attitudes Toward and Beliefs about Obese Persons. International Journal of Eating Disorders 10(5):599–607.
Anderson-Fye, Eileen P.
 2004 A "Coca-Cola" Shape: Cultural Change, Body Image, and Eating Disorders in San Andres, Belize. Culture, Medicine, and Psychiatry 28(4):561–595.
Aron, Arthur, Elaine N. Aron, and Danny Smollan
 1992 Inclusion of Other in the Self Scale and the Structure of Interpersonal Closeness. Journal of Personality and Social Psychology 63(4):596–612.
Becker, Anne E.
 1995 Body, Self and Society: The View from Fiji. Philadelphia: University of Pennsylvania Press.
 2004 Television, Disordered Eating and Young Women in Fiji: Negotiating Body Image and Identity during Rapid Social Change. Culture, Medicine and Psychiatry 28(4):533–559.
Bessenoff, Gayle R., and Jeffery W. Sherman
 2000 Automatic and Controlled Components of Prejudice toward Fat People: Evaluation versus Stereotype Activation. Social Cognition 18(4):329–353.
Bleich, Sara N., Kimberly A. Gudzune, Wendy L. Bennett, Marian P. Jarlenski, and Lisa A. Cooper
 2013 How Does Physician BMI Impact Patient Trust and Perceived Stigma? Preventive Medicine 57(2):120–124.
Bombak, Andrea
 2014 Obesity, Health at Every Size, and Public Health Policy. American Journal of Public Health 104(2):e60–e67.

Bordo, Susan

1993 Unbearable Weight: Feminism, Western Culture and the Body. Berkeley: University of California Press.

Brewis, Alexandra

2011 Obesity: Cultural and Biocultural Perspectives. NJ: Rutgers University Press.

2014 Stigma and the Perpetuation of Obesity. Social Science and Medicine 118:152–158.

Brewis, Alexandra A., and Amber Wutich

2012 Explicit versus *Implicit* Fat *Stigma*. American Journal of Human Biology 24(3):332–338.

Brewis, Alexandra A., Amber Wutich, Ashlan Falletta-Cowden, and Isa Rodriguez-Soto

2011 Body Norms and Fat-Stigma in Global Perspective. Current Anthropology 52(2):269–276.

Brown, Peter J., and Melvin Konner

1987 An Anthropological Perspective of Obesity. Annals of the New York Academy of Science 499:29–46.

Brown, Peter J., and Jennifer Sweeney

2009 The Anthropology of Overweight, Obesity, and the Body. AnthroNotes 30(1):6–12.

Campos, Paul, Abigail Saguy, Paul Ernsberger, Eric Oliver, and Glenn Gaesser

2006 The Epidemiology of Overweight and Obesity: Public Health Crisis or Moral Panic? International Journal of Epidemiology 35(1):55–60.

Caprio, Sonia, Stephen R. Daniels, Adam Drewnowski, Francine R. Kaufman, Lawrence A. Palinkas, Arlan L. Rosenbloom and Jeffrey B. Schwimmer

2008 Influence of Race, Ethnicity, and Culture on Childhood Obesity: Implications for Prevention and Treatment. A Consensus Statement of Shaping America's Health and the Obesity Society. Diabetes Care 31(11):2211–2221.

Carels, Robert A., and Dara R. Musher-Eizenman

2010 Individual Differences and Weight Bias: Do People with an Anti-Fat Bias Have a Pro-Thin Bias? Binge Eating 7(2):143–148.

Carryer, Jenny

1997 Embodied Largeness: A Feminist Exploration. *In* Bodily Boundaries, Sexualised Genders, Medical Discourses. Marion De Ras and Victoria Grace, eds. Pp. 99–109. New Zealand: Dunmore Press.

Edmonds, Alexander

2011 Pretty Modern: Beauty, Sex, and Plastic Surgery in Brazil. Durham: Duke University Press.

Farmer, Paul

1999 Infections and Inequalities: The Modern Plagues. Berkeley: University of California Press.

2005 Pathologies of Power. Berkeley: University of California Press.

Foster, Gary D., Thomas A. Wadden, Angela P. Makris, Duncan Davidson, Rebecca Swain Sanderson, David B. Allison, and Amy Kessler

2003 Primary Care Physicians' Attitudes about Obesity and its Treatment. Obesity Research 11(10):1168–1177.

Harvey, Emma L., and Andrew Hill

2001 Health Professionals' Views of Overweight People and Smokers. International Journal of Obesity and Related Metabolic Disorders 25(8):1253–1261.

Hatzenbuehler, Mark L., Jo C. Phelan, and Bruce G. Link

2013 Stigma as a Fundamental Cause of Population Health Inequalities. American Journal of Public Health 103(5):813–821.

Krieger, Nancy, Dana Carney, Katie Lancaster, Pamela D. Waterman, Anna Koshelava, and Mahzarin Banaji

2010 Combining Explicit and Implicit Measures of Racial Discrimination in Health Research. American Journal of Public Health 100(8):1485–1492.

Leatherman, Tom, and Alan H. Goodman

2011 Critical Biocultural Approaches in Medical Anthropology. *In* A Companion to Medical Anthropology. Merrill Singer and Pamela I. Erickson, eds. Pp. 38–45. Oxford: Wiley-Blackwell.

Levine, James A.

2011 Poverty and Obesity in the U.S. Diabetes 60(11):2667–2668.

Pérez-Cueto, Federico J. A., Ana Bayá Botti, and Wim Verbeke
  2009 Prevalence of Overweight in Bolivia: Data on Women and Adolescents. Obesity Reviews 10(4):373–377.
Popenoe, Rebecca
  2004 Feeding Desire: Fatness, Beauty, and Sexuality among a Saharan People. London: Routledge.
Puhl, Rebecca
  2010 Obesity Stigma: Important Considerations for Public Health. American Journal of Public Health 100(6):1019–1028.
Puhl, Rebecca M., and Chelsea A. Heuer
  2009 The Stigma of Obesity: A Review and Update. Obesity Research 17(5):941–964.
Puhl, Rebecca, Joerg Luedicke, and Jamie Lee Peterson
  2013 Public Reactions to Obesity-Related Health Campaigns: A Randomized Controlled Trial. American Journal of Preventative Medicine 45(1):36–48.
Schwartz, Marlene B., Lenny R. Vartanian, Brian A. Nosek, and Kelly D. Brownell
  2006 The Influence of One's Own Body Weight on Implicit and Explicit Anti-Fat Bias. Obesity 14(3):440–447.
Schwartz, Marlene B., Heather O. Chambliss, Kelly D. Brownell, Steven N. Blair, and Charles Billington
  2003 Weight Bias among Health Professionals Specializing in Obesity. Obesity Research 11(9):1033–1039.
Sobo, Elisa
  1994 The Sweetness of Fat: Health, Procreation, and Sociability in Rural Jamaica. In Many Mirrors: Body Image and Social Meaning. Nicole Sault, ed. Pp. 132–154. New Brunswick, NJ: Rutgers University Press.
Teachman, Bethany A., and Kelly Brownell
  2001 Implicit Anti-Fat Bias among Health Professionals: Is Anyone Immune? International Journal of Obesity 25(10):1525–1531.
Townend, Louise
  2009 The Moralizing of Obesity: A New Name for an Old Sin? Critical Social Policy 29(2):171–190.
Trainer, Sarah
  2012 Negotiating Weight and Body Image in the UAE: Strategies Among Young Emirati Women. American Journal of Human Biology 24(3):314–324.
Vantanian, Lenny R., P. Herman, and J. Polivy.
  2005 Implicit-and-Explicit Attitudes toward Fatness and Thinness: The Role of the Internalization of Societal Standards. Body Image 2:371–381.
Vartanian, Lenny R., and Joshua M. Smyth.
  2013 Primum Non Nocere: Obesity Stigma and Public Health. Journal of Bioethical Inquiry 10(1):49–57.
Wott, Carissa B., and Robert A. Carels
  2010 Overweight Stigma, Psychological Distress and Weight Loss Treatment Outcomes. Journal of Health Psychology 15(4):608–614.
World Health Organization (WHO)
  2013 Obesity and Overweight, Fact sheet No 311. http://www.who.int/mediacentre/factsheets/fs311/en/, accessed September 28, 2014.
Wutich, Amber, Alissa Ruth, Alexandra Brewis, and Christopher Boone
  2014 Stigmatized Neighborhoods, Social Bonding, and Health. Medical Anthropology Quarterly 28(4)556–577.

THE REPRODUCTION OF POVERTY AND POOR HEALTH IN THE PRODUCTION OF HEALTH DISPARITIES IN SOUTHERN PERU

Thomas Leatherman
University of Massachusetts

Kasey Jernigan
University of Massachusetts

It is a common starting assumption for analyses of health disparities that poverty and poor health occur together and mutually influence one another. While earlier research tended to focus on how poverty leads to poor health, over the past two decades it has become more common to focus on the social and economic costs of illness and disease. Yet, the majority of this research has not employed an ethnographic lens and is limited in accounting for local level factors that shape vulnerability and resilience to illness and its impact on lives and livelihoods. This paper illustrates how the inequality and health dialectic plays out among rural producers in the district of Nuñoa in the southern Peruvian Andes. Using a critical biocultural approach attending to global–local interactions, relations of power and human agency, and that is grounded in ethnographic realities, we explore connections between vulnerability and resiliency in the reproduction of poverty and poor health. While the direct costs of healthcare can be catastrophic to a household's economy in extreme cases, indirect costs to labor power and household production create for many a greater cumulative loss that limits resilience in the face of future illness and other problems. The way illness impacts lives and livelihoods in the reproduction of poverty and poor health is shaped by people's access to land, labor power, and cash reserves, so that these effects are experienced unevenly and with different long-term implications among vulnerable populations.

INTRODUCTION

It has become increasingly common to recognize and acknowledge that health disparities are a product of social inequalities, and that poverty, inequalities, and illness are co-constitutive across time and space; mutually influencing one another in a negative synergistic relationship (Farmer 1999; Hamoudi and Sachs 1999; Singer 2011; Wagstaff 2002). Indeed, international development agencies place health at the center of poverty reduction strategies (Calvo et al. 2000; Department for International Development [DFID] 1999; Peters et al. 2008; Russell 2004; World Health Organization [WHO] 2002), recognizing that the urban and rural poor are often caught in a self-perpetuating poverty–illness nexus across multiple generations—"part of a larger cycle, where poverty leads to ill

ANNALS OF ANTHROPOLOGICAL PRACTICE 38.2, pp. 284–299. ISSN: 2153-957X. © 2015 by the American Anthropological Association. DOI:10.1111/napa.12057

health and ill health maintains poverty" (Peters et al. 2008:161). At the root of this poverty-illness nexus are structural inequalities that underlie intergenerational vulnerabilities to heightened exposure to stressors, diminished coping capacity, and weakened resilience (Leatherman 2005). Yet at the local level, considerable variation exists in how specific conditions, histories, and lived experience make some people more or less vulnerable to the synergies of poverty and poor health. Focusing an ethnographic lens on local contexts of inequalities and lived vulnerabilities is needed to uncover this variation. Because most studies examining poverty and health have sought broad patterns of association using large-scale databases, this sort of attention to local level vulnerabilities, lived experiences, and impacts of illness and disease on local biologies is relatively rare. While broad patterns of associations are important to assess the dimensions of relationships between economics and health, contextualized case studies are equally important for understanding why some individuals and households disproportionately suffer from illness and its impacts on their livelihoods and social lives. A critical biocultural analysis that exposes global–local interactions and that is grounded in ethnographic realities can make these connections between vulnerability, resiliency, and the reproduction of poverty and poor health that others do not.

In this paper, we present a case study based on earlier research in highland Peru that examined influences of poverty on poor nutrition and health and the impacts of illness on food production and household livelihoods. We expand the focus here to include multiple measures of health, production, household economy, social responses to illness, and impacts of illness—and how these interact in the reproduction of poverty and poor health in the specific local context of rural producers in the southern Andes of Peru. An analysis of how poverty and inequalities become embodied as poor health or "biological insult" and in turn, how "local biologies" play a role in the reproduction of poverty is relevant for the urban and rural poor in multiple global contexts.

BACKGROUND

Until the last two decades, it has been relatively rare to examine health and household-level economic measures as a bidirectional relationship. It was a given that poverty was correlated with poor health, but the relationship was largely seen as unidirectional with poverty as the independent variable and nutrition, illness, and disease as the dependents. Some studies did focus on the way health care expenditures could impoverish a family and how worker absenteeism lowered manufacturing or other industry productivity. Less common were explorations of the multiple ways undernutrition and illness created and exacerbated economic crises for poor households. Among rural producers relying on their own physical labor to produce crops or earn wages to feed their families, the potential for poor nutrition and health to impact work, production, and household economies seemed rather obvious (Leatherman 1998b), but relatively little work examined this relationship.

There were clearly exceptions. Almost four decades ago, Gerald Spurr and colleagues (1975) published one of the first studies linking reduced working capacity and poor endurance in physically demanding occupations to lowered productivity and lower wages.

They demonstrated relationships between undernutrition (stunting as well as iron deficiency anemia), reduced working capacity, and lowered productivity among sugarcane cutters in Columbia. Lowered productivity led to less earnings and less money to purchase food and other basic needs and this had the potential to further compromise nutrition and health. Additionally, in their work with school-aged boys, Spurr and colleagues illustrated how these relationships span generations, by linking chronic marginal malnutrition and reduced body size in youths to reduced work capacity and productivity as adults engaged in moderate to heavy physical work (Spurr 1988; Spurr et al. 1983).

In support of these early findings, Martorell and colleagues (2010) reviewed the impact of nutrition interventions carried out by the Institute of Nutrition of Central America and Panama from 1969 to 1977. Follow-up studies in 1988–89 and 2002–04 demonstrated that nutrition intervention in early life had positive impacts on adult human capital and productivity. Men with better childhood nutrition earned 46 percent higher wages at the time of the re-studies. Thus in low income countries where economic productivity relies on strenuous human labor, the broader implications of these findings for health and household economies are obvious. Moreover, poor health in the present often begets poor health in the future, and a larger cycle of poverty and poor health is set in motion—a cycle that can span generations.

As work on the social and economic costs of illness emerged, malaria was one of the diseases frequently studied because of its prevalence in farming populations, as well as its debilitating impacts due to lost work and costs of medication. As a general rule of thumb, observe Sachs and Malaney, "where malaria prospers most, human societies have prospered least" (2002:681). Although there is debate about the most appropriate quantification methods, the economic burden of malaria is evident in whichever method employed. In resource-poor settings, malaria imposes high and regressive cost burdens on patients and their families, with poor households spending a higher proportion of their income on healthcare than better-off households; in some estimates up to 28 percent of annual incomes (Ettling et al. 1994; Russell 2004).

However, the direct costs of preventing and treating malaria (as a single disease) can be relatively low compared to the indirect costs to work and current and future earning potential for households in which the primary wage earner is sick or must forgo work to care for sick children. Some estimates suggest that indirect costs make up more than 75 percent of total household malaria costs (Asenso-Okyerea and Dzator 1997; Ettling and Shepard 1991; Russell 2004; Shepard et al. 1991), and these costs can span generations. In Kenya, for example, primary school children miss an estimated 11 percent of school days per year due to malaria (Leighton et al. 1993), and in other estimates between 13 and 50 percent of school absences were attributed to the disease (Brooker et al. 2000; Sachs and Malaney 2002). Research on the long-term social and economic burden of malaria has linked malaria-related school absenteeism to increased failure rates, repetition of school years, and higher dropout rates (Sachs and Malaney 2002). Other work has examined the potentially severe consequences of malaria on cognitive development and learning ability (Al Serouri et al. 2000; Holding and Snow 2001; Shiff et al. 1996), and developmental impacts on very low birth weight children (McCormick et al. 1992). These effects on child development speak to the long-term impacts on livelihoods and intergenerational transmission of costs of disease.

More recent research on health and household economy has focused on HIV/AIDS where costs in lost life, lost labor, caring for the sick and orphaned, lost livelihoods and incomes, and costs of medication are cumulatively catastrophic for many households. Russell (2004) cites long-term studies in Tanzania and Thailand, where the direct costs of HIV/AIDS were estimated at 50–100 percent of annual incomes. Treatment costs and funeral costs were important contributors to this burden. While the direct costs are extremely high, the indirect costs are equally so since HIV/AIDS impacts the labor of adults and leaves households with little to no means of livelihood. Similarly, Arrehag et al., in a major case study from Malawi, conclude that:

> HIV/AIDS acts as a forceful vehicle for impoverishment at the individual and household level and results in increased income and asset inequality. Poor households with small economic buffers are particularly exposed to the economic consequences of HIV/AIDS. For these, illness and death in the family due to AIDS often entails economic disaster as they are forced to sell off precious productive assets such as land and cattle to cope, with landlessness and destitution as a result. It is clear that HIV/AIDS leads to increased destitution and increased asset and income inequality. (2006:5)

In a "critical" biocultural anthropology, it is important to draw connections between the reproduction of poverty and poor health to the larger macrosocial contexts that shape exposure and constrain agency. A recent issue of the *Annals of Anthropological Practice* edited by Mazzeo and Rödlach (2011) does that by presenting a series of papers that together effectively demonstrate the links among macroeconomic policies, patterns of migration and exposure to HIV/AIDS, and other diseases in southern Africa; what Singer (2011:9) calls a "perfect epidemiological storm." The resulting syndemic of HIV/AIDS and related diseases that in turn leads to sickness and death, increased demands for care for the sick and orphaned, diminished household production, greater food insecurity, and costs of treatment serves to (re)produce household poverty and reinforce patterns of migration and exposure to the disease. As Singer notes in a powerful conclusion to his paper on the HIV/AIDS syndemic:

> In other words, while the social distance from the comfortable office suites of the World Bank and the International Monetary Fund in Washington, D.C. to the crudely dug grave of a poor man or woman who dies of AIDS/malnutrition in an obscure village in southern Africa is seemingly enormous, and hence highly disguisable and deniable, they are united by a fairly straight and deadly line of political economic micro–macro connection. (2011:21–22)

MODELS AND META-ANALYSES

There have been several meta-analyses in the past decade of the direct and indirect economic impacts of illness on households. McIntyre and colleagues (2006) synthesized the findings of 62 studies from low- to middle-income countries (LMIC), and Russell (2004) examined the costs of three key maladies: tuberculosis, malaria, and HIV/AIDS.

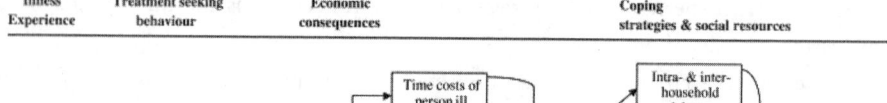

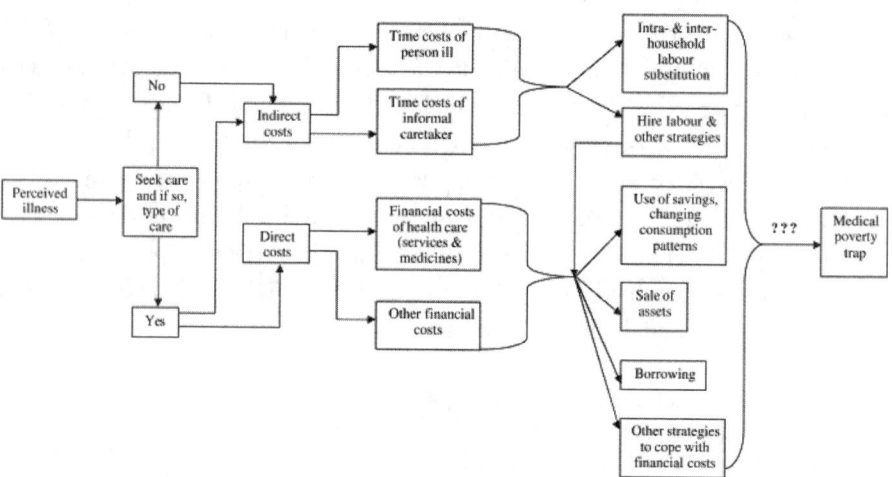

FIGURE 1. Simplified flowchart of key issues relating to the economic consequences of illness. *Source*: McIntyre et al. (2006:860).

   Both reviews employ similar analytical frameworks to organize the data presentations and analyses (see Figure 1, from McIntyre et al. 2006:860). They begin with recognition and identification of perceived illness and then move to treatment-seeking behavior, and the direct and indirect costs of care and caretaking, and finally address the costs of coping strategies employed to deal with the impacts of illness. They differentiate between direct costs associated with health-seeking behaviors (transport, fees for services, hospitalization, purchase remedies, etc.) and indirect costs due to lost labor, lost earning potential and productivity, and the costs associated with coping strategies such as hiring extra workers to compensate for lost labor, or selling assets to cover direct costs of healthcare. While direct costs can be catastrophic, indirect costs are often found to be greater. A major factor contributing to both direct and indirect costs of illness in their analyses is poor quality of healthcare, its costs, and frequently its ineffectiveness in reaching the poor, further aggravated by increasing burdens of chronic illness on health care systems in some of the poorer regions of the world (Goudge et al. 2007). Households might forgo treatments or otherwise limit health care utilization and expenditures when they cannot meet costs, or they might employ strategies to finance healthcare (e.g., borrowing, reducing expenditure on other basic needs). Either option can diminish health or livelihoods and lead to greater poverty over the short and long run (Bebbington 1999; Davies 1993; Goudge et al. 2007; Goudge and Govender 2000). A key concern is how these cumulative costs lead households into a "medical poverty trap" or depletion of household assets leading to impoverishment.

   Their analyses make it clear that the costs of illness are important forces producing and maintaining poverty. What is not clear is variation in these costs and how and why in different instances people might be more or less vulnerable or resilient to the effects of illness on household economies. An ethnographic case study can provide a useful approach lens through which to examine these variations, processes, and relationships between illness and household economies. Using McIntyre and colleagues' (2006) analytic framework as a point of departure to explore the reproduction of poverty and illness, we provide a case study drawn from earlier research with farmers and herders of the Nuñoa District in the southern Peruvian Andes—households whose livelihoods are based on small-scale agricultural production for home consumption, meat and wool production largely for sale, and a variety of other income-generating strategies (mostly unskilled manual labor). While details of the research findings can be found elsewhere (see, e.g., Leatherman 1992, 1996, 1998a; Thomas et al. 1988), the emphasis here is on illustrating how poverty and inequalities become embodied as poor health and, in turn, how these "local biologies" play a role in the reproduction of poverty.

A CASE STUDY FROM THE SOUTHERN PERUVIAN ANDES

This case study is drawn from research conducted between 1983 and 1985 in Nuñoa Peru (Leatherman 1996; Thomas et al. 1988). The objectives of the research were to analyze patterns of nutrition and illness, the consequences of and responses to illness among households living in different social and economic contexts, and how these consequences contributed to ongoing levels of health and nutrition (Leatherman 1996, 1998a, 1998b, 2005). Put simply, we were examining the reproduction of poverty and poor health among small-scale producers (Leatherman 2005).

The reproduction of poverty and poor health in highland Peru is shaped by intersection of three axes of vulnerability: exposure to risk, constrained agency, and consequences and resiliency. This framing of spaces of vulnerability can also be applied to the earlier examples of malaria and HIV/AIDS, as well as other diseases and contexts. The most vulnerable individuals and groups are exposed to more insults, have the most limited coping capability, suffer the greatest impacts, have the least resiliency, and thus, are at the greatest risk for perpetuation of conditions of vulnerability (Leatherman 2005; Watts and Bohle 1993). Outcomes of this reproduction of poverty and poor health in spaces of vulnerability are often described with terms we are familiar with, such as *vicious cycles*, *persistent inequalities*, or *medical poverty traps*. In the study described here, we use the term *household disintegration* (Deere 1990:267) to describe a process where families in poor health cannot reproduce the very means of production to maintain their livelihood as farmers and herders.

Research design and methods have been published in detail elsewhere (Leatherman 1996; Thomas et al. 1988), but briefly, we conducted informal interviews, participant observation, and seasonal surveys of more than 90 rural households (about 450 individuals). We collected data on a range of social and economic household characteristics including: household demography; economic strategies and activities; diet and nutrition; perceived illness and impacts of illness on work; annual inputs (e.g., land, labor, and seed) and returns in subsistence based farming production; and utilization of family and nonfamily labor for farming. In addition, we collected information on the relationship between illness and work from a time allocation study of a subsample of 40 households (Leatherman 1992).

Historical and Political Economic Contexts

Nuñoa is a region with a deep history that experienced relative prosperity under the Incan state, suffered the devastation of conquest and colonization, and was the site of large export-oriented haciendas, a subsequent failed agrarian reform, and more recently, a civil war between forces of *Sendero Luminoso* and the Peruvian state. This very global history imposed a legacy of structural violence that resulted in some of the worst health conditions in Peru—and among the worst in Latin America and global south. At the time of the Spanish conquest of Peru, Nuñoa was a productive region with lands across a series of vertical ecozones. Early chroniclers noted its relative wealth but also its decline due in large part to reordering of settlement and productive relations by the Spanish and the impact of abusive labor practices of the Spanish colonial *Mita*, a form of forced labor contributions to the mining industry through which the Spanish sought to extract wealth. Indeed, Melissa Dell (2010) has performed an economic analysis arguing that those parts of the southern Peruvian Andes such as Nuñoa that were impacted by the *Mita* labor practice in the late 16th through early 18th centuries continue to suffer from greater poverty and health disparities today, due in part to lower levels of economic development.

The district has long been a center for alpaca production and by the 1800s had been organized into larger haciendas, smaller landholdings, and a few indigenous *ayllus*. Historically, little was invested in the town or district infrastructure by the national, regional, or local governments. In the 1980s, this district, along with much of the central and southern Andes, was extremely poor, with inadequate and substandard infrastructure in terms of transportation, markets, economic opportunities, and healthcare. For instance, throughout this part of the Andes, there was roughly one physician for every 10,000 people (Aramburu and Ponce Alegre 1983). There was one clinic in the capital of the district staffed by a doctor performing a rural residency shortly after completing medical school, a nurse obstetrician, and several auxiliary nurses. Only local auxiliary nurses spoke any Quechua, and the clinic was small, dark, cold, poorly staffed with resources (e.g., no IV stands) and few medicines, and altogether uninviting (Morse and Stoner 1986). The town government was largely run by a major (and advisors) and one town clerk, on a shoestring budget.

An agrarian reform established in the late 1960s and implemented in the 1970s concentrated landholdings to an even greater extent but did provide better conditions for its *socios*—families formerly tied to haciendas whose members became members of the cooperative. But, it also increased landlessness among many rural households that did not acquire a place in one of the newly formed cooperatives. These households were often forced to rent land or work in share-cropping arrangements and relied to a greater extent on local wage work and the outmigration of older teens and adults in search of work to supplement limited agro-pastoral production. Another effect associated with increased landlessness and greater reliance on wage work was a decline in labor reciprocity, historically a key mechanism through which households obtained extra-family workers to meet labor needs in strenuous and time-sensitive production tasks. These changes—land inequities, declining reciprocity, outmigration of young adults and adolescents for work—importantly shaped the spaces of vulnerability and contributed to substantial poverty, inequality, hunger, malnutrition, and illness. Indeed, within Peru and even in Latin America, this region continually reports some of the highest rates of poverty, infant mortality, and chronic undernutrition. It is within these contexts that we are examining costs of illness.

Consequences of Illness in the Reproduction of Poverty

Utilizing McIntyre and colleagues' (2006:860) framework (Figure 1), we begin with the identification of illness and health-seeking behavior and then address direct and indirect costs of illness and costs associated with coping strategies. A key point we wish to make with the case study is that, on the one hand, strong associations between poverty and poor health are clearly evident, but, on the other, there are myriad factors that shape short- and long-term consequences of illness on individual household economies and that create different sorts of dialectical relationships between poverty and poor health.

Experience of illness

In our work, as in others (see, e.g., Alonzo 1979; Crandon-Malamud 1993), it was clear that the identification of illness and treatment choice involves a negotiation process among individuals, families, and social networks. The reading of symptoms, deciding whether to be sick, and if so, what sort of illness and what sort of treatment might be sought is dependent, in part, on social class, gender, ethnicity, and whether one can afford to be sick both in terms of cost of treatment and time lost to work or other critical activities. Many households dealt with common problems related to minor illness without assuming a sick role. When mothers were asked whether their young children were sick in previous weeks, the answer was frequently no, even though children exhibited cough, congestion, runny nose, watery eyes, and frequent diarrhea. Similarly, it appeared that many chose not to be sick because they were unable to afford treatment or to seek treatment, or because they had important work to complete during planting or harvest.

As one example, harvest time was often a time of social gatherings as well as work. The work was not as strenuous as planting and weeding, the result more immediate and positive, and it was important to have as many workers available as possible to harvest crops in a timely manner. In seasonal surveys of illness, we found harvest time the period of fewest sickness events and workdays lost due to sickness. The onset of harvest season is associated with the cessation of rains, the onset of colder temperatures, and limited food availability due to diminished food stores. The symptoms reported during this season were somewhat less but not in line with decrease of reported sickness events and work lost. Thus, it appeared people tended to choose not to be sick during harvest. Some individuals also reported no work lost due to illness during the strenuous planting season, but later reported sickness and extended bed-rest following the planting. That is, they worked through an illness during the critical planting production cycle only to suffer a more prolonged sickness later.

We also observed that some families redefined chronic illness as essentially nontreatable as it progressed over time. Chronic illness in Nuñoa was often seen as incurable and out of the control of the patient or health specialist. Such problems were often defined/labeled as *desgracias* (the term can have many meanings, including disgrace, sadness, misfortune) rather than *enfermedades* (disease/illness) or *dolores* (pains/sore-ness). The idea of illness as *desgracia* speaks to the social meanings and vulnerabilities linked to health problems such as social transgressions, social stigma, problems within the family or *compadres*, and failure to meet obligations to spirits. Thus, *desgracias* were often associated with a profound loss of control over one's health and well-being. Illness labels often changed as a problem progressed from an acute to a chronic state, which sometimes meant reclassifying an *enfermedad* as a *desgracia.* For example, a set of persistent symptoms classified as *gripe* or flu (an *enfermedad)* in October might be relabeled in May as *machu huayru* (old winds; a *desgracia),* for which there were few treatment options. It appeared (but was difficult to document) that this shift in explanatory model and treatment strategy happened more commonly and quickly in poorer households that could not afford costs associated with prolonged treatment. Such strategies implied reduced direct costs but perhaps greater indirect costs due to illness.

Direct costs of health care
A key theme in examining consequences of illness on household economies is that the direct costs of healthcare carries the potential of great impoverishment. We found that in 91 illness episodes recorded across 47 families, 78 percent were treated with home remedies (*remedios caseros*), primarily herbal teas. Yet, for the 22 percent who sought some more specialized form of healthcare, the cost of a visit to the clinic and cost of medications averaged approximately US$5, or about one week's wages for an unskilled laborer in Nuñoa. This helps explain in part why so few sought care of this sort. For problems requiring surgery or other treatment in the regional hospital, the costs were truly catastrophic. Hospitalization entailed not only paying a fee for service, but having a family member on hand to watch over and care for the patient, as well as buy them food and medicines prescribed by but rarely available in the clinic or hospital. It often meant borrowing money or selling assets (animals and land), migrating out in search of work, and risking long-term debt or loss of livelihood. While not an everyday event, we saw several cases of households going into debt from borrowing money, and others where herds and land were sold off. Ultimately, some left the countryside for towns or cities and entered into a wage labor market, but often this only accentuated the precariousness of livelihoods. For example, in one case a father and his teenaged son from a newly landless family migrated out for wage work, leaving his wife and four younger children behind. While they were gone, two of the younger children fell ill. His wife, lacking local social networks of support, was unable to leave the children unattended to seek work, and they all barely survived on food handouts. When the father and son returned, they found one child near death, all malnourished, and the mother seriously ill. They spent all of the earnings from the work they did while away on the purchase of food and medicine for the family and, in fear of leaving town again, remained permanently in the

town living on temporary wage-work that paid US$1 per day (Leatherman 1996). The unfortunate reality is that households such as these—landless and getting by on irregular wage work—were those at greatest risk for illness, least able to cope with its affects, and at greatest risk of impoverishment.

As noted earlier, many individuals avoided adopting a sick role especially during critical production periods; and in more severe cases, many just decided that they could not afford to be ill. These decisions carry costs as well; they are just not so easy to measure. Thus, other than in more severe cases where people sought expensive healthcare out of the district, we more frequently observed illness impacting household economies through diminished livelihoods and earning potential.

Indirect costs to labor and livelihoods

In what McIntyre and colleagues (2006) call "indirect" costs of illness, we measured costs in terms of lost labor, time, costs of obtaining extra help, and reduced home food production. While these are not easily translatable into monetary losses, they reflect enhanced vulnerability as the household bears the triple burdens of health care costs, income losses, and diminished home food production.

One measure of illness and its impacts was work lost due to illness. For any given two-week recall, almost 60 percent of households surveyed reported adult work disruption due to illness, amounting to a loss of between four to five workdays. This varied by season, gender, class, and community—women reported more work lost than men, and poorer families reported more work lost than others. For example, households in one of the poorest farming-herding communities in the district lost an estimated seventy-five adult workdays per year—the equivalent of a 20 percent loss of adult labor time over the course of a year.

Time allocation studies provided additional information on time lost in illness. Households decreased time put into production and wage work by 14 percent and in more strenuous household tasks (e.g., collecting wood or water) by nine percent. This overall decrease was shaped by the intrahousehold allocation of labor in times of illness. Sick adults on average decreased time in production activities by 13 percent and by ten percent for the more strenuous daily household tasks. Healthy adults increased time in care-taking and food preparation and reduced wage work and subsistence production activities accordingly (about a ten percent shift). This implies a 23 percent loss of adult time in production activities. Given the high degree of outmigration and a high dependency ratio in farming families (only ten percent of the population was between the ages of 15–25 years), younger children were pulled out of school to help out in production and household work. They increased time spent on production activities by ten percent and on household maintenance tasks by 14 percent, resulting in proportionally reduced time at school (>20 percent) and in other nonwork activities. What this meant in practical terms was that a child who was repeatedly pulled out of school to help out in production tasks or family chores often never completed primary school and never attended secondary school. This reduced their earning potential and ability to escape poverty in the future—particularly as the child participants of this study are now adults living and working in an economy where education has become important to finding steady and decent-paying jobs.

Lost time in work translates to lost cash earnings and decreased household food production. We found that on average, households with severe or chronic illness compared to those with relatively fewer and less severe bouts, reported planting 50–60 percent fewer fields, spending 34 percent more time working to cultivate each field (presumably at a slower pace), and 23 percent lower yields per field planted. These are significant losses to household livelihoods, and especially for poorer families that were more vulnerable to illness and the impacts on work and production due to constrained coping responses. But, the averages mask how different dimensions of poverty—whether one was labor poor, cash poor, or land poor—led to different coping capacities and hence effects on livelihoods.

Unless one had a large family, meeting labor needs required seeking outside help by engaging in labor reciprocity or by paying workers in cash or produce. Yet reciprocity was not widely available, particularly to families in sickness who could not easily repay the labor. A poorer family without major illness normally relied on family labor for 78 percent of agricultural labor inputs and utilized nine percent reciprocal and 12 percent paid labor. In illness, they decreased family labor only by three percent, decreased hired labor by one percent, and increased reciprocal labor by four percent. In other words, they made minor shifts in labor allocation but, operated with roughly the same workers, were not able to fully replace the sick individual's labor, and often simply spent more time performing basic agricultural tasks (hence lower productivity). Wealthier families in good health normally used 62 percent household labor, 35 percent hired labor, and only two percent reciprocal labor. In illness, they decreased the contribution of household labor by 29 percent, used no labor reciprocity, and increased the relative percent of hired labor by 31 percent. This meant far greater monetary costs in terms of hiring labor and lower productivity, but also ensured greater overall food production and less chance of future food insecurity and nutritional stress. Thus, the wealthier household's ability to compensate for lost work in sickness by hiring extra-family labor led to higher short-term indirect costs but greater long-term security.

On average, families in sickness but with secure access to land through ownership or usufruct rights tended to plant the same number of fields although with lower levels of productivity. However, the landless or semi-landless tended to cut back the number of fields they planted and reap smaller harvests. In order for a landless or semi-landless family to plant fields of potatoes, they were required to rent land or enter into a share-cropping arrangement, borrow or buy seed and fertilizer, and pay for any extra-family labor required. For those without cash reserves who paid in produce, this often meant that after seed, labor, and land costs were extracted from the harvest the remaining potatoes would provide only a few months of food. A debilitating episode of illness would lead to greater costs for hiring workers or lower productivity. Thus, many of the landless or near-landless households dealing with illness decided the investment in land and additional labor was risky and simply planted fewer fields and produced less. Some even chose not to plant at all, and turned instead to irregular wage work and other income-generating activities to meet basic household needs.

Poor households then lived in a space of vulnerability, where they were exposed to greater food insecurity, undernutrition, and illness, had the fewest options with which to cope—either through seeking treatments or obtaining extra labor to cover for sick individuals—and suffered the greatest impacts on food production and other earnings. They were at the greatest risk for what Carmen Diana Deere termed "household disintegration."

> If net household income is not sufficient to insure simple reproduction . . . the peasant household . . . could disintegrate in several ways. The inability to guarantee normal levels of consumption might result in *declining nutrition or lowered health* (italics added) . . . the lowered quality of labor power . . . might affect the productive capacity of the household in the next cycle. . . .The peasant household . . . might also disintegrate as a result of a decision to sell or rent all of its means of production. (1990:267)

Clearly the direct and indirect costs of illness on livelihoods over time have the capacity to lead to household disintegration. But, how this relationship plays out varies by access to land, labor, and cash reserves, and different strategies for coping with illness imply different short-term and long-term costs. For example, selling assets and shifting livelihood strategies to greater engagement in local wage work was sometimes a logical choice and a necessity, but could mean an even deeper spiral into poverty and continued poor health. Landless or near landless households relying on unskilled wage work to meet household livelihood needs were among the poorest households in the district and experienced the highest levels of illness and work lost (Leatherman 1998a). We have argued elsewhere (Leatherman and Thomas 2009) that the ever-present potential for household disintegration in contexts of chronic poverty and illness, and diminished resilience and hope, was an important context for the revolution that dominated much of Peru for the last two decades of the 20th century and directly impacted lives and livelihoods in Nuñoa from 1986 to 1992 (Leatherman and Thomas 2009).

CONCLUSION

Similar to McIntyre et al. (2006), Russell (2004), and a growing body of literature on economic costs of illness, we saw illness as major factor in the production and reproduction of poverty. One goal of this paper has been to provide an ethnographically grounded case study that demonstrates the social and economic costs of illness in the broader production and reproduction of poverty and poor health in the Andes. Poverty, inequalities, malnutrition, and illness are mutually constitutive. As such, they cannot be understood as independent–dependent relationships but rather as a complex dialectic. A second goal was to demonstrate that, while poverty creates conditions for illness, and the costs of illness exacerbate and reproduce contexts of poverty, how this plays out is not homogenous, standard, or predictable. Factors such as access to land, labor power, social networks, and sources of income strongly shaped the poverty–illness nexus in Nuñoa.

Identifying these local level contexts that underlie variation in vulnerability and resilience is only possible in ethnographically grounded research.

Many of the problems we describe from the 1980s are evident today. Indeed, a recent study of 40 farming and herding communities in northern and southern Peru (including the district of Nuñoa) examined factors that moved households into and out of poverty (Kristjanson et al. 2007). They found that economic diversification and animal husbandry were the best ways to move out of poverty, and that among the many factors that can push people deeper into poverty, *illness* was the most important. As we have argued here understanding *how* illness impacts livelihoods and (re)produces poverty demands attention to local contexts, lived experience, and constrained human agency. This is where an ethnographically grounded biocultural analysis is important. If our goal is to dismantle conditions that diminish health and constrain agency and break cycles of persistent inequality and illness, a critical biocultural analysis that exposes global–local interactions and grounds analysis in local environments and biologies can shed much light on vulnerability and resilience among rural producers and the reproduction of inequalities and health.

REFERENCES CITED

Al Serouri, Abdel Wahed, Sally M. Grantham-McGregor, Brian Greenwood, and Anthony Costello
   2000 Impact of Asymptomatic Malaria Parasitaemia on Cognitive Function and School Achievement of Schoolchildren in the Yemen Republic. Parasitology 121(4):337–345.
Alonzo, Angelo A.
   1979 Everyday Illness Behavior: A Situational Approach to Health Status Deviations. Social Science & Medicine Part A: Medical Psychology & Medical Sociology 13:397–404.
Aramburu, Carols E., and Ana Ponce Alegre
   1983 Familia y Trabajo en el Peru Rural. Lima, Peru: Instituto Andino de Estudios en Población y Desarrollo.
Arrehag, Lisa, Stefan de Vylder, Dick Durevall, and Mirja Sjöblom
   2006 The Impact of HIV/AIDS on Livelihoods, Poverty and the Economy of Malawi. Sida Studies No. 18. Stockholm, Sweden.
Asenso-Okyerea, W. Kwado, and Janet A. Dzator
   1997 Household Cost of Seeking Malaria Care: A Retrospective Study of Two Districts in Ghana. Social Science & Medicine 45(5):659–667.
Bebbington, Anthony
   1999 Capitals and Capabilities: A Framework for Analyzing Peasant Viability, Rural Livelihoods and Poverty. World Development 27(12):2021–2044.
Brooker, Simon, Helen Guyatt, Judy Omumbo, Rima Shretta, Lesley Drake, and John Ouma
   2000 Situation Analysis of Malaria in School-aged Children in Kenya—What Can be Done? Parasitology Today 16(5):183–186.
Calvo, Christina Malmberg, Monica Das Gupta, Christiaan Grootaert, Ravi Kanbur, Victoria Kwakwa, and Nora Lustig
   2000 World Development Report 2000/2001: Attacking Poverty. Washington, DC: World Bank Press. http://documents.worldbank.org/curated/en/2000/09/17408018/world-development-report-20002001-attacking-poverty, accessed June 11, 2014.
Crandon-Malamud, Libbett
   1993 From the Fat of Our Souls: Social Change, Political Process and Medical Pluralism in Bolivia. Berkeley, CA: University of California Press.

Davies, Susanna
   1993   Are Coping Strategies a Cop Out? IDS Bulletin 24(4):60–72.
Deere, Carmen Diana
   1990   Household and Class Relations: Peasants and Landlords in Northern Peru. Berkeley, CA: University
          of California Press.
Dell, Melissa
   2010   The Persistent Effects of Peru's Mining Mita. Econometrica 78(6):1863–1903.
Department for International Development (DFID)
   1999   Better Health for Poor People. International Development Target Strategy Paper. London.
          http://www.hivpolicy.org/Library/HPP000147.pdf, accessed September 13, 2014.
Ettling, Mary, Deborah A. McFarland, Linda J. Schultz, and Lester Chitsulo
   1994   Economic Impact of Malaria in Malawian Households. Tropical Medicine and Parasitology 45(1):74–
          79.
Ettling, Mary, and Donald S. Shepard
   1991   The Economic Cost of Malaria in Rwanda. Tropical Medicine Parasitology 42:214–218.
Farmer, Paul
   1999   Infections and Inequalities: The Modern Plagues. Berkeley, CA: University of California Press.
Goudge, Jane, and Veloshnee Govender
   2000   A Review of Experience Concerning Household Ability to Cope with the Resource Demands
          of Ill Health and Health Care Utilization. EQUINET Policy Series 3. South Africa: Cen-
          tre for Health Policy, Wits University and Health Economics Unit, University of Cape Town.
          http://www.equinetafrica.org/bibl/docs/POL3POVgoudge.pdf, accessed June 11, 2014.
Goudge, Jane, Tebogo Gumede, Lucy Gilson, Steve Russell, Stephen M. Tollman, and Anne Mills
   2007   Coping with the Cost Burdens of Illness: Combining Qualitative and Quantitative Methods in
          Longitudinal, Household Research. Scandinavian Journal of Public Health 35(69 Suppl.):181–185.
Hamoudi, Amar A., and Jeffrey D. Sachs
   1999   Economic Consequences of Health Status: A Review of the Evidence. CID Working Pa-
          per no. 30. Cambridge, MA: Center for International Development at Harvard University.
          http://academiccommons.columbia.edu/catalog/ac:123665, accessed June 11, 2014.
Holding, Penny A., and Robert W. Snow
   2001   Impact of Plasmodium Falciparum Malaria on Performance and Learning: Review of the Evidence.
          American Journal of Tropical Medicine and Hygiene 64(1,2S):68–75.
Kristjanson, Patricia, Anirudh Krishna, Maren Radeny, Judith Kuan, Gustavo Quilca, Alicia Sanchez-Urrelo,
    and Carlos Leon-Velarde
   2007   Poverty Dynamics and the Role of Livestock in the Peruvian Andes. Agricultural Systems 94(2):294–
          308.
Leatherman, Thomas L.
   1992   Illness as Lifestyle Change. MASCA Research Papers in Science and Archeology 9:83–89.
   1996   A Biocultural Perspective on Health and Household Economy in Southern Peru. Medical Anthropol-
          ogy Quarterly 10(4):476–495.
   1998a Changing Biocultural Perspectives on Health in the Andes. Social Science & Medicine 47(8):1031–
          1041.
   1998b Illness, Social Relations, and Household Production and Reproduction in the Andes of Southern
          Peru. In Building a New Biocultural Synthesis: Political-economic Perspectives on Human Biology.
          Alan H. Goodman and Thomas L. Leatherman, eds. Pp. 245–267. Ann Arbor, MI: University of
          Michigan Press.
   2005   A Space of Vulnerability in Poverty and Health: Political Ecology and Biocultural Analysis. Ethos
          33(1):46–70.
Leatherman, Thomas L., and R. Brooke Thomas
   2009   Structural Violence, Political Violence and the Health Costs of Civil Conflict: A Case Study from
          Peru. In Anthropology and Public Health: Bridging Differences in Culture and Society. 2nd edition.
          Robert A. Hahn and Marcia C. Inhorn, eds. Pp. 196–218. New York: Oxford University Press.

Leighton, Charlotte, Rebecca Foster, John Ouma, Joseph Wang'ombe, Okokon Ekanem, William Brieger, Mary Ettling, and Samir Zaman
  1993 Economic Impacts of Malaria in Kenya and Nigeria. Major Applied Research Paper No. 6, Health Financing and Sustainability (HFS) Project. Bethesda, MD: Abt Associates, Inc. http://pdf.usaid.gov/pdf_docs/pnabs294.pdf, accessed June 11, 2014.

Martorell, Reynaldo, Paul Melgar, John A. Maluccio, Aryeh D. Stein, and Juan A. Rivera
  2010 The Nutrition Intervention Improved Adult Human Capital and Economic Productivity. Journal of Nutrition 140(2):411–414.

Mazzeo, John, Alexander Rödlach, and Barrett P. Brenton
  2011 Introduction: Anthropologists Confront HIV/AIDS and Food Insecurity in Sub-Saharan Africa. Annals of Anthropological Practice 35(1):1–7.

McCormick, Marie C., Jeanne Brooks-Gunn, Kathryn Workman-Daniels, JoAnna Turner, and George J. Peckham
  1992 The Health and Development Status of Very Low-Birth-Weight Children at School Age, Journal of the American Medical Association 267(16):2204–2208.

McIntyre, Diane, Michael Thiede, Göran Dahlgren, and Margaret Whitehead
  2006 What Are the Economic Consequences for Households of Illness and of Paying for Health Care in Low- and Middle-Income Country Contexts? Social Science & Medicine 62(4):858–865.

Morse, Lucinda, and Bradley Stoner
  1986 Utilization and Effectiveness of Health Services in an Andean Community. Abstracts of the 85th Annual Meeting, Philadelphia, PA: American Anthropological Association (AAA), p. 239.

Peters, David H., Anu Garg, Gerry Bloom, Damian G. Walker, William R. Brieger, and M. Hafizur Rahman
  2008 Poverty and Access to Health Care in Developing Countries. Annals of the New York Academy of Sciences 1136(1):161–171.

Russell, Steven
  2004 The Economic Burden of Illness for Households in Developing Countries: A Review of Studies Focusing on Malaria, Tuberculosis, and Human Immunodeficiency Virus/Acquired Immunodeficiency Syndrome. American Journal of Tropical Medicine and Hygiene 71(Suppl. 2):147–155.

Sachs, Jeffrey, and Pia Malaney
  2002 The Economic and Social Burden of Malaria. Nature 415(6872):680–685.

Shepard, Donald S., Mary B. Ettling, Ulrich Brinkmann, and Rainer Sauerborn
  1991 The Economic Cost of Malaria in Africa. Tropical Medicine Parasitology 42(3):199–203.

Shiff, Clive, William Checkley, Peter Winch, Zul Premji, Japhet Minjas, and Pros Lubega
  1996 Changes in Weight Gain and Anaemia Attributable to Malaria in Tanzanian Children Living Under Holoendemic Conditions. Transactions of the Royal Society of Tropical Medicine and Yygiene 90(3):262–265.

Singer, Merrill
  2011 Toward a Critical Biosocial Model of Ecohealth in Southern Africa: The HIV/AIDS and Nutrition Insecurity Syndemic. Annals of Anthropological Practice 35(1):8–27.

Spurr, Gerald B.
  1988 Marginal Malnutrition in Childhood: Implications for Adult Work Capacity and Productivity. In Capacity for Work in the Tropics. K. J. Collins and Derek F. Roberts, eds. Pp. 107–140. Cambridge: Cambridge University Press.

Spurr, Gerald B., Mario Barac-Nieto, and Michael G. Maksud
  1975 Energy Expenditure Cutting Sugar Cane. Journal of Applied Physiology 39:990–996.

Spurr, Gerald B., Julio C. Reina, Hans W. Dahners, and Mario Barac-Nieto
  1983 Marginal Malnutrition in School-aged Colombian Boys: Functional Consequences in Maximum Exercise. American Journal of Clinical Nutrition 37(5):834–847.

Thomas, R. Brooke, Thomas L. Leatherman, James W. Carey, and Jere D. Haas
  1988 Biosocial Consequences of Illness Among Small Scale Farmers: A Research Design. In Capacity for Work in the Tropics. K. J. Collins and Derek F. Roberts, eds. Pp. 249–276. Cambridge: Cambridge University Press.

Wagstaff, Adam
    2002 Poverty and Health Sector Inequalities. Bulletin of the World Health Organization 80(2):97–105.
Watts, Michael J., and Hans G. Bohle
    1993 The Space of Vulnerability: The Causal Structure of Hunger and Famine. Progress in Human
          Geography, 17(1):43–67.
World Health Organization (WHO)
    2002 Improving Health Outcomes of the Poor. The Report of Working Group 5 of the Commis-
          sion on Macroeconomics and Health. World Health Organization. http://whqlibdoc.who.int/
          publications/9241590130.pdf, accessed June 11, 2014.

SYNDEMIC SUFFERING IN SOWETO: VIOLENCE AND INEQUALITY AT THE NEXUS OF HEALTH TRANSITION IN SOUTH AFRICA

EMILY MENDENHALL
Walsh School of Foreign Service, Georgetown University and Developmental Pathways for Health Research Faculty of Health Sciences, University of the Witwatersrand

This article examines the roles of structural and interpersonal violence in individual experiences of health transition in South Africa, focusing on women's narratives of distress and diabetes as well as epidemiology. Over the past decade marked increases in noncommunicable diseases, including type 2 diabetes, have transitioned in South Africa to afflict those who concurrently face great mental health burdens and the world's largest HIV and AIDS and tuberculosis epidemics. First, this article considers how social and health problems cluster among impoverished populations through a discussion of syndemics theory. Drawing from the VIDDA Syndemic employed to describe the experience of Mexican immigrant women living with diabetes and depression in urban United States, this analysis demonstrates how violence plays a unique role as a perpetuator of suffering through structural, social, psychological, and even biological pathways. Second, data around stress and structural violence, gun violence, and gender-based violence that emerged from a small study of urban South African women with type 2 diabetes are presented to discuss how violence functions as a cofactor of the syndemic of diabetes and depression in this context. This analysis emphasizes the role of historical and social contexts in how conditions such as depression and diabetes are distributed epidemiologically and experienced individually. Finally, this article argues that the utility of understanding the role of violence in health transition may be a fundamental source of intervention to mitigate the effects of the double burden of diseases on socially and economically marginalized populations in middle-income countries such as South Africa.

INTRODUCTION

"They have burgled into my house on two occasions and I have once been mugged while on the road. I still live in fear ever since. I live behind lock and key and I always have my dog loose. I even feel uncomfortable as I walk on the street and somebody is walking or running behind me. I always stop and let them pass."

—*Sister, 60-year-old women in Soweto*

Sister's comment demonstrates how fear and violence can shape the everyday lives of people living in Soweto, a township of Johannesburg, South Africa. Like many regions

ANNALS OF ANTHROPOLOGICAL PRACTICE 38.2, pp. 300–316. ISSN: 2153-957X. © 2015 by the American Anthropological Association. DOI:10.1111/napa.12058

of the world, the reign of violence within urban townships is not surprising, given the great wealth disparities. The historical legacy of violence in South Africa from political violence of the apartheid era to structural violence measured in the rampant epidemics of HIV and AIDS and tuberculosis among the poor has profoundly shaped disease and suffering, contributing to extraordinary health disparities (Coovadia et al. 2009). While the role of such violence has been examined in detail by cultural and medical anthropologists, such as Fassin's (2007) research on the politics and experiences of AIDS in South Africa, few have considered how the complex dynamics of violence and health shape health transitions marked by increased incidence and prevalence of chronic and noncommunicable diseases rapidly occurring in townships such as Soweto. This article considers the role of violence, in its visible and less-visible forms, in individual experiences of health transition, focusing how such factors shape the depression–diabetes syndemic among urban Black South Africans.

South Africa provides an excellent case study for health transition. Despite abysmal progress toward improving mortality of mothers and children, a substantial reduction in life expectancy as a result of HIV and AIDS, and an underperforming health system, the aging population, and increase in relevant risk factors in rural and urban areas have contributed to substantial increases in type 2 diabetes (hereafter, "diabetes") and other noncommunicable diseases (Mayosi et al. 2012). Although increasing in rural areas, the most vulnerable spaces associated with noncommunicable diseases are poor urban settings (Mayosi et al. 2009). For instance, in 2007, diabetes prevalence was estimated to be 3.1 percent at the population level with the expectation of significant escalation in the next two decades (Mash et al. 2007). Yet, diabetes prevalence among Blacks in urban centers already is estimated to be much higher: recent studies estimate 13.1 percent diabetes prevalence among urban Blacks in the Cape (Peer et al. 2012) and 14.1 percent diabetes prevalence among urban Black women in Soweto—Johannesburg (Crowther and Norris 2012). These data indicate that diabetes prevalence may be much higher among socially and economically disadvantaged groups who are in tandem disproportionately afflicted by diseases of poverty, including HIV (Karim et al. 2009) and depression (Tomlinson et al. 2009), as well as poor access to good health care (Mayosi et al. 2012).

Diabetes escalation among impoverished groups in South Africa fosters increased potential for co-occurring depression. This is because depression is closely linked with socioeconomic disadvantage (Kessler and Bromet 2013) as well as physical illness (Patel and Kleinman 2003). Indeed, a recent review indicates that more than one in three (36 percent) people with diabetes in low- and middle-income countries may have co-occurring depression (Mendenhall et al. 2014). Meta-analyses from high-income countries indicate that prevalence of depression among those with diabetes is lower, between 20 and 25 percent, and that those who are poor, women, older age, overweight, and smoke are most likely to have these coconditions (Ali et al. 2006; Anderson et al. 2001; Golden et al. 2007). Furthermore, they suggest that depression and diabetes maintain a bidirectional relationship, where diabetes contributes to depression, and vice versa (Egede and Ellis 2010; Golden et al. 2008; Knol et al. 2006; Leone et al. 2012; Mezuk et al. 2008). Thus, through the lens of the depression–diabetes syndemic, opportunities for understanding the intersection of "diseases of poverty" and "diseases of modernization" become realized.

This article is divided into three parts. First, how social and health problems cluster among impoverished populations will be examined critically through a discussion of syndemics theory. Drawing from the VIDDA Syndemic employed to describe the co-occurrence and synergistic interaction of violence, immigration, depression, diabetes, abuse among Mexican immigrant women in urban United States (Mendenhall 2012), this analysis will demonstrate how violence plays a unique role as a perpetuator of suffering through structural, social, psychological, and even biological pathways. Second, the impact of violence and inequality on health will be examined via structural and interpersonal pathways that emerged from the literature as well as the research. Four pathways through which violence afflicts the women living with diabetes in the urban South African township known as Soweto will be presented to underscore how violence functions as a cofactor of the syndemic of diabetes and depression in this group. This analysis will provide an in-depth discussion of the role of historical and social contexts in how conditions such as depression and diabetes are distributed epidemiologically and experienced individually. The section also will demonstrate how contextual nuances shape syndemic interactions, which are evident socially and may influence women's physical health experiences. The final section discusses the utility of understanding the role of violence in health transition in order to consider how the social and psychological factors associated with such violence may be a fundamental source of intervention to mitigate the effects of the double burden of diseases on socially and economically marginalized populations in middle-income countries such as South Africa.

SYNDEMICS OF SOCIAL INEQUALITY, DEPRESSION, AND DIABETES

This article employs the term *syndemic* to consider the impact of macro- and micro-level social factors on disease and suffering among impoverished populations. Syndemics often develop within contexts of great health inequality, fueled by structural violence, poverty, and stress, and contribute to significant burden of disease within a population (Singer 2009b). Syndemics weave these social realities into explanations of how health inequalities come to be, emphasizing how social problems contribute to and exacerbate the clustering of two or more diseases in a population in which there is some level of biological interaction that worsens the health consequences of both diseases (Singer 2009b). However, instead of focusing solely on the biological aspects of disease interactions, syndemics demand that we evaluate the biosocial dynamics that shape clustering, formation, and progression of disease (González-Guarda 2009) in a specific time and place. Thus, the syndemics construct may be defined by a synergistic interaction of social, contextual, and disease-related factors that escalate the burden of suffering and disease on marginalized groups in a way that exceeds the impact of any single factor (Singer 2009a, b; Singer et al. 2006).

It is important to describe the biological and biomedical realities underlying the depression–diabetes dyad in order to understand the unique circumstance of syndemic clustering of these two diseases. Depression and diabetes maintain a bidirectional relationship, which can be abbreviated into two hypotheses (Golden et al. 2008). The first hypothesis is that diabetes itself is stressful and may contribute to depression. An established literature shows significant associations of depression with poor glycemic control and diabetes complications (deGroot et al. 2001). The second hypothesis is that people with depression may have increased risk for diabetes via biological and behavioral pathways. Biological pathways include (1) neurohormonal processes associated with counter-regulatory release and action of stress hormones; (2) alterations in glucose transport function; and (3) increased immunoinflammatory activation (Golden et al. 2007; Musselman et al. 2003). These biological responses contribute to insulin resistance and β islet cell dysfunction, which ultimately can lead to diabetes. Additionally, depression may lead to unhealthy behaviors associated with diabetes, including overeating, physical inactivity, smoking, alcohol consumption, and poor medicine adherence, and these behaviors may be mediated by antidepressant medication (Golden et al. 2008). These complex biological, behavioral, and biomedical pathways demonstrate how these two diseases are linked beyond social context. Yet, they do not explain why they cluster among certain populations.

Indeed, social inequality plays a fundamental role in why and how depression and diabetes cluster among poor populations, although the social problems that contribute to such clustering may differ based on social context (Weaver and Mendenhall 2014). This is particularly important for low- and middle-income country contexts where diabetes incidence is undergoing a socioeconomic reversal as it increases among middle-income and working-class populations and decreases among the affluent (Popkin et al. 2012). Structural inequalities, such as poor access to healthy foods and safe spaces to be physically active, therefore have a profound role in people's risk for diabetes as do social influences, such as chronic stress and what foods people's acquaintances consume. Diabetes transitions therefore provide opportunities for increased comorbid depression, as poverty is closely linked with depression (cf. Lund et al. 2010). Because poor populations often have more untreated depression and poor diabetes care, this also can result in disproportionate numbers of people who suffer and die from complications from one or both conditions (cf. Cowie et al. 2010). Such complications contribute to a negative feedback loop, whereby health complications associated with untreated depression, diabetes, and their overlap contribute to further economic and social hardship. Thus, social inequality manifest in problems such as structural violence, food access, and social distress plays a fundamental role in the depression–diabetes syndemic among poor populations.

The VIDDA Syndemic

The most comprehensive analysis of the syndemic interactions of the depression–diabetes dyad regards the "VIDDA Syndemic" (Mendenhall 2012) that was constructed to understand social factors interacting with depression and diabetes among Mexican immigrant women in Chicago. VIDDA emphasizes the structural, social, and psychological factors that come together with biology to emphasize that diabetes is not simply an *endpoint* as it is in biomedicine. Rather, it is the confluence of factors of structural violence, immigration, depression, diabetes, and abuse that come together in the lives of Mexican immigrant women as a singular force, or "VIDDA," to shape their disease and suffering. These factors bring to light the various dimensions of structural and political problems (e.g., structural violence and immigration-related criminalization and discrimination), interpersonal problems (e.g., emotional, physical, and sexual abuse), depression, and diabetes that contribute to the disproportionate morbidity and mortality attributed to diabetes among people of Mexican descent in the United States (Mendenhall 2012, 2015). However, the syndemic analysis underscores the fact that it is not diabetes itself that causes elevated health burden among this population; rather, the multiplicity of social distress, depression, and diabetes in the lives of these women shape their health and social well-being.

Violence plays a central role in the VIDDA Syndemic, traversing structural, political, and individual, emotional spheres of life and livelihoods among the Mexican immigrant women interviewed (Mendenhall 2012). For instance, women described how living in extreme poverty either in the United States or Mexico compromised their health during their childhoods, through adolescence, and well into adulthoods. The structural dimensions of their suffering involved not only living conditions but also healthy lifestyles and a sense of security. While the push-pull of economic livelihood was fundamental for first-generation Mexican immigrant women's decisions to immigrate to the United States, some women were unsure if they had indeed achieved happier, healthier lives. The breakdown of social and familial networks as a result of immigration and the constant fear and anxiety of living in the United States as an undocumented migrant were also major stressors interlinked with expressions of psychological distress and problems with diabetes. They were also expressed in women's stories of interpersonal abuse, as lack of legal, social, and even familial protection were fundamental aspects of many women's narratives of child sexual abuse, wife battering, emotional manipulation, and verbal insult. Women's narratives of abuse often remained private memories for much of their lives, leading them to harbor negative emotions that continued, in most cases for decades, to cause prolonged emotional distress. Thus, VIDDA was interwoven to shape these women's health as a single, integrated force.

The vulnerable spaces through which the VIDDA Syndemic exists are historically and contextually situated, but there are some important findings that can be applied to other contexts. Contemporary narratives of Mexican immigrant women cannot be dissociated from U.S.-Mexico economic and immigration policies that shaped their motivation to migrate or marginalization through race and class in the city. Nor can their experiences be dissociated from the stress women experienced as a result of their migration experiences or marginalization resulting from immigration and social circumstances of living in Chicago upon arrival. Moreover, their stories are squarely rooted within metanarratives of families broken due to migration and rooted within the unique time and space of urban United States. However, economic inequalities, problems associated with finding and maintaining a job in order to achieve economic security, and lack of power to negotiate working conditions or pay among laborers have been linked with an increase in gender-based violence in the domestic sphere (Maskovsky and Susser 2009) as well as health inequalities among the poorest members of society (Wilkinson 1996). Such experiences became realized through women's narratives of extreme physical, sexual, or verbal acts of violence that occurred upon migrating to Chicago for which they rarely received treatment—physical or psychological (Mendenhall 2012). These various forms of structural and interpersonal violence were significant factors in women's depression (directly) and diabetes (both directly and indirectly). In these ways, violence was revealed as an important cofactor in the depression–diabetes dyad.

Methods

The remainder of the article attends to the syndemic cofactors associated with depression–diabetes dyad among Black women living in urban South Africa. Methods for the present study have been explained in depth elsewhere (Mendenhall and Norris 2015). The qualitative research presented in this article is embedded within the larger Birth to Twenty (Bt20) cohort located in Soweto, a township of Johannesburg, South Africa. These women were first enrolled in Bt20 in 1989 as caregivers, mostly mothers, of Bt20 children; social, economic, psychological, and biological measures of health of both caregivers and children were measured over two decades. I identify the women in this article as "Black," a political category instated during apartheid, and in doing so recognize that there are important cultural nuances linked with ethnicity in South Africa. The women participating in the study, however, represent numerous sending communities around South Africa; most of them moved to Soweto during apartheid, some as a result of displacement from other parts of the city and others seeking economic opportunities. Most women had lived in Soweto for many years by the time of the interview and therefore I adopt the political term, but not without recognizing its problematic underpinnings.

The women invited to participate in the present study self-reported having type 2 diabetes two years before this study was conducted in November and December 2012. After providing informed consent, 27 women participated in a 60–90 minute in-depth qualitative interview about stress and diabetes followed by the administration of the Center for Epidemiological Studies Depression Scale (CES-D) (Radloff 1977), a self-report survey of previously diagnosed disorders, and a brief sociodemographic questionnaire. All interviews were audio-recorded and women were compensated 50 ZAR (around 5.88 USD) for transportation costs. All data collection received clearance by the University of the Witwatersrand Human Ethics Committee (Clearance number M121059).

The qualitative interviews were transcribed and those conducted in Sesotho and Zulu ($n = 8$ of 27) were translated into English. Systematic content analysis was utilized to evaluate emergent themes around stress and diabetes. On average women reported 4.8 (SD ±2.1) stressors; the most common emergent themes (described in depth in Mendenhall and Norris 2015) were street violence (74 percent), interpersonal violence (59 percent), living with an alcoholic husband (33 percent), the stress of caring for grandchildren (59 percent), loss of a family member to AIDS or other sicknesses (56 percent), financial stress (48 percent), and diabetes-related stress (30 percent). For the purposes of this article, these emergent themes are applied to demonstrate how structural and interpersonal forms of violence shape women's lives in contexts of health transitions observed in the depression–diabetes syndemic.

Stress and the Structural Violence of Soweto

Structural violence can be understood to be a theoretical orientation and analytic tool to examine how political-economic systems place particular persons or groups in situations of extreme vulnerability that compromise their health (Bourgois 2001; Farmer 1997a; Galtung 1969). In the South African case, the historical legacy of apartheid and the hegemonic practices of inequality instituted through education and public policy in postapartheid leadership can be closely linked to the unequal distribution of health (Coovadia et al. 2009). For instance, despite being a middle-income country, South Africa's health indicators reflect the health burden of a low-income country. This is most evident in the poverty-related diseases such as maternal deaths and undernutrition that remain widespread. Since the launch of the Millennium Development Goals in the 1990s, South Africa is one of 12 nations where maternal mortality has actually increased, despite its relative wealth (Chopra et al. 2009). It is also evident in that South Africa constitutes 17 percent of the global burden of HIV infection and one of the world's worst tuberculosis epidemics (Karim et al. 2009). The Black population bears the brunt of these concomitant epidemics, which are largely due to social, economic, and environmental conditions cultivated by apartheid. Conditions such as overcrowded squatter settlements, migrant labor, and underdeveloped health services for Black people have fostered a favorable environment for HIV and tuberculosis transmission in this population (Karim et al. 2009). Thus, the remarkable health burden found in South Africa is rooted in social and structural inequalities.

Structural violence also plays a fundamental role in the emerging diabetes epidemic among South Africans, and particularly among those who are poor. The Bt20 data indicates that 14.1 percent of the cohort presents with diabetes (Crowther and Norris 2012) and 40 percent with psychological distress (Mendenhall et al. 2013). Distress among those with diabetes is around 50 percent (Mendenhall et al. 2013). The narratives of impoverished women living with diabetes who participated in this study described two key pathways through which structural violence shaped their social and health problems: via the social impact of living in a community overburdened by the AIDS virus, and their struggle to manage their chronic illness via purchasing and preparing healthy foods and accessing reliable and affordable diabetes care.

First, it was not the affliction of living with both HIV and diabetes that was at the center of women's narratives, as one might assume for women living in an area where one in four are HIV infected. In fact, none of the women reported HIV-positive status (which may be a byproduct of social stigma more than anything else). Instead, this study underscores how HIV and AIDS is both a visible and "invisible" (Bourgois 2009) outcome of social inequality and perpetrator of stress in everyday life. Its visibility is measured not only in the physical marks of disease in the body but also in the commonness of death and burial in low-income South African communities (cf. Andrews et al. 2006). As the following quotes demonstrate, attending to funerals was a weekly event in the lives of many of my interlocutors, as was caring for grandchildren in the loss of their children to AIDS, which was often a major cause of stress.

> "I think [the diabetes is] due to the worries that I have faced in my life. In my family I am the only one who is old that is left and that causes stress to me. I was in Swaziland last week to bury another family member. All of them die and leave their kids behind to take care of themselves. Just yesterday I received a call about somebody passing on again. I have now had to carry the burden of having to take care of the surviving offspring." 63-year-old woman in Soweto

> "I am also not a social grant recipient at the same time I have two granddaughters from my first eldest daughter who has since passed away. They are dependent on me but they are very naughty because they know that granny cannot cope with running after them all the time. This then brought about a lot of stress for me and I would cry a lot. I tried to get them to understand that it was hard for me to take care of them, and I could use some cooperation on their part. This whole ordeal stresses me. I have resorted to just drinking a lot of water and sleeping it off instead of confronting them." 60-year-old woman in Soweto

Although less visible, these respondents demonstrate how the virus has lingering effects on family members left behind, including those who suffer from chronic illness. This stress plays an important role in the depression–diabetes syndemic because many women preference their grandchildren's health and social well-being to their own. The link of this stress to the AIDS epidemic must be recognized as a factor in women's health as women begin to face new epidemic problems of insulin resistance within their own bodies, while continuing to care for the social consequences of the AIDS that afflicted the bodies of their children. Thus, the structural violence of HIV in the lives of women living with diabetes in Soweto is more social than biological.

Second, structural violence also played a fundamental role in women's ability to achieve expectations of controlling diabetes due to poor access to affordable and healthy foods (Altman et al. 2009) as well as health care (Mayosi et al. 2012). A growing literature underscores the relative import of the built environment in shaping the nutritional health and risk for noncommunicable diseases such as diabetes, known as *food deserts*, although much of this research stems from poor populations in high-income countries (cf. Walker et al. 2010). The South African context presents unique challenges as "geographies of food retail" (Battersby 2012) differ from high-income countries insofar as people in townships often depend on local markets, with unstable pricing, spaza shops, and neighbors for the majority of food consumption, leading to high caloric, low nutritional diets. Moreover, in tandem with a rapid upsweep of fast food chains, Soweto families often pick up their food in neighborhood food stalls that are quick, cheap, and unhealthy. In addition to fried foods and chips, the local food choice is pap, a cheap, filling, but not very nutritious starch, which the majority of women reported to eat daily. Indeed, many women noted that pap was an essential food in that if they did not eat "pap" then they did not "eat." High sodium flavorings also are added to foods made in the home and on the street.

Although most women recognized the importance of managing diabetes with diet, they often described difficulty when attending to curtail their diets to eat the foods apart from pap that their physicians recommended:

"They advised us to eat only a little portion of pap at the clinic. Due to a lack of funds however I cannot afford to forego most of the other foods that I should stop eating." 54-year-old woman in Soweto

"I am not troubled much by being a diabetic serve for the fact that I do not have the money to buy the necessary food that I should be eating. The right food is very costly." 48-year-old woman in Soweto

We have coined the ability to buy foods, but inability to buy foods recommended for diabetic health needs as "diabetes food insecurity" (Mendenhall and Norris 2015). This concept of diabetes food insecurity cannot be dissociated from the apartheid's legacy of segregation that shaped the poorly nutritious "geographies of food retail" in communities such as Soweto, cultivating structural impediments to individuals' access to purchase the foods necessary to live healthily with a chronic illness.

As people become wealthier in the rapidly transforming townships such as Soweto, meats become staples and markers of status. Men in particular eat few vegetables and prefer pap and meats—a food choice linked with colonial and apartheid legacies of political and structural violence. However, these food choices are also linked with a preferred larger body size (Mash et al. 2007), which is juxtaposed to those who are "sick" or wasting as a result of HIV and AIDS. This has played a role in the extraordinary escalation of obesity in Soweto—today 70 percent of the women in the Bt20 cohort study are overweight, two-thirds are obese (Richter et al. 2004), and around 40 percent of those who are obese have diabetes (Crowther and Norris 2012).

Complicated histories of diabetes care emerged from women's narratives, unveiling mistrust of private health care providers as well as systemic issues associated with public hospitals. Despite one in three women reporting access to health insurance, most sought care at their community health clinic located near their home in Soweto or Baragwanath Hospital. In this way, they chose the public option over the private one, despite the systemic barriers that characterize public hospitals:

"I wouldn't mention the doctors at the private hospitals because they accumulate money; they will treat all your diseases as long as you pay them and pop money into their pharmacies. But here at Bara, I have the panic attacks the minute I know that the following day I'm going to see the doctor, in so much that even my sugar level would rise because of that." 60-year-old woman in Soweto

"Seeing the doctor requires some patience and I have become used to the long queues. I get there at about 07h00 only to see the doctor at 12 noon. The waiting is cumbersome but there isn't much that one can do but to wait for your turn. They will eventually check your feet and chest amongst other things." 48-year-old woman in Soweto

Women's ability to access consistent and quality medical care not only fueled problems of treatment "compliance" (Farmer 1997b), which shallow pockets to purchase foods, medicines, and transport to the clinic may prove difficult. But also stymied clinical and public engagement around diabetes pointed to a problem of education around diabetes; in many cases women expressed confusion about treatment modalities as they often compared and contrasted their knowledge around diabetes with their knowledge of AIDS (see Mendenhall and Norris 2015). Indeed, both factors may have had an impact on their choice of treatment facility as well as trust in their community clinic. Moreover, this may be a reflection of the limited extra-institutional education around diabetes at the community level and decades-long education programs around HIV and AIDS.

Interpersonal violence: Fear and insecurity in the private and public spheres

The prominence of interpersonal violence provides another compelling argument for the role of violence in shaping health disparities, a problem that is profoundly gendered and higher in South African when compared to many other regions of the world (Murray et al. 2012). For instance, the rate of female homicide by intimate partners in South Africa is six times the global average, and limited governmental resources are expended to mitigate this problem or support women and children who suffer from it (Seedat et al. 2009). Moreover, nearly half of deaths attributed to injury result from some form of violence, four and a half times global measures (Peden et al. 2002). These acts of violence are not only gender-based and hidden from view in the domestic sphere, such as child sexual abuse or wife battering, but also include more public acts, such as street violence, often through the use of guns. These more public acts become "normalized" forms of violence in society, which are repeated so often in everyday life that, over time, they become routine (Bourgois 2009; Scheper-Hughes 1993).

The role of domestic violence in women's health was underscored in the recent Global Burden of Disease 2010 study as a major cause of morbidity in southern Africa (Murray et al. 2012). Therefore, it was not surprising that 60 percent of women reported at least one form of physical, sexual, verbal, and emotional abuses, and many experienced more than one form. For example, one woman said, "I have basically been abused throughout all of my life." Two-thirds of these women reported depressive symptoms (CESD $\geq$ 16) (Mendenhall and Norris 2015).

Most instances of abuse were specific types of abuse, such as one woman who said, "He [my husband] used to hit before" and another who said,

> "I was never appreciated and at times he [my husband] would hit me for my cooking. He would also accuse me of promiscuity. He would at times refuse to look after his kids and claim that there weren't his. That on its own was abusive." 48-year-old woman in Soweto

Spousal battering commonly was associated with an alcoholic husband. Although many women spoke proudly of staying in their marriage due to cultural expectations around gender and marriage, many women left their marriages, and this was largely due to abuse and infidelity.

EM: "What are the challenges in your life that are most stressful?"

P: "I can say that it was my husband. We fought a lot and he had a drinking problem. We would fight over children and every other thing."

EM: "Did he ever hit you?"

P: "Yes he did when he was drunk; I even use false teeth now. My life was very hard. He once had an affair with another woman and tried to kick me out of the house. [. . .] I got a tip off from somebody that I knew and followed the whole thing up. My life was never the same from that day onwards. It took a turn for the worst." 78-year-old woman in Soweto

The most severe cases of abuse were often sexual abuse during childhood:

"I have been sexually abused as a child. I grew up in an extended family with all my cousins, and I wasn't aware at the time that I was being raped because I was just a kid playing hide and seek with a cousin. I only realized that I was violated at a later stage when I was all grown up. I couldn't have said anything to the elders." 50-year-old woman in Soweto

The everyday violence against women revealed in these stories further the analysis of other public health scholarship (cf. Murray et al. 2012) that underscores the role of interpersonal violence in people's mental and physical health. By recognizing the insidious acts of violence that frame women's memories and cultivate psychological distress, we can understand how such social problems may indeed shape health problems.

Acts of senseless interpersonal violence in the street also fostered extreme stress: three-quarters of the women interviewed reported violence in the public sphere to be a central part of their lives. This violence was defined broadly, from burglary to losing a family member to gun violence. Some women reported that their husbands were shot during the apartheid struggle decades before the interview, as is described by the following 59-year-old woman in Soweto:

"My husband, he was shot in the head . . . I found that he [my husband] was not in the bed, and I did not hear him when he woke up and gone out. I went to my two sons' bedroom because through their window you can see the tuck-shop light. I asked my younger son where his father was and he said he didn't know. The older one usually go out at about six to prepare, that's why I asked this little one. It was dark in the tuck-shop and I thought maybe the bakery truck had come early . . . When I opened the kitchen door I found him lying there, I didn't hear a thing. Then I screamed."

Almost every woman interviewed reported more recently being victim to violence associated with *tsotsis* (gangsters), including some extreme cases such as a woman who reported she finally had to put iron bars on her home after tsotsis forced their way in once to steal a television and another time to rape her children.

Such severe acts of violence had profound effects on women's lives, and we might assume that such experiences affect their mental health. For example, a 53-year-old woman described the direct impact of senseless violence in the loss of her son:

"The passing away of my son still affects me although it was two years ago. He was my first born. He was gunned down on his way from work."

However, in most cases women described violence as a general fear that people maintained in their everyday lives, as opposed to linked with specific incidences:

"There used to be too much violence and a lot of burglaries in the neighborhood. There were tsotsis attacking people on the street and in houses. As a new member in the community at the time, I felt that the whole neighborhood was against me and my family. The area we are living was relatively new and people thought that mostly affluent people lived there and we were evidently not meeting the standard. People would come and steal. Not necessarily my house but my neighbors." 60-year-old woman in Soweto

Although this small study could not claim causality between such extreme forms of suffering and mental health, it is difficult to deny the strong association between violence and the high rates of mental distress within the study population. Across the sample at large 40 percent of the women enrolled in Bt20 reported psychological distress (Mendenhall et al. 2013). Such distress was markedly worse among women with multiple physical morbidities, as more than half of the study population who reported three or more diseases also reported mental distress (Mendenhall et al. 2013). As all the women interviewed for the present study had type 2 diabetes, and most had one or more comorbidities, it may be presumed that the data presented today represent the social experiences of those living with one or more chronic illness. What is surprising is that, despite the physical and medical challenges the women interviewed must face, it was the social stressors that were placed at the center of their narratives, begging us to recognize how social inequality shapes psychological and physical health in tandem. Indeed, the data demonstrate how the structural violence of AIDS and obesity, gender-based violence, and gun violence shape women's everyday lives and play a fundamental role in stress that is central to the depression–diabetes syndemic.

CONCLUSION

The structural and interpersonal forms of violence described in this study reveal the important roles of political-economic and social inequalities in health transition in South Africa. They show how the structural dimensions of everyday life, highlighted here through the guise of AIDS and interpersonal experiences, which become visceral components of individual, emotional worlds, are situating factors that shape how people live in the world and understand health and social well-being. Indeed, grief and stress linked with such violence may play a role in the high prevalence of psychological distress among women residing in Soweto. And we must not underestimate the toll that such stress takes on the body, particularly as the incidence of obesity and type 2 diabetes rises in Soweto—with diabetes now reaching 14 percent of the population (Crowther and Norris 2012). As in other middle-income countries, escalation of noncommunicable diseases among middle income and working poor presents greater challenges with regard to depression, poor access to medical care, and diabetes-related complications (Leone et al. 2012). Thus, understanding how these stressors manifest in the mind and body is a fundamental factor in syndemic theory as social factors are equally vital for intervention as psychological and biological ones.

The unique structural and interpersonal factors that shape women's life experiences and become syndemic with depression and diabetes are inherently a problem of context. When juxtaposed to the syndemic violence in Chicago, the social and physical toll of the HIV and AIDS epidemic reveals itself as pivotal to understanding how women in sub-Saharan Africa will engage with chronic, co-occurring noncommunicable diseases. The women in this study indicated that diabetes not only has less legitimacy as a form of suffering within Soweto when compared to AIDS, but also women hold less local knowledge around strategies for care and treatment. As diabetes incidence continues to escalate among the middle class and working poor in South Africa, as well as other low- and middle-income countries (Leone et al. 2012; Mendenhall et al. 2014), the knowledge gap around the severity of diabetes and capability to manage the disease and live healthy, normal lives must be a central part of public health education. Moreover, recognizing how the social life of HIV and AIDS permeates into other illness experiences of those affected (and perhaps doubly infected) by AIDS must be recognized as part of the diabetes narrative that women experience and retell in a context of such high AIDS burden.

Yet, stress manifest in deeply personal, prolonged suffering associated with interpersonal violence—in the private and public spheres—must be recognized to compound the effects of structural violence on mental and physical health across contexts. There is evidence that stressful and traumatic experiences, such as childhood abuse, may be associated with the development of depression (Felitti et al. 1998) and diabetes (Lee et al. 2014). Such experiences often are situated within contexts of chronic poverty that further cultivate one's propensity for mental disorders (Lund et al. 2010) and diabetes (Weaver and Mendenhall 2014). Thus, we may understand the syndemic relationship of violence, depression, and diabetes to maintain some form of biological underpinnings that transcend culture and context. Nevertheless, social realities of structural and interpersonal violence that become realized in women's stories reveal how other diseases may be co-constructed within the depression–diabetes syndemic through social pathways, such as HIV and AIDS. Such findings underscore how social problems apart from the purview of biomedicine may play a role in how people perceive and experience the emergence of diabetes in Soweto.

In contexts of health transition, how diseases of poverty and modernization come together in our dynamic world must be realized as interwoven and interacting. This is important not only on a social level but also a biological one. By recognizing how social factors shape the depression–diabetes dyad epidemiologically, such as through cultural and social variants of modernization contributing to the socioeconomic reversal of diabetes incidence from the affluent to the poor, and individually, such as the everyday realities of structural and interpersonal violence in Soweto, we can better understand not only how a syndemic truly emerges but also the social and psychological variants that underlie and interface with diseases in transition.

NOTE

Acknowledgments. This article was developed by way of a postdoctoral research fellowship with the MRC/Wit's Developmental Pathways for Health Research Unit with the support of Dr. Shane Norris (University of the Witwatersrand Faculty of Health Sciences). This study would have been impossible without the commitment of Mama Hunadi Shawa who scheduled interviews and conducted interviews in Zulu and Sesotho, and of Meikie Hlalele who assisted with two Zulu interviews.

REFERENCES CITED

Ali, S., M. A. Stone, J. L. Peters, M. J. Davies, and K. Khunti
  2006 The Prevalence of Co-Morbid Depression in Adults with Type 2 Diabetes: A Systematic Review and Meta-Analysis. Diabetic Medicine 23:1165–1173.
Altman, Miriam, Tim Hart, and Peter Jacobs
  2009 Household Food Security Status in South Africa. Agrekon 48(4):345–361.
Anderson, Ryan J, Kenneth E. Freedland, Ray E. Clouse, Patrick J. Lustman
  2001 The Prevalence of Comorbid Depression in Adults with Diabetes. Diabetes Care 24(6):1069–1078.
Andrews, Gail, Donald Skinner, and Khangelani Zuma
  2006 Epidemiology of Health and Vulnerability among Children Orphaned and Made Vulnerable by HIV/AIDS in Sub-Saharan Africa. AIDS Care 18(3):269–276.
Battersby, Jane
  2012 Beyond the Food Desert: Finding Ways to Speak About Urban Food Security in South Africa. Geografiska Annaler: Series B, Human Geography 94(2):141–159.
Bourgois, Philippe
  2001 The Power of Violence in War and Peace: Post-Cold War Lessons from El Salvador. Ethnography 2(1):5–37.
  2009 Recognizing Invisible Violence. *In* Global Health in Times of Violence. B. Rylko-Bauer, L. Whiteford, and P. Farmer, eds. Pp. 17–40. Santa Fe, NM: School for Advanced Research Press.
Chopra, Mickey, Emmanuelle Daviaud, Robert Pattinson, Sharon Fonn, and Joy E. Lawn
  2009 Saving the Lives of South Africa's Mothers, Babies, and Children: Can the Health System Deliver? Lancet 374:835–846.
Coovadia, Hoosen, Rachel Jewkes, Peter Barron, David Sanders, and Diane McIntyre
  2009 The Health and Health System of South Africa: Historical Roots of Current Public Health Challenges. Lancet 374:817–834.
Cowie, Catherine C., Keith F. Rust, Danita D. Byrd-Hold, Edward W. Gregg, Earl S. Ford, Linda S. Geiss, Kathleen E. Bainbridge, and Judith E. Fradkin
  2010 Prevalence of Diabetes and High Risk for Diabetes Using A1C Criteria in the U.S. Population in 1988–2006. Diabetes Care 33(3):562–568.
Crowther, Nigel J., and Shane A. Norris
  2012 The Current Waist Circumference Cut Point Used for the Diagnosis of Metabolic Syndrome in Sub-Saharan African Women Is Not Appropriate. PLoS One 7(11):e48883.
De Groot, Mary, Ryan Anderson, Kenneth E. Freedland, Ray E. Clouse, and Patrick J. Lustman
  2001 Association of Depression and Diabetes Complications: A Meta-Analysis. Psychosomatic Medicine 63:619–630.
Egede, Leonard E., and Charles. Ellis
  2010 Diabetes and Depression: Global Perspectives. Diabetes Research and Clinical Practice 87:302–312.
Farmer, Paul
  1997a On Suffering and Structural Violence: A View from Below. *In* Social Suffering. A. Kleinman, V. Das, and M. M. Lock, eds. Berkeley: University of California Press.
  1997b Social Science and the New Tuberculosis. Social Science and Medicine 44(3):347–358.
Fassin, Didier
  2007 When Bodies Remember: Experiences and Politics of AIDS in South Africa. Berkeley: University of California Press.

Felitti, Vincent J., Robert F. Anda, Dale Nordenberg, David F. Williamson, Alison M. Spitz, Valarie Edwards, Mary P. Koss, and James S. Marks

    1998 Relationship of Childhood Abuse and Household Dysfunction to Many of the Leading Causes of Death in Adults: The Adverse Childhood Experiences (ACE) Study. American Journal of Preventive Medicine 14(4):245–258.

Galtung, John

    1969 Violence, Peace, and Peace Research. Journal of Peace Research 6(3):167–191.

Golden, Sherita Hill, Hochang Benjamin Lee, Pamela J. Schreiner, Ana Diez Roux, Annette L. Fitzpatrick, Moyses Szklo, and Constantine Lyketsos

    2007 Depression and Type 2 Diabetes Mellitus: The Multiethnic Study of Atherosclerosis. Psychosomatic Medicine 69:529–536.

Golden, Sherita Hill, Mariana Lazo, Mercedes Carnethon, Alain G. Bertoni, Pamela J. Schreiner, Ana V. Diez Roux, Hochang B. Lee, and Constantine Lyketsos

    2008 Examining a Bidirectional Association between Depressive Symptoms and Diabetes. Journal of the American Medical Association 299(23):2751–2759.

González-Guarda, Rosa

    2009 The Syndemic Orientation: Implications for Eliminating Hispanic Health Disparities. Hispanic Health Care International 7(3):114–115.

Karim, Salim S. Abdool, Gavin J. Churchyard, Auarraisha Abdool Karim, and Stephen D. Lawn

    2009 HIV Infection and Tuberculosis in South Africa: An Urgent Need to Escalate the Public Health Response. Lancet 374:921–933.

Kessler, Ronald C., and Evelyn J. Bromet

    2013 The Epidemiology of Depression across Culture. Annual Review of Public Health 34:119–138.

Knol, M. J., J. W. R. Twish, A. T. F. Beekman, R. J. Heine, F. J. Snoek, and F. Pouwer

    2006 Depression as a Risk Factor for the Onset of Type 2 Diabetes Mellitus. A Meta-Analysis. Diabetologia 49(5):837–845.

Lee, Chious, Vera Tsenkova, and Deborah Carr

    2014 Childhood Trauma and Metabolic Syndrome in Men and Women. Social Science & Medicine. 105:122–130.

Leone, Tiziana, Ernestina Coast, Shilpa Narayanan, and Ama de Graft Aikins

    2012 Diabetes and Depression Comorbidity and Socioeconomic Status in Low and Middle Income Countries (LMICs): A Mapping of the Evidence. Globalization and Health 8(39):1–10.

Lund, Crick, Alison Breen, Alan J. Flisher, Ritsuko Kakuma, Joanne Corrigall, John A. Joska, Leslie Swartz, and Vikram Patel

    2010 Poverty and Common Mental Disorders in Low and Middle Income Countries: A Systematic Review. Social Science and Medicine 71:517e528.

Mash, Robert J., Elma De Vries, and Isaac Abdul

    2007 Diabetes in Africa: The New Pandemic. Report on the 19th World Diabetes Congress, Cape Town, December 2006. African Family Practice 49(6):44–55.

Maskovsky, Jeff, and Ida Susser

    2009 Introduction: Rethinking America. In Rethinking America: The Imperial Homeland in the 21st Century. J. Maskovsky and I. Susser, eds. Boulder: Paradigm.

Mayosi, Bongani M., Alan J. Flisher, Umesh G. Lalloo, Freddy Sitas, Stephen M. Tollman, and Debbie Bradshaw

    2009 The Burden of Non-Communicable Diseases in South Africa. Lancet 374:934–947.

Mayosi, Bongani M., Joy E. Lawn, Ashley van Niekerk, Debbie Bradshaw, Salim S. Abdool Karim, Hoosen M. Coovadia, and Lancet South Africa Team

    2012 Health in South Africa: Changes and Challenges since 2009. Lancet 380(9858):2029–2043.

Mendenhall, Emily

    2012 Syndemic Suffering: Social Distress, Depression, and Diabetes among Mexican Immigrant Women. Walnut Creek, CA: Left Coast Press.

2015 Beyond Co-Morbidity: A Critical Anthropological Perspective of Syndemic Depression and Diabetes in Cross-Cultural Contexts. Medical Anthropology Quarterly, forthcoming. DOI: 10.1111/maq.12210

Mendenhall, Emily, and Shane A. Norris

2015 When HIV Is Ordinary, Diabetes New: Remaking Suffering in a South African Township. Global Public Health, forthcoming 10(4).

Mendenhall, Emily, Shane A. Norris, Rahul Shidhaye, and Dorairaj Prabhakaran

2014 Depression and Type 2 Diabetes in Low- and Middle-Income Countries: A Systematic Review. Diabetes Research and Clinical Practice 103:276–285.

Mendenhall, Emily, Linda Richter, Alan Stein, and Shane A. Norris

2013 Psychological and Physical Co-Morbidity among Urban South African Women. PLoS One 8(10):e78803.

Mezuk, Brian, William Eaton, Sandra Albrecht, and Sherita Hill Golden

2008 Depression and Type 2 Diabetes over the Lifespan: A Meta-Analysis. Diabetes Care 31(12):2383–2390.

Murray, Christopher J. L., Theo Vas, Rafael Lozano, Mohsen Naghavi, Abraham D. Flaxman, Catherine Michaud, Majid Ezzati, Kenji Shibuya, Joshua A. Salomon, Safa Abdalla, Victor Aboyans, Jerry Abraham, Ilana Ackerman, Rakesh Aggarwal, Stephanie Y. Ahn, Mohammed K. Ali, Mohammad A. AlMazroa, Miriam Alvarado, H. Ross Anderson, Laurie M. Anderson, Kathryn G. Andrews, Charles Atkinson, Larry M. Baddour, Adil N. Bahalim, Suzanne Barker-Collo, Lope H. Barrero, David H. Bartels, Maria-Gloria Basáñez, Amanda Baxter, Michelle L. Bell, Emelia J. Benjamin, Derrick Bennett, Eduardo Bernabé, Kavi Bhalla, Bishal Bhandari, Boris Bikbov, Aref Bin Abdulhak, Gretchen Birbeck, James A. Black, Hannah Blencowe, Jed D. Blore, Fiona Blyth, Ian Bolliger, Audrey Bonaventure, Soufiane Boufous, Rupert Bourne, Michel Boussinesq, Tasanee Braithwaite, Carol Brayne, Lisa Bridgett, Simon Brooker, Peter Brooks, Traolach S. Brugha, Claire Bryan-Hancock, Chiara Bucello, Rachelle Buchbinder, Geoffrey Buckle, Christine M. Budke, Michael Burch, Peter Burney, Roy Burstein, Bianca Calabria, Benjamin Campbell, Charles E. Canter, Hélène Carabin, Jonathan Carapetis, Loreto Carmona, Claudia Cella, Fiona Charlson, Honglei Chen, Andrew Tai-Ann Cheng, David Chou, Sumeet S. Chugh, Luc E. Coffeng, Steven D. Colan, Samantha Colquhoun, K. Ellicott Colson, John Condon, Myles D. Connor, Leslie T. Cooper, Matthew Corriere, Monica Cortinovis, Karen Courville de Vaccaro, William Couser, Benjamin C. Cowie, Michael H. Criqui, Marita Cross, Kaustubh C. Dabhadkar, Manu Dahiya, Nabila Dahodwala, James Damsere-Derry, Goodarz Danaei, Adrian Davis, Diego De Leo, Louisa Degenhardt, Robert Dellavalle, Allyne Delossantos, Julie Denenberg, Sarah Derrett, Don C. Des Jarlais, Samath D. Dharmaratne, Mukesh Dherani, Cesar Diaz-Torne, Helen Dolk, E. Ray Dorsey, Tim Driscoll, Herbert Duber, Beth Ebel, Karen Edmond, Alexis Elbaz, Suad Eltahir Ali, Holly Erskine, Patricia J. Erwin, Patricia Espindola, Stalin E. Ewoigbokhan, Farshad Farzadfar, Valery Feigin, David T. Felson, Alize Ferrari, Cleusa P. Ferri, Eric M. Fèvre, Mariel M. Finucane, Seth Flaxman, Louise Flood, Kyle Foreman, Mohammad H. Forouzanfar, Francis Gerry R. Fowkes, Marlene Fransen, Michael K. Freeman, Belinda J. Gabbe, Sherine E. Gabriel, Emmanuela Gakidou, Hammad A. Ganatra, Bianca Garcia, Flavio Gaspari, Richard F. Gillum, Gerhard Gmel, Diego Gonzalez-Medina, Richard Gosselin, Rebecca Grainger, Bridget Grant, Justina Groeger, Francis Guillemin, David Gunnell, Ramyani Gupta, Juanita Haagsma, Holly Hagan, Yara A. Halasa, Wayne Hall, and Diana Haring

2012 Disability-Adjusted Life Years (DALYs) for 291 Diseases and Injuries in 21 Regions, 1990–2010: A Systematic Analysis for the Global Burden of Disease Study 2010. Lancet 380:2197–2223.

Musselman, Dominique L., Ephi Betan, Hannah Larsen, and Lawrence S. Phillips

2003 Relationship of Depression to Diabetes Types 1 and 2: Epidemiology, Biology, and Treatment. Biological Psychiatry 54:317–329.

Patel, Vikram, and Arthur Kleinman

2003 Poverty and Common Mental Disorders in Developing Countries. Bulletin of the World Health Organization 81:609e–615e.

Peden, Margie, Kara S. McGee, and Gyanendra Sharma

2002 The Injury Chart Book: A Graphical Overview of the Global Burden of Injuries. Geneva: World Health Organization.

Peer, Nasheeta, Krisela Steyn, Carl Lombard, Estelle V. Lambert, Bavinisha Vythilingum, and Naomi S. Levitt
   2012   Rising Diabetes Prevalence among Urban-Dwelling Black South Africans. PLoS One 7(9):e43336.
Popkin, Barry M., Linda S. Adair, and Shu Wen Ng.
   2012   Global Nutrition Transition and the Pandemic of Obesity in Developing Countries. Nutrition Reviews 70(1):3–21.
Radloff, Lenore Sawyer
   1977   The CES-D Scale. Applied Psychological Measurement 1(3):385–401.
Richter, Linda M., Shane A. Norris, and Thea De Wet
   2004   Transition from Birth to Ten to Birth to Twenty: The South African Cohort Reaches 13 Years of Age. Paediatric and Perinatal Epidemiology 18:290–301.
Scheper-Hughes, Nancy
   1993   Death without Weeping: The Violence of Everyday Life in Brazil. Berkeley: University of California Press.
Seedat, Mohamed, Ashley van Niekerk, Rachel Jewkes, Shahnaaz Suffla, and Kopano Ratele
   2009   Violence and Injuries in South Africa: Prioritising an Agenda for Prevention. Lancet 374:1011–1022.
Singer, Merrill
   2009a Desperate Measures: A Syndemic Approach to the Anthropology of Health in a Violent City. *In* Global Health in Times of Violence. B. Rylko-Bauer, L. Whiteford, and P. Farmer, eds. Pp. 137–156. Santa Fe, NM: School for Advanced Research.
   2009b Introduction to Syndemics: A Systems Approach to Public and Community Health. San Francisco: Jossey-Bass.
Singer, Merrill, Pamela I. Erickson, Louise Badiane, Rosemary Diaz, Dugeidy Ortiz, Traci Abraham, and Anna Marie Nicolaysen
   2006   Syndemics, Sex and the City: Understanding Sexually Transmitted Disease in Social and Cultural Context. Social Science & Medicine 63(8):2010–2021.
Tomlinson, Mark, Anna T. Grimsrud, Dan J. Stein, David R. Williams, and Landon Myer
   2009   The Epidemiology of Major Depression in South Africa: Results from the South African Stress and Health Study. South African Medical Journal 99(5):368–373.
Walker, Renee E., Christopher R. Keane, and Jessica G. Burke
   2010   Disparities and Access to Healthy Food in the United States: A Review of Food Deserts Literature. Health and Place 16:876–884.
Weaver, Lesley Jo, and Emily Mendenhall
   2014   Applying Syndemics and Chronicity: Interpretations from Studies of Poverty, Depression, and Diabetes. Medical Anthropology 33(2):1–17.
Wilkinson, Richard C.
   1996   Unhealthy Societies: The Afflictions of Inequality. London: Routledge.

BIOSKETCHES

Mauro C. Balieiro is Professor of Psychology and Director of the Center for Applied Psychology, Paulista University, Ribeirão Preto, Brazil. His research interests focus on culture and psychology, and particularly cultural risk factors associated with depression. He is currently engaged in research incorporating psychodynamic concepts into biocultural models of subjective well-being in Brazil. He has also carried out research examining cultural models of depression in Brazil.

Alexandra Brewis (Slade) is President's Professor of Medical Anthropology and Director of the School of Human Evolution and Social Change at Arizona State University. Her current research interests are focused on understanding the biocultural complexities of contemporary global food and water issues, including the growing obesity "epidemic." She has previously conducted extended field-based projects in the Pacific Islands, Mexico, and the US focused on complex health problems that intersect culture and biology, including infertility, ADHD, and depression. Brewis has authored 3 books including *Obesity: Cultural and Biocultural Perspectives* (2011, Rutgers University Press) and an array of articles within anthropological, health, and environmental disciplines.

William W. Dressler is Professor of Anthropology at the University of Alabama. His research interests focus on the relationship of culture and behavior, as described by the concept of cultural consonance, and how cultural consonance is associated with health outcomes. Currently he is conducting research on gene-culture interactions in relation to subjective well-being in Brazil. He is committed to the further theoretical and empirical development of a biocultural perspective.

Craig Hadley is an associate professor in anthropology at Emory University, specializing in food insecurity, public health nutrition, cultural epidemiology, and related population issues. He has conducted research in Ethiopia, Tanzania, Australia, and the United States. He is currently studying the relationship between food prices, nutritional wellbeing and food insecurity. (chadley@emory.edu)

David Himmelgreen is Professor and Chair of Anthropology at the University of South Florida. Himmelgreen specializes in nutritional anthropology with a focus on food insecurity, under- and over-nutrition, growth and development, diet-related chronic diseases, and HIV/AIDS prevention. He has conducted research in Costa Rica, the U.S., Lesotho, India, and Puerto Rico. With funding from the National Science Foundation, Himmelgreen is currently conducting research on food choices and decision-making in low-income U.S. households at risk of food insecurity. Himmelgreen has published over 80 academic papers, edited volumes, book chapters, and book reviews.

Morgan Hoke is a biocultural anthropologist. She received her B.A. in Anthropology and Hispanic Studies from Columbia University in 2008. She is currently a doctoral candidate at Northwestern University. Her work focuses on illuminating the

ANNALS OF ANTHROPOLOGICAL PRACTICE 38.2, pp. 317–319. ISSN: 2153-957X. © 2015 by the American Anthropological Association. DOI:10.1111/napa.12066

interconnectedness of political economy, culture, and biology through the study of the embodiment of socio-economic inequalities in highland Peru. Her current research centers on the interrelationships among increasing inequalities, the influences of early growth, and understandings of infant health.

Kasey Jernigan, MPH, is a PhD student in the Department of Anthropology at the University of Massachusetts Amherst. She earned her MPH in Epidemiology from the University of Oklahoma Health Sciences Center. Her research is in the areas of critical biocultural anthropology and participatory action research with Indigenous communities and considers how health and heritage are understood and enacted in everyday life contexts. Kasey is a Ford Foundation Fellow and a Native American Research Centers for Health (NARCH) Fellow.

Thomas Leatherman is Professor and Chair of Anthropology at the University of Massachusetts, Amherst. He is a biocultural anthropologist whose work addresses social change, inequalities, and health in Latin America and the U.S. Work in the Yucatan of Mexico focused on the "coca-colonization" of diets within a tourism-based economy. Long-term research in the southern Peruvian Andes focused on the co-constitutive nature of poverty, nutrition and illness as part of the structural and political violence manifested in a 20-year civil war (1980–2000). Recent work examines shifts in national and regional economies, food security and health in post-conflict Andean Peru.

Thomas McDade, PhD, is a Professor in the Department of Anthropology at Northwestern University, and a Faculty Fellow of the Institute for Policy Research, both at Northwestern. He is a biological anthropologist specializing in human population biology, and he has conducted research in Bolivia, Ecuador, Kenya, Mexico, Samoa, the Philippines, and the US. Much of this work focuses on integrated, biocultural approaches to understanding the health effects of stress, and the long term effects of early environments on human biology, development, and health.

David Meek (PhD University of Georgia, 2014) is an environmental anthropologist, critical geographer, and education scholar with an area specialization in Brazil. Professor Meek theoretically grounds his research in a synthesis of political ecology, critical pedagogy, and place-based education. His interests include: sustainable agriculture, social movements, and environmental education. Dr. Meek's work has been conducted using a combination of traditional anthropological and cartographic methods, such as GIS, remote sensing and historic aerial photography. Meek has carried out research on sustainable agriculture education within Brazil's Landless Workers' Movement. (ddmeek@ua.edu).

Emily Mendenhall, PhD, MPH, is an Assistant Professor of Global Health in the Science, Technology, and International Affairs (STIA) Program at Georgetown University's School of Foreign Service. Emily has conducted cross-cultural research on the syndemics of poverty, depression, and diabetes in vulnerable populations residing in urban United States, India, Kenya, and South Africa. This research culminated in a book entitled "Syndemic Suffering: Social Distress, Depression, and Diabetes among Mexican Immigrant Women" and more than two dozen peer-reviewed articles. She also co-edited "Global Mental Health: Anthropological Perspectives" and the Global Health Narratives series of books for youth (www.GHN4C.org).

Rosane P. Ribeiro is Associate Professor of Maternal and Child Health and Public Health, Faculty of Nursing, University of São Paulo-Ribeirão Preto. Her research has focused on factors associated with the diagnosis and treatment of eating disorders in Brazil, including especially cultural and psychological influences on anorexia nervosa and bulimia. She is currently carrying our research comparing cultural models of food among patients with eating disorders.

Ernesto Ruiz received his doctoral degree in biological anthropology from the University of South Florida. His research focuses on nutritional health and child growth and development within the context of food insecurity and increasing consumerism. For his dissertation he examined the relationship between cultural consonance, food security status and indicators of child growth and development. Ernesto has also carried out ethnographic and bioanthropological fieldwork exploring the genetic ancestry and cardiovascular health of an East-Indian derived population on the Caribbean coast of Costa Rica.

José Ernesto dos Santos is Associate Professor of Medicine, Faculty of Medicine of Ribeirão Preto, University of São Paulo. His research interests encompass eating disorders, lipid metabolism, genomic medicine, and cultural influences in disease risk. He is currently involved on research on gene-culture interaction in relation to subjective well-being in Brazil. He is committed to the translation of medical anthropological research into clinical practice.

Lesley Jo Weaver, Ph.D., M.P.H., is an assistant professor in the Department of Anthropology at the University of Alabama. Weaver works primarily in India and Brazil, using methods drawn from biology, epidemiology, and cultural anthropology to explore how and why we knowingly make health choices that produce suboptimal outcomes. Weaver's specific research interests include type 2 diabetes and depression/anxiety in urban North India, food insecurity and depression in rural Brazil, and social stigma toward people with Hansen's disease (leprosy) in India.

Amber Wutich is a faculty member of Arizona State University's Anthropology and Global Health programs. She has been awarded the Carnegie CASE U.S. Professor of the Year Award for Arizona and ASU's Award for Excellence in Classroom Performance. Her research examines the nexus of injustice, resource insecurity, and adaptability, focusing on water and food in Bolivia, Paraguay, and the U.S. She directs the Global Ethnohydrology Study, a multi-year, cross-cultural study of water knowledge and management. She is Associate Editor of the journal Field Methods and on the faculty of the National Science Foundation's research methods programs in cultural anthropology.

CORRIGENDUM

In [1], the following error was published in Table 3.

The headings of the last two columns were incorrect. The last column contains the Oxygen isotope data but it is labeled as C isotopes and the second last column is labeled as O isotopes but contains the Carbon isotope data:

TABLE 3. Concentrations and Pb, Sr, N, C, O Isotope Data for Teeth, Rib and Hair from the Victim

	Pb (ppm)	$^{206}Pb/$ ^{204}Pb	$^{207}Pb/$ ^{204}Pb	$^{208}Pb/$ ^{204}Pb	$^{208}Pb/$ ^{206}Pb	$^{207}Pb/$ ^{206}Pb	$^{206}Pb/$ ^{207}Pb	$^{87}Sr/$ ^{86}Sr	δ^{15} N (‰, vs. AIR)	δ^{13} C (‰, vs. VPDB)	δ^{18} O (‰, vs. VPDB)	δ^{13} C (‰, vs. VPDB)
Sixth rib	9	18.311	15.602	38.065	2.07872	0.85207	1.1736	0.708589				
First molar	11	18.298	15.587	38.009	2.07730	0.85188	1.1739	0.709713			−10.23	−5.07
Lower right canine	29	18.215	15.576	37.926	2.08232	0.85521	1.1693	0.709487				
Third molar	2	18.269	15.593	38.056	2.08305	0.85352	1.1716	0.708459			−8.13	−3.72
Hair (bulk)	9	18.587	15.630	38.153	2.05266	0.84088	1.1892	0.708113				
Hair A (root)	22	18.563	15.638	38.184	2.05702	0.84240	1.1871	0.708419	10.28	−15.95		
Hair B (tip)	7	18.520	15.630	38.142	2.05956	0.84396	1.1849	0.707962	10.56	−17.18		

The online version of the table has been corrected on 15 December 2015 after first online publication and the corrections are marked by the symbol^.

TABLE 3. Concentrations and Pb, Sr, N, C, O Isotope Data for Teeth, Rib and Hair from the Victim

	Pb (ppm)	$^{206}Pb/$ ^{204}Pb	$^{207}Pb/$ ^{204}Pb	$^{208}Pb/$ ^{204}Pb	$^{208}Pb/$ ^{206}Pb	$^{207}Pb/$ ^{206}Pb	$^{206}Pb/$ ^{207}Pb	$^{87}Sr/$ ^{86}Sr	δ^{15} N (‰, vs. AIR)	δ^{13} C (‰, vs. VPDB)	$^\wedge$C (‰, vs. VPDB)	$^\wedge$O (‰, vs. VPDB)
Sixth rib	9	18.311	15.602	38.065	2.07872	0.85207	1.1736	0.708589				
First molar	11	18.298	15.587	38.009	2.07730	0.85188	1.1739	0.709713			−10.23	−5.07
Lower right canine	29	18.215	15.576	37.926	2.08232	0.85521	1.1693	0.709487				
Third molar	2	18.269	15.593	38.056	2.08305	0.85352	1.1716	0.708459			−8.13	−3.72
Hair (bulk)	9	18.587	15.630	38.153	2.05266	0.84088	1.1892	0.708113				
Hair A (root)	22	18.563	15.638	38.184	2.05702	0.84240	1.1871	0.708419	10.28	−15.95		
Hair B (tip)	7	18.520	15.630	38.142	2.05956	0.84396	1.1849	0.707962	10.56	−17.18		

The author apologizes for this error.

REFERENCE

1. Kamenov, G. D., Kimmerle, E. H., Curtis, J. H. and Norris, D. (2014) Georeferencing a Cold Case Victim With Lead, Strontium, Carbon, and Oxygen Isotopes. *Annals of Anthropological Practice* 38, 137–154.

ANNALS OF ANTHROPOLOGICAL PRACTICE 38.2, p. 320. ISSN: 2153-957X. © 2015 by the American Anthropological Association. DOI:10.1111/napa.12059

Save Time and Let the Research Come to You

Sign up for new content alerts for all of your favorite journals:

- ✓ Be the first to read Early View articles
- ✓ Get notified of Accepted Articles when they appear online
- ✓ Receive table of contents details each time a new issue is published
- ✓ Never miss another issue!

Follow these 3 easy steps to register for alerts online:

1 Log into **Wiley Online Library**. If you are not already a registered user, you can create your profile for free.

2 Select "**Get New Content Alerts**" from Journal Tools on the top left menu on any journal page or visit the Publications page to view all titles.

3 Submit your preferences and you are done. You will now receive an email when a new issue of the journal publishes.

wileyonlinelibrary.com

12-46060